Finland's National Theatre 1974–1991

This study analyses the Finnish National Theatre's activities throughout the decades during which the post-war generation with its new societal and theatrical views was rising to power, and during which Europe, divided by the Iron Curtain, was maturing to break the boundaries dividing it.

Pirkko Koski summarises the activities of the Finnish National Theatre as a cultural factor and as a part of the Finnish theatre field during 1970s and 1980s. Alongside this she examines the general requirements, resources, and structures for activity, including artists, places, geographical position, performances, and the analysis of societal conditions.

This book will be of great interest to scholars and students of European theatre and history.

Pirkko Koski is Professor emeritus in the Department of Philosophy, History, and Art Studies at the University of Helsinki.

Routledge Advances in Theatre & Performance Studies

This series is our home for cutting-edge, upper-level scholarly studies and edited collections. Considering theatre and performance alongside topics such as religion, politics, gender, race, ecology, and the avant-garde, titles are characterized by dynamic interventions into established subjects and innovative studies on emerging topics.

Deburau
Pierrot, Mime, and Culture
Edward Nye

Performance at the Urban Periphery
Insights from South India
Cathy Turner, Sharada Srinivasan, Jerri Daboo, Anindya Sinha

Australian Metatheatre on Page and Stage
An Exploration of Metatheatrical Techniques
Rebecca Clode

Functions of Medieval English Stage Directions
Analysis and Catalogue
Philip Butterworth

Live Visuals
History, Theory and Practice
Steve Gibson, Donna Leishmann, Stefan Arisona, Atau Tanaka

The Celestial Dancers
Manipuri Dance on Australian Stage
Amit Sarwal

For more information about this series, please visit: https://www.routledge.com/Routledge-Advances-in-Theatre–Performance-Studies/book-series/RATPS

Finland's National Theatre 1974–1991

The Two Decades of Generational Contests, Cultural Upheavals, and International Cold War Politics

Pirkko Koski

Translated by
Kayleigh Töyrä

LONDON AND NEW YORK

First published 2022
by Routledge
2 Park Square, Milton Park, Abingdon, Oxon OX14 4RN

and by Routledge
605 Third Avenue, New York, NY 10158

Routledge is an imprint of the Taylor & Francis Group, an informa business

© 2022 Pirkko Koski

The right of Pirkko Koski to be identified as author of this work has been asserted in accordance with sections 77 and 78 of the Copyright, Designs and Patents Act 1988.

All rights reserved. No part of this book may be reprinted or reproduced or utilised in any form or by any electronic, mechanical, or other means, now known or hereafter invented, including photocopying and recording, or in any information storage or retrieval system, without permission in writing from the publishers.

Trademark notice: Product or corporate names may be trademarks or registered trademarks, and are used only for identification and explanation without intent to infringe.

British Library Cataloguing-in-Publication Data
A catalogue record for this book is available from the British Library

Library of Congress Cataloging-in-Publication Data
A catalog record has been requested for this book

ISBN: 978-0-367-47689-2 (hbk)
ISBN: 978-0-367-49849-8 (pbk)
ISBN: 978-1-003-04766-7 (ebk)

DOI: 10.4324/9781003047667

Typeset in Bembo
by Taylor & Francis Books

Contents

List of figures vii
Acknowledgements ix

1 Introduction 1

SECTION I
Operational frames 17

2 The Finnish National Theatre and the changing field of theatre 19
3 Experiencing, conveying, and interpreting 30
4 The creators of artistic direction 38
5 A national landmark renewed and replenished 53

SECTION II
Programming, performances, and the national agenda 63

6 The national mission driving the National Theatre's programming 65
7 Highs and lows in the context of the domestic repertoire 76
8 Finnish history without a nationalist slant 96
9 Significant literary works as national interpretations 111
10 Modern dramatic classics 127
11 New Eastern European drama 145
12 New plays from the West 160
13 Social upheaval on the national stage 177

14	Popular and commercial elements and National Theatre press debates	187
15	The advent of the small and the young	196
16	Theatre company visits from East and West	204
17	Conclusion: The National Theatre during a time of transition	217

Bibliography 224
Index 231

Figures

2.1	New Theatre Director Kai Savola, 1973	20
3.1	The Main Stage audience from the stage	35
4.1	Valeri Levental and Anatoli Efros with the *Cherry Orchard* ensemble, 1983	48
4.2	Declan Donnellan	49
5.2	The Small Stage of the Finnish National Theatre	56
5.3	The Willensauna Stage of the National Theatre	58
5.4	The Omapohja Stage of the National Theatre	60
6.1	Actors on the National Main Stage, *Kolmekymmentä hopearahaa*, 1982	73
7.1	*Tohvelisankarin rouva* 1985. Tea Ista and Yrjö Järvinen	80
7.2	*Nummisuutarit* 1984, Seppo Pääkkönen as Esko. photograph Leena Klemelä.	82
7.3	*Mr Puntila and His Man Matti* 1975. Kauko Helovirta with Maija Karhi, Marjukka Halttunen, Ansa Ikonen and Eeva-Kaarina Volanen	85
7.4	*Juurakon Hulda* 1986. Jarno Hiilloskorpi, Karin Pacius and Simo Tamminen	88
8.1	*Yks perkele yks enkeli* 1985. Seppo Pääkkönen and Martti Järvinen	101
8.2	*Tie talvisotaan*, 1989	106
9.1	*King Lear* 1983. Veijo Pasanen and Risto Mäkelä. Photograph by Johnny Korkman	116
9.2	*Macbeth* 1986. Markku Maalismaa and the ensemble	117
9.3	*The School for Wives*. 1976. Set design by Miklós Köllö	119
10.1	*Cherry Orchard* 1983. Paula Siimes, Terhi Panula, and Soila Komi	131
10.2	*Man and Superman* 1982. Ismo Kallio and Risto Järvinen	133
10.3	*The Death of a Salesman* 1984. Eeva-Kaarina Volanen and Pentti Siimes	135
11.1	*Viimeistä seuraava yö* 1976. Hannes Häyrinen and Antti Litja (The Pope and Bruno)	149
11.2	*Vastaanotto* 1978. Antti Litja and Pekka Autiovuori	152
12.1	*Donna* 1980. Kyllikki Forssell	167
12.2	*Amadeus* 1981. Jussi Jurkka	172

viii *List of figures*

12.3 *Masterclass* 1986. Risto Aaltonen, Jarno Hiilloskorpi, Pentti Siimes and Leif Wager Photograph by Johnny Korkman 175
13.1 *Johnny Johnson* 1975. Pentti Siimes and the ensemble 178
13.2 *Caligula* 1980. Hannu Lauri and Risto Mäkelä. 183
14.1 *Parisian Life* 1981. Ahti Jokinen, Jarno Hiilloskorpi, Karin Pacius, Maija Karhi and Jouko Keskinen 191
15.1 *Orphans* 1988. Tapani Perttu, Petteri Sallinen and Markku Maalismaa 199
15.2 *Lintu vai kala* 1990. Anna-Leena Härkönen and Mari Rantasila 201

Acknowledgements

Over the course of writing this book I have been grateful to receive a lot of direct and indirect support that has assisted me throughout my writing process. During these challenging times of COVID-19, many of my colleagues have had the unenviable task of surmounting unprecedented obstacles in their work, which made me rather reluctant to burden them with detailed questioning of my own. Consequently, the actual process of bringing this book to life has been somewhat more lonesome than usual, and a lot of my gratitude and acknowledgements reach further back in time to encompass a much wider academic process that has ultimately culminated in this book.

Nevertheless, I have still enjoyed significant direct support, for which I am very grateful. First, I would like to thank the Finnish National Theatre Archives and its archivist Laura Saloniemi, archivist Eeva Mustonen from the Theatre Museum Archives, and the Museum's database researcher Pälvi Laine, for continuing to help me to locate a variety of source material that has been integral to my work, with this year being no exception. I would also like to thank the production photographers for their co-operation. I am especially grateful to the Finnish National Theatre's retired Director Maria-Liisa Nevala for her insightful comments when it came to narrowing down which productions to focus on and which aspects of Finnish culture would interest a wider audience. I have also greatly enjoyed working with the text's translator, Kayleigh Töyrä, whose knowledge of both the Finnish and English languages and culture made for a fruitful and flexible collaborative. In contrast to my own historical and personal appreciation of the events depicted, the period covered in this book is merely history for Kayleigh and her generation – a fact that pushed me to reassess and re-examine my study from a fresh perspective. A consistent and comforting presence throughout the different life stages of the text has been my husband Heikki, who has acted as both a reader throughout the text's genesis as well as helping with framing its social context.

The book I published in Finnish in 2019 on the activities of the Finnish National Theatre during this same era also forms a significant part of this book's textual background, although I have re-angled my questioning and chosen different productions for analysis. The support that I received throughout the writing of that previous text stood me in good stead when it came to writing this book. I would like to thank the Finnish National Theatre's historical committee and especially its president Professor Seppo Zetterberg, as well as its member Doctor Docent Mikko-Olavi Seppälä. I have also re-visited some of the interviews that I undertook at that time, especially the information supplied by Finnish National Theatre Director Kai Savola. Working with the Finnish publisher SKS in 2019 led to new ways of working that have benefitted me in writing this book.

Even though all national theatre, Finnish national theatre included, is an international phenomenon, national theatre studies are invariably received differently outside the theatre's country of origin. During my own academic career, I have striven to analyse the Finnish theatrical world while simultaneously actively engaging with international academic circles; endeavouring to marry the national with the international has been central to my work, and I owe a debt of gratitude to the many people who have helped me on that journey. Regardless of the final language that they were written in, I have been able to present most of my research papers in international research contexts, significantly to the Historiography working group of the International Federation for Theatre Research and the Association of Nordic and Baltic Theatre Scholars. Running the International Centre for Advanced Theatre Studies (ICATS) summer school for a decade in collaboration with other academics, notably Bruce McConachie, Janelle Reinelt, Freddie Rokem, Steve Wilmer, and William Worthen, and working with international students indelibly changed the way that I approach all my research. The exhaustive list of people who have influenced me throughout these activities would naturally be long and significant, but my debt of gratitude in this case is particularly tangible: in this book I have referred to many of my published and unpublished papers that are indebted to conversations that have come out of these groups, the conversations themselves often influencing the papers' academic frame of reference and their research hypotheses.

I would like to extend a special thank you to my publisher and thank them for this opportunity to write about the Finnish National Theatre during these decades of significant cultural change and shift. This study functioned as a fascinating bridge between my present and my own personal archive as I delved into a period that dealt with a time before the beginning of my actual research career, when my professional activities were centred around museums, archives, and writing theatrical reviews. Writing for an international audience allowed a suitable level of distance from a subject matter to which I am very close in so many ways (my memory also functioned in much the same way as my own recollections from three decades ago were disjointed and rather hazy). The book's final form owes much to the helpful input that I received from editor Swati Hindwan, whose answers to my questions were always accurate, prompt, and encouraging.

1 Introduction

The subject of this book is the Finnish National Theatre (Suomen Kansallisteatteri) during the two decades preceding the end of the Cold War. During this era, the 1960s generation with their new ideas on society and theatre matured and took hold; simultaneously, a Europe divided by the Iron Curtain matured and broke out of its restrictive chains. Nations and their national theatres faced up to the challenges of a world in flux.

The end of the 1960s ushered in a period of unrest in Europe and the rest of the world, culminating in the collapse of the Iron Curtain. As a country uniquely caught between East and West, these changes deeply affected Finland, permanently altering Finnish society and its power structures. The unrest bled into the theatrical world. In order to maintain the distinctive position it had held in Finnish theatrical culture for the past century, the Finnish National Theatre attempted to meet the demands of contemporary society without losing sight of its unique national mission. The aim of my study is to describe the choices made by the Finnish National Theatre and examine its artistic output and social and cultural position during these turbulent times.

The Finnish National Theatre: tradition and turbulent times

The roots of the Finnish National Theatre go back to the 1800s, to a time when national theatres emerged all over Europe, reflecting an ethos of cultural nationalism. The Finnish National Theatre is part of a group of Central and Eastern Europe national theatres that were part of national projects to disrupt the stranglehold of French, German or Russian language, aesthetics, or politics within the borders of their countries. Similarly, in countries such as Ireland and Norway, national theatres played a part in the ongoing cultural nationalist project and were intrinsic to the formation of a coherent national identity.[1]

The Finnish National Theatre has its own unique characteristics. It was founded when Finland was part of the Russian Empire as an autonomous Grand Duchy, after Sweden had lost Finland to Russia in 1809. Linguistic and political powers within the borders of Finland were split, and the Finnish-speaking majority did not hold the keys to power in either arena. In Finland, the language of the elite and the language used, e.g. in law and education was not Russian,

DOI: 10.4324/9781003047667-1

but Swedish; the power structures inherited from Sweden were not demolished. According to constitutional expert Pekka Hallberg it was essential that 'throughout the period of Russian autonomy state and legislative powers were based in Finland and not outside the country's borders'.[2] Therefore, the language of power was still Swedish, and the Finnish language continued to be oppressed. First begun in the 1860s, the initiatives to equalise the status of Finnish and Swedish in Finland had to wait for almost half a century to be finally fully realised in the 1922 parity law. Many of the Finnish language national institutions founded in the 1800s, the Finnish National Theatre included, were part of this linguistic struggle, and at the same time both Finnish and Swedish-speaking Finland were working towards Finnish sovereignty.

The Finnish National Theatre was first founded in 1872 under the name of the Finnish Theatre (Suomalainen Teatteri) to challenge Russia's political power and the hegemony of the Swedish language in Finland. The Theatre was proof that Finnish-speaking Finland aspired to be on par with other established national cultures. When the Theatre moved into its new National Romantic theatre building in 1902, it was renamed the Finnish National Theatre. As the 1900s progressed, the Finnish language attained its dominant position. Once Finland became independent in 1917, the country was also freed from external political oppression. Even after these changes, the Finnish National Theatre had to continuously justify its position as a national artistic institution and cultural producer. The Theatre could not rely on a formalised national position, owing to its private limited company status, though it did rely on public funding. It was administratively independent, but in order to be nationally legitimised widespread public support was paramount. Generally, the word 'national' was taken to imply 'public', and in that spirit the Theatre's activities were scrutinised from many different angles and camps. In the 1970s the Finnish National Theatre's historical legitimacy seemed unproblematic, but once its original aims were reached, new justifications for its continued existence were needed.

Throughout its history, the National Theatre Directors consistently remained in post for a long time, guaranteeing stability in the Theatre's artistic activities and output. Arvi Kivimaa (b. 1904) started as Theatre Director in 1950, retiring in 1974 after leading the Finnish National Theatre for over two decades. He revamped the Theatre's repertoire after the war and cultivated Finland's international theatrical connections. During his time as Director, the 1960s generation matured into adults, Finland became more urbanised, and the number of Finnish people studying in higher and tertiary education grew exponentially. Finland had lost the war to the Soviet Union, but the country had been spared occupation and after paying off its war debts, Finland managed to stay relatively apart from Europe's redrawn borders and border zones. Finland's democratic society and market economy fostered strong international ties and an affinity with the Nordics, Western Europe, and the United States, though maintaining its political position would prove to be a constant challenge for Finland.[3] Finland was culturally and economically tied to the West, but its political position was undermined by the Agreement of Friendship, Cooperation, and Assistance (the YYA treaty)[4] that it had signed with the Soviet Union. In the event of a potential war, Finland would have been forced to in effect become a Soviet buffer zone against the West. Keeping the peace was paramount to Finland. Officially Finland was wary about openly criticising the Soviet Union, but memories of the war(s)[5] were still fresh, and Finnish attitudes towards its Eastern neighbour were generally guarded. Finland's cultural and political atmosphere was built on contradictory principles, presenting challenges when it came to defining and enacting its national dramatic mission.

Despite his successes, in his later years Arvi Kivimaa failed to establish common ground with the younger generation who were coming in and changing the field of theatre. The Finnish National Theatre's leadership reacted to the mounting criticism by choosing a new Theatre Director: Kai Savola (b. 1931) who was the Director of Tampere's Työväen Teatteri (Tampere Workers' Theatre, TTT). This study covers Savola's era as the Theatre Director of the Finnish National Theatre that began in August 1974 and ran until the end of 1991.

In studies of recent Finnish history, the 1970s and 1980s are frequently grouped together into their own cohesive historical period, labelled as the era of the welfare state. In this period, art and economic policy intertwined when it came to governance and finances, and the 1960s generation with their more radical social agenda ascended into prominence.[6] Despite the continuity, these two Cold War decades differed from each other as well, something that the theatrical experience clearly exemplifies. In the 1970s the atmosphere became markedly more politicised. During the following decade, political abuses of power made people more sceptical about politicians and political parties, and the media's power over public opinion grew.[7] The economic fluctuations of the time period affected certain elements of the Finnish National Theatre's activities, but did not significantly alter its foundations.

The Finnish National Theatre had to continuously differentiate itself from the rest of the Finnish theatrical system. There were over thirty publicly funded professional repertoire theatres around the country that were joined by a few small private theatres founded after the war, and a few professional group theatres that had first entered the scene in the 1960s. Finnish-language and Swedish-language theatres worked side-by-side, and the Svenska Teatern (Helsinki Swedish Theatre) was seen as the unofficial national theatre for the Swedish-speaking minority. Owing to its history, Tampere's TTT was in a unique position: it was the only remaining professional workers' theatre that had survived from the old system where most cities had both a workers' and a bourgeois theatre. Finland also had a number of amateur theatres led by professionals, a host of large summer theatres, and a few radio and TV theatres.[8] The Finnish National Theatre's position was bolstered by its heritage, its location in the country's capital, an emerging public support that set it apart from other theatres, the Theatre's size, and its larger-than-average resources.

During the period covered in this study, social turbulence was characterised by intergenerational differences and the different ways in which generations responded to social change. Matti Virtanen, who has studied the Finnish nationalist movement, claims that going through a period of social change creates a way for generations to bond together, though this in of itself is not enough to mobilise a generation. Social change is experienced in a multitude of ways. Different generations experience the same event at different ages. Mobilisation creates factions. Historians Timo Soikkanen and Vesa Vares also highlight the fact that people join these key experiences at different times, and – if they are mobilised – might also "leave" one faction and take up a vanguard of influence in the ensuing, younger faction. Factions become tied to tradition in a double-bind; the relationship with their own generation remains intact, but tradition itself is layered with different age groups, and people mobilised at different stages.[9] The social activities of the different generations and their relationship with tradition were projected onto the Finnish National Theatre, partly explaining the social and political tensions that developed around the Theatre. Also, in theatre research the year 1968 is delineated as a period boundary: post-war theatre made way for contemporary theatre and the emerging ascendancy of postmodernism, interculturalism, postcolonialism, and the postdramatic.[10]

The turbulence of Finnish society and its theatrical milieu was connected with the international social movement of the late 1960s that divided generations. The Vietnam War, race riots, the Biafra famine, and the occupation of Czechoslovakia all led to demonstrations in Finland. In a country like Finland that was caught between two superpowers the Cuban missile crisis increased the tangible threat of war. 1968 became the defining generational experience for the 1960s generation, and the symbol of the ideological activation of the youth. Social change made people more interested in the left and generally more open to adopting a community-minded way of thinking. The left-leaning youth movement also gave birth to a minor Marxist-Leninist student movement who supported Soviet power politics; this radical left-wing faction became dogmatised in the 1970s.[11]

Some of the theatrical movers and shakers of the late 1960s had briefly worked at the Finnish National Theatre under Arvi Kivimaa's direction without fully becoming part of the Theatre's tradition.[12] Some of the theatre practitioners got caught up in leftist extremism, but despite a small vocal minority, the majority of people preferred to remain outside of these politics. The 1960s generation attained little or transient power at the National Theatre. Even though the National Theatre did not want to embrace the radicalised left-wing faction when it came to its own artistic output, the Theatre did not have sufficient power to define its own position in the cultural and theatrical field of its day. Clashes were inevitable. In the 1980s, the new youth movement activated itself against the 1960s generation, moving closer to the Finnish National Theatre's traditional emphasis on the independence of artistic expression.

A divided Europe had to wait until the end of the 1980s to undergo its biggest political changes, though the foundations for the Cold War shift had been steadily developing over the preceding decades. In the 1970s and the 1980s, alongside traditional ties to the West, the National Theatre built relationships across the Iron Curtain to the East. These relationships were in keeping with the principle of peaceful coexistence, but their artistic content was in direct contrast with the Finnish authorities' cautious approach. The Finnish National Theatre's approach also differed from that of many people in the theatre field of the time who openly supported Soviet and East German cultural politics. In contrast, the Finnish National Theatre's collaborations with Eastern Europe revolved around an emphasis on dramatic values and an artistic framework that in some cases contradicted the prevailing politics of both the country of origin and destination.[13] The Finnish National Theatre was an independent agent whose approach to the East followed Western modes of thought.

Social commentary was not an alien concept to the Finnish National Theatre's new Director, Savola, who had worked at the Union of Workers' Stages and Tampere's TTT. In Savola's vision one can sense a preoccupation with social issues through the lens of the individual. In this way he mirrored the values of the post-war liberal intelligentsia, in contrast to the more strident political demands made by the 1960s generation. Savola was chosen as the Theatre Director of the Finnish National Theatre, owing to a desire to eschew the radical left-wing faction and avoid signing on a politically radical leader. Savola's reputation was based on his knowledge of drama and his theatrical expertise, not his political activities.

National stature and fulfilling the national mission

The Finnish state was an important financial backer of the Finnish National Theatre, but the government had no official recourse to decision-making inside a private theatre. The ownership of the Finnish National Theatre was national only in the sense that it was governed by people of high social standing who had inherited their positions and were committed to improving national culture.

As Marvin Carlson has shown, national theatres cannot be grouped into one coherent monolith. Rather, national theatres tend to share certain characteristics: an impressive building in the capital city, government-level support and financial backing, and a repertoire that emphasises national works. Even the most entrenched national theatres tend to differ on one or two of these generalised definitions.[14] S. E. Wilmer explains how national theatres were often created to advance the cause of a cultural nationalist movement. National theatres play a significant role in building a national identity and showcasing cultural achievements, something that the Finnish National Theatre has certainly achieved. Wilmer also explains how national theatres embody their own unique contexts, reflecting 'a specific originating movement, location, set of goals, language, history, and mythology, as well as the idiosyncratic beliefs of its individual founding members'.[15] Many of these, as well as the ability to adapt over time, are especially pertinent when analysing the Finnish National Theatre through the ages.

In *Theatre & Nation* (2010), Nadine Holdsworth references Steven Grosby's distinction between 'house' and 'home': how the "spirit" of past generations and a historical moment converge in order to create a territory with a spatial concept, the homeland.[16] Applying these concepts to the Finnish National Theatre leads us to consider the role of the National Theatre as a carrier of cultural tradition and how the people who operated within its orbit (audience included) participated in the formation of a coherent national experience. Even in the 1970s the National Theatre's unique standing anchored in tradition was understood to be its natural state. However, social change meant that the image of what constituted "national" shifted, so the "spirit" of the Theatre was also expected to change.

In Benedict Anderson's *Imagined Communities* (1981[1995]), the definition of "national" as an "imagined community" can be leveraged to expose the national theatre as a construction whose national standing is missing a *natural* legitimate right, legitimacy.[17] It had to keep re-proving its own exceptionality for each era. Media researchers Mikko Lehtonen and Anu Koivunen have turned Anderson's definition on its head by seeing the nation, Finnish people included, as a type of political catalogue created by art producers. Essentially, producers of art modify the heterogeneous population into an idealised and consistent portrait of Finnishness by excluding those who do not fit the picture.[18] Leveraging this definition, The Finnish National Theatre expressed its own policy and its own unique character as a national institution through its strategy and artistic programming. Adapting the ideas of Michel de Certeau, the Theatre's *strategic* function meets the *tactical* needs of the audience, and encompassing both tells of 'the difference or similarity between the production of the image and the secondary production hidden in the process of its utilization'.[19] The Theatre's "imagined" image of its target audience and its needs was central to the Theatre's attempts at legitimising its position. Audience reception (audience here including professional reviewers) also played a significant role when it came to finding justifications for the Theatre's national function.

In *The National Stage* (1992) Loren Kruger defines the two concepts of *national theatre* and *popular national theatre* and sees the line between these two as slippery.[20] The cultural nationalist roots of the Finnish National Theatre mean that the oscillation between national and popular outlined by Kruger has been instrumental in shaping the Theatre's function and public image. The cultural elite who originally founded the Theatre felt that they were representing the Finnish nation and were seeking legitimation for their function from the Finnish people, at the same time as the publicised programming emphasised high art. The target group, the "people", also became activated and felt that they had a right to express their views if their theatre did not meet their expectations.[21]

Kruger also defines the concept of *theatrical nationhood* as predicated on something that is essential to the theatrical experience: encounters. This differs from Anderson's concept of an 'imagined community'. The fact that theatrical expression is anchored in a deep sense of presence leads to the fact that an outsider can be made to conform to a concept of the national, simultaneously participating in *defining* the national. Kruger posits that 'this national assembly, rather than the linguistic or cultural consistency of the repertoire, is the essential point of theatrical nationhood'.[22] David Wiles posits that the personal encounter inherent to theatre, *the performance*, challenges the discursive and textual elements of Anderson's arguments. According to Wiles 'the very nature and purpose of theatre' is 'to create communities, and most forms of pre-modern theatre minimized the audience's awareness that it embodied a community that transcended familial and neighbourly relations'.[23] In the case of the Finnish National Theatre this transcendence is fruitful when taking into account the expectations set by its history, governance, and audiences. The Finnish audience collectively experienced events that were alien to them, and in dialogue with the performers, these events became familiar and were sometimes even "nationally" adopted. At the same time it is evident that the Finnish National Theatre was also discursively defined, divorced from a sense of belonging and personal encounters.

The Finnish National Theatre represented a type of 'cosmopolitan conviviality': a combination of the national and the international. Even though at times the National Theatre promoted ideas that could be seen as nationalist when emphasising its national policy in Finland, the Theatre always strived for international collaboration in the name of cultural exchanges and high art. The concept of what constitutes high art has naturally shifted with the times. As Holdsworth writes, 'the focus on identity – for our purposes, national identity – is destabilised, and instead cultural practices arising out of cohabitation and interaction take on primary significance'. The theatre can bring people together 'to create work that relies on the collision and integration of different perspectives and skills'. In this heightened place 'the qualities of listening, looking and responsiveness are highly regarded activities in both making and watching theatre'.[24] The theatre does not simply reflect its surroundings, but through its creative function it can also 'contribute to the creation of the nation'.[25]

Finnish folklorist Pertti J. Anttonen has studied the diverse ways in which cultural identity was formed in the Finnish context. According to Anttonen, when studying tradition one must also take into account the impact of transnational politics and economic structures, as well as the interplay between centres and peripheries. 'It is in the context of a variety of competing ideologies, political processes, and social and commercial networks, that vernacular cultural production, the constitution of local cultural and territorial identity as well as the construction of local history and historical imaginations, take place'.[26] At the same time, one can ask whether national approval in theatre was primarily based on artistic merit with "national" content only being a secondary consideration. What roles did upholding tradition and renewing dramatic arts play? These are the questions that this book aims to answer.

In *Theatre & Nation* (2010), Holdsworth sets up a cultural and geographic boundary by positioning herself 'as a Western, monoglot English-speaker'; she primarily chooses plays from the United Kingdom, the United States, and Australia as subjects of her study. 'It would be fair to say that a completely different book on theatre and the nation would emerge from a writer coming from a non-Western perspective or with expertise in that field', Holdsworth writes.[27] Her musings on the relationship between the theatre and the nation can be applied to theatre more generally, but the boundaries set up by Holdsworth leave liminal spaces unexplored. When it comes to examining the relationship between theatre and the nation, many Continental and Northern Europe national theatres, the Finnish National Theatre included, share their own unique characteristics, but they do not represent a non-Western viewpoint. When it came to the Finnish National Theatre, more was required of it than other theatres in Finland, though it was impossible to determine to any great accuracy what this intangible requirement was.

My own national position inevitably emphasises the exceptionality of Finland's geographic position, its small population, and the uniqueness of the Finnish language. In Finland, being caught between cultures has played a big part in forming the Finnish national agenda. Ideological and theoretical movements, as well as those that directly impact theatre and dramatic culture, have transcended geographic and linguistic boundaries. The Finnish theatre system has been heavily influenced by the theatre history of the entire European continent. Right from the beginning the Finnish National Theatre defined itself by placing the Theatre within an international context. The ideological basis for the Theatre can be traced back to Germany, and its general aim was to place the emerging Finnish nation on an equal footing with other established national cultures. Internationality was intrinsic to the Finnish National Theatre, so changes to international borders that characterised these historical eras are pertinent to the Finnish National Theatre's story.

National Theatres in a Changing Europe (2007), edited by Wilmer, presents a wide range of national theatres as its subject, while simultaneously interrogating the concept of 'national' from different perspectives. In his article 'National Theatres: Then and Now' Carlson zooms in on the institution of the national theatre in the East, West, and across the continents. Carlson also considers how to define the concept of 'national', namely its cultural status and place in a country's culture as a whole, before examining the move towards transnationalism.[28] One of the aims of my study is to bring new case studies to light by presenting specific geographically and contextually bound examples from Finland.

The differences between national theatres also touch on the politics of power. Financial instability made the National Theatre dependent on contemporary decisions on public spending on culture, despite the Theatre being independently governed and owned. Simo Häyrynen posits that cultural politics operate on an axis of power in function of fluctuating resources where change causes tension between 'the spiritual mores of the time and the mechanisms that uphold the institutional continuity of power'.[29] Finnish cultural projects like the desire to change governance structures were also directed at the Finnish National Theatre, impacting its activities. During the 1970s the Theatre was caught up in the intergenerational power struggle swirling around artistic institutions. As Pentti Haapala states, power can only be maintained by constantly renewing it. When change is a society's central driving force, change can also be used to understand society.[30] In order to justify its national status the Finnish National Theatre also needed to change. Through its ability to adapt and change, this history of the Finnish National Theatre is also an analysis of how to maintain power by renewing structures and functional frameworks.

Researching theatre history

My study examines the theatrical institution and the way in which it fulfils its core function, producing dramatic works for an audience. National theatres as an institution and a concept have been frequently examined, especially in the 1990s and the decade that followed. This coincided with a period when wider questions about nations and what the term 'national' constituted were topical in social studies and the arts. Those studies have focused on the cultural role performed by national theatres, the development of a national artistic function, as well honing in on productions that were deemed 'national'. Even though their questions have been specifically addressed in the context of national theatres, the research methodologies leveraged mirror those used in other studies into theatre history. While examining the history of the Finnish National Theatre, my research methodologies have been informed by other studies pertaining to the institution of theatre, the theatrical event, theatrical context, as well as general source criticism. I especially lean on the models that look at the interplay between structure and dramatic output.[31]

The widest angle of my research work looks at the institution of theatre itself. In his book *Taide instituutiona ja järjestelmänä* (The Arts as an Institution and a System) (1998) Erkki Sevänen interrogates the artistic institution within the framework of a system. As well as the interplay between a dramatic work and its reception, Sevänen looks at individual creative institutions in the context of the artistic institution, as well as how they interact with wider art and cultural politics.[32] Sevänen's scope is similar to my study in terms of the breadth of its scope. By adapting the definitions by Juhani Niemi to a dramatic institution like the National Theatre, the Theatre can be understood as a system of structures, concepts, and theories inside which drama as a performing art becomes possible. Niemi divides institutions into two separate parts: 1) the structure or organisation; and 2) the functional contract undertaken inside that structure. Questions of art are conditional on the agreements between writers, performers, and researchers, and the receiver: the audience.[33] Studying the National Theatre adds its own national viewpoint to these models.

In his book *The Cambridge Introduction to Theatre Historiography* (2009) Thomas Postlewait describes historic theatrical events using a model where both the creators and receivers of the event are in constant dialogue with each other, as well as constantly interacting with their surrounding traditions and society.[34] In general terms, this is exactly how institutions tend to function too. The interplay between tradition and the prevailing world is a tension that can be brought to bear on the backgrounds and functions of leaders, staff, and artists of the National Theatre. Tensions arise throughout the different stages of the theatrical process such as when choosing theatre programming or adapting a text for performance; societal weak spots also tend to have an impact on dramatic decisions. When studying a theatrical event, the difference between a historic and contemporary approach is defined by their objects, the evidentiary material; though, theoretical frameworks and methods are shared. '[N]either from an epistemological nor from a methodological point of view does it make sense to draw a strict borderline between our various research activities [...] such as theatre historiography and performance analysis [...]', Erika Fischer-Lichte has written.[35]

When creating a functional model for analysing a performance as an event, Willmar Sauter further classifies the contexts impacting the experiences of the performer and the receiver. According to Sauter, the specific contexts surrounding a theatrical event are: *conventions, structures, concepts, cultural* factors, as well as *life world*. These contextual factors are in a two-way relationship with the facilitators and actors of the event, a relationship that Lehtonen describes in his own work using the word con-text.[36] Performance activities are core to a theatre's function and they have their own contexts that extend from the internal workings of the theatre to the surrounding societal framework. These contexts support the continuity of the theatrical institution and their deeper contextual meanings become more pronounced when analysing the repertoire and individual performances. Both the institution as a whole and an individual theatrical event share a multiplicity of diverse stakeholders.

Applying cultural theorist Doreen Massey's model, a site is a place for encounters where social relationships transform over time and themselves in turn interact with the history of the site. Massey posits that time is a dimension of change whereas space is a dimension of parallel multiplicity. We produce both simultaneously, and both space and time are essential to one another.[37] Lehtonen sees spatial experiences as concurrent and highly porous processes; structural mechanisms that are made up when local, national, and transnational functions overlap.[38] When applied to an institution's history, this space for encounters becomes part of a temporal movement that also encompasses the theatre's functional structures, its agents and operatives, its output, and its ideological emphasis. The connections with the surrounding environment also change and shift, as Dwight Conquergood writes in *The Performance Studies Reader* (2004): 'Our understanding of "local context" expands to encompass the historical, dynamic, often traumatic, movements of people, ideas, images, commodities, and capital'.[39] In *Unsettling Space* (2006) Joanne Tompkins connects the experience of a space with cultural memory and the forming of an identity and brings this perspective to bear on national Australian theatre. According to Tompkins, 'space does not exist on its own: it interacts with social conditions and with supporting discourses including cultural nationalism, self/other, and time, among many'.[40]

There has been a diverse range of prestigious space and place studies on theatre and performance over the past few decades, and different studies have brought a variety of perspectives to framing the theatre as "a place for encounters". Carlson's work on this topic starting from his *Places of Performance* (1989) creates a fruitful basis for spatial analysis and has influenced my appraisal of the Finnish National Theatre on many levels. 'Theatre historians need to develop a more sophisticated understanding and methodology for studying theatre in terms of its all spatial codes – aesthetic, semiotic, social, political, geographical, and ethical. The ways we think not only *about* space but also *with* the ideas of space are crucial to our historical investigation', writes Carlson.[41] He has also looked at the significance of time by highlighting the different functions of memory and by emphasising the beginning of the word, re-member. Temporal changes are stored in both collective and individual memories as features. Carlson describes theatre as a memory machine in his *The Haunted Stage* (2001): 'We are able to "read" new works [...] only because we recognize within them elements that have been recycled from other structures of experience that we have experienced earlier'.[42] This recycling extends to the entire dynamics of theatrical production. The theatre as a "place of memory" both for individuals and a culture is significantly enriched by this recycling.[43] Recycling also plays a big part when it comes to ideas such as the recognition of a national concept.

Approaching the past: sources

A past theatrical event that is anchored in its specific performance context can retrospectively only be accessed through indirect means: sources. Source criticism demands you understand the legalities of storing information, something that Postlewait gives an excellent primer and reminder on in 'The theatrical event and its conditions: a primer with twelve cruxes'.[44] One of the special characteristics of theatre history is the fact we are also trying to reach past events from an aesthetic viewpoint. Still, as Fischer-Lichte reminds us: 'As an aesthetic work the object is not available to the historian: she/he is bound to deal with documents on it only – the work itself is gone and lost forever'[45]. When a performance unfolds in dialogue with its audience, the audience experience of a theatrical event is underlined, and at the same time the performer's analysis of their own work becomes especially significant. Universally accepted historical materials and methods enable the study of theatre, but a theatre historian is often forced also to rely on sources that historians have dismissed as inconclusive sources of information. In my own study, newspaper reviews and other press material, photographic material, multiple memoirs, and memory recall have all become particularly important sources of information.

Material that includes aesthetic judgements contains research and criticism, the powerful *filters* [46] of the theatre institution, that have the power to not only define art, but also influence art itself and general attitudes towards it. Therefore, when using this kind of material as a source alongside other historical material, the central question about power dynamics remains. During the period in question, there are no comprehensive historical accounts of the Theatre, and research articles are based on the same materials as this book, so the question about power is particularly relevant to press criticism. The press material is extensive, and it simultaneously describes productions, as well as commenting on and evaluating them.

Maaria Linko, in her reception studies, divides reception into four parts: audience, critics, researchers, and a fourth 'productive reception'. Productive reception moves the conversation from the primary performance to the secondary texts that spring up around it. In the context of performance studies, it is possible to separate out the impact of experts (theatre critics), 'the general public' (audience numbers and audience feedback and surveys), and the actions of cultural political leaders on the development of a theatrical function and its output.[47] All these disparate groups saw performances at the National Theatre.

When newspaper reviews and critiques offer the most detailed view of an event in question, their overall reliability as a source warrants scrutiny. In Finland, theatre critics represented their own institutional tradition that was particularly strong and wide-ranging. Theatre reviews often directly or indirectly also referenced audience reactions or preferences. All these reservations affect a (historic) material's ability to function as a reliable source, and they also highlight the need for a transparent approach to source criticism and selection.

Production photographs provide another form of expansive source material related to past performances, though the primary function of these photographs was to serve the press writing stories about the shows; they only accidentally or in an ancillary way function as performance documentation. According to National Theatre photographer Leena Klemelä, a production photograph is deeply embedded within a specific performance, it is not an independent work of art. Klemelä also recognises the power of an image when attached to a certain review or a critique: a single picture can crystallise the performance's idea in the right (or wrong) direction, pictorial representations can entice people to visit the theatre, or picture can even help set the scene in terms of ambience. A theatrical photo is also connected to the photographer's personal way of viewing performance through a camera lens.[48] Barbara Hodgdon acknowledges the saying 'a picture is worth a thousand words', but recognises that it is only fulfilled if viewing *that* picture leads people to think about *those* words. A photo of a performance enacts a form of visual dialogue with the actual performance itself, but it is partial, fragmented, and also fundamentally divorced from the performance itself too. When attempting to interpret a historic event, a photo needs to be accompanied by a description that fills in the gaps; as archive material, a photo is like a recorded impression that can resurrect feelings about the play.[49]

In this study, production photographs have helped shape the analysis of the performances discussed. When these photographs were originally published as part of newspaper reviews and critiques they also helped fill in the "gaps" left by the written descriptions of the performances. In the archives of the National Theatre, newspaper reviews are organised by performance. The general picture of the performances covered in this study is a combination of archived performance reviews and images. This is not explicitly mentioned unless the source requires a clarification or it is situated elsewhere than the archive storing all the clippings for that specific performance.[50]

Because of the ephemeral nature of theatrical performances, interviews from people who witnessed the performance can help build a sequence of events that simply cannot be found in any other sources. Actors are closest to the performance and their memories and impressions are important, though they also often become mixed up with the numerous events that happened during their careers. However, interviews can be a great way to find out more about the context behind the events documented, and in their subjectivity they speak of a need to always analyse events from different points of view. Theatre Director Savola's views and impressions of the time have been an important source for my study. As well as conducting my own interviews, I have used interview recordings from the archive and published memoirs. The exalted status of the National Theatre is evident in the number of memoirs and artist biographies published by and about its staff. National Theatre actors were also frequently featured and interviewed in the papers and press of the time. The advantage of this older press material over the interviews conducted in the present-day is their proximity to the events, but a potential drawback is the insertion of a writer's interpretation that could be alienating, disjointing, or even irrelevant.

Experiences also shape the researcher, in this case my relationship with national Finnish concepts and the Finnish National Theatre. During the period I cover in this study I was working as a theatre critic and I wrote about dozens of National Theatre productions, and about as many productions at other theatres of the time, though my reviews only amount to a fraction of the overall column inches and reviews dedicated to the Finnish National Theatre in the press. While I wrote for a national social-democratic paper, I was primarily the director at the Theatre Museum and not a critic, a perfect example of the porousness of the Finnish critical tradition. I was also born on the fringes of my generation and I did not strongly attach myself to either of the generational groups around me. Reading my own criticism and reviews has taught me that other than a few exceptions, my connection to my writing back then has been severed. The wider problematics of a researcher's position and viewpoint are harder to analyse, but they are something that all researchers face.

The Finnish National Theatre during a time of rupture: the structure of this work

I will be looking at the Finnish National Theatre from the 1970s until the year 1991 in two modes: as a national institution whose national status partly enabled and fostered its artistic output, and the ways in which the dramatic texts staged at the Theatre reflected its mission. The temporal shift spans both parts.

The first part looks at the National Theatre's structure and the ways it organised itself, its procurement contracts, and general factors affecting its dramatic output.[51] The first chapter situates the Finnish National Theatre in the cultural and theatrical contexts of its time and examines the expectations placed on its output and activities. The next chapter introduces key interpreters of National Theatre activities and the audiences who participated in the Theatre's function through public writing or by buying a theatre ticket. The chapter about the Theatre's artists aims to give an overview of the Theatre's staff, simultaneously helping the reader to paint a more accurate picture of the key players mentioned in the upcoming descriptions of the Theatre's programming. The Finnish National Theatre's historically significant building and the staging solutions adopted by the Theatre in this era played a significant and relational role when it came to forming the Theatre's artistic output. The building is intimately tied up with appraisals of the Theatre's national significance.

The second part of my study is organised around drama, using the actual performances of the plays as my material. The Finnish National Theatre is a repertoire theatre, justifying the need to frame my analysis in function of the plays themselves. When analysing performances – to borrow Fischer Lichte – '[it] can be assumed that the fundamental structure of drama, its organisation into names of roles and speech text, is given its signature in the issue of identity'. At the same time it must be noted 'that it is not the drama which makes theatre into an art, but only the performance; that it is the performativity of theatre which fundamentally differentiates it from literature or the fine arts'.[i] In this study, theatre is acknowledged as the performing arts, though structurally analysed inside the frames of established dramatic boundaries.

The first chapter of this section examines the conventions and expectations attached to artistic activity. In this chapter I also attempt to elucidate how the Finnish National Theatre's traditional role as a drama theatre is a defence for a specific way of narrating history. The next six chapters describe the National Theatre performance activities in relation to the Theatre's traditional programming mandate that states that the Theatre's aim is to produce international and national classic texts, as well as significant contemporary drama. The division also attempts to bring to the fore the centrality of the tensions between East and West to this study and its time period. The next chapters examine the Finnish National Theatre's role as a font for topical social issues, the high art demands placed on the Theatre by critics, and the significance of the advent of the new generation in power when it came to the reconciliation of the Theatre's public image. The final chapter depicts visits to the Finnish National Theatre from international theatre practitioners, as well as the National Theatre's visits abroad.

Some of the material in this book has been taken (with the permission of the Finnish publisher) from my Finnish-language book *Suomen Kansallisteatteri ristipaineissa* (*The Finnish National Theatre Caught in Cultural Crossfires*) (SKS 2019).

Notes

1 Carlson 2008, 22; Wilmer 2008, 13–16.
2 Hallberg 2019, 35–36.
3 Meinander 2019, 29, 87, 92–93.
4 In accordance with the final peace treaty signed in 1948, the Soviet Union and Finland signed the YYA treaty, whereby Finland agreed to become a buffer zone for attacks against the Soviet Union. Finland also agreed to enter negotiations as soon as a perceived threat became imminent. Finland also committed to refraining from commenting on the relationship between the Soviet Union and the United States. Finland was not part of the Warsaw Treaty and did not participate in the SEV Treaty. Finland interpreted the YYA not as a military pact, but as a commitment to defend itself.
5 The Soviet Union attacked Finland in November 1939 and after a war that lasted for a hundred days a temporary peace treaty was signed that stipulated that Finland had to give up some of its territories. The Finnish population left the lost territories and settled elsewhere in Finland. Finland initiated the war again in June 1941. Finland lost the Continuation War (1941–1944) that it had fought with support from Germany against the Soviet Union, culminating in a truce. The articles of peace specifically stipulated the removal of the German troops from Lapland, and the peace treaty was followed by a short 'Lappish War' against the Germans.
6 e.g. Haapala 2006, 94–95; Sevänen 1998, 371.
7 Hallberg 2019, 183.
8 Cf. Wilmer and Koski 2006, 129–131.
9 Virtanen 2001, 24–27, 354; Soikkanen and Vares 1998, 39. The basis of these studies is Karl Mannerheim's generational study.
10 Balme 2008, 108–109.
11 Cf. Meinander 2019, 176–178, 187–193.
12 For example, Ralf Långbacka (b. 1932) was a director between 1963 and 1965. His Brechtian-influenced productions were praised, but Långbacka did not get on with the Theatre's Director. Långbacka was a major influence on Finnish theatre over a span of many decades.
13 The Finnish National Theatre stood for the free movement of art, as exemplified by the staging of Václav Havel's plays *Unveiling* and *Audience* as the 1978 *Vastaanotto* production. Havel was a notorious Czechoslovakian dissident.
14 Carlson 2008, 21–22.
15 Wilmer 2008, 15, 9.
16 Cft. Holdsworth 2010, 15.
17 Cf. Anderson 1995, 4.
18 Lehtonen and Koivunen 2010, 235.
19 de Certeau 1984, XIII.
20 Kruger 1992, 3–4; cf. also Koski 2008b, 21.
21 Quote linked to Adolf Ivar Arvidson from the 1860s: 'We are not Swedes, we don't want to become Russians, so let's be Finns' that has lived on in cultural memory is a good example of how people "imagine" and define Finnishness.
22 Kruger 2008, 37–39 (quotation p. 39).
23 Wiles 2001, 8.
24 Holdsworth 2010, 71–72.
25 Holdsworth 2010, 79–80.
26 Anttonen 2005, 112–113.
27 Holdsworth 2010, 10.
28 Carlson 2008, 21–33.
29 Häyrynen 2015, 10–13. Häyrynen bases his study on theorists such as Pierre Bourdieu.

30 Haapala 2010, 21–22.
31 The range of historiography and texts that affected my study. E.g. In *Presenting the Past. Essays in Performance Historiography* (2010), edited by Charlotte M. Canning and Thomas Postlewait, the authors state their purpose as 'to help historians to construct the historical conditions, institutions, attitudes, and values that provide the spatial and temporal coordinates for the historical actions and events' (pp. 2, 7.) In *Theorizing Practice. Redefining Theatre History* (2003) edited by W. B. Worthe and Peter Holland, the collection of essays celebrates the different perspectives of its academics. In *New Readings in Theatre History* (2003) Jacky Bratton reminds us that we should be asking 'present-minded questions' but avoiding 'present-minded answers'. *Theatre, History and Historiography: Ethics, Evidence and Truth* (2016) edited by Claire Cochrane and Joanna Robinson, discusses processes and challenges of various histories in different countries and from different viewpoints.
32 Sevänen 1998, 11–12.
33 Niemi 1991, 13, 16. Niemi writes about literary institutions.
34 Postlewait 2009, 18–19.
35 Sauter 2000, 33; Fischer-Lichte 1997, 346.
36 Sauter 2000, 9–11.
37 Massey 2008, 14–15.
38 Lehtonen 2013, 11–14, 20.
39 Conquergood 2004, 311.
40 Tompkins 2006, 15.
41 Carlson 2010, 205, 208.
42 Carlson 2001, 4.
43 Carlson 2001, 3–4.
44 Postlewait 2009, 225–269.
45 Fischer-Lichte 1997, 344.
46 Niemi 1991, 16–17: The *filterers* who assessed the Theatre also influenced notions of the Theatre as an institution. The message goes both ways.
47 Linko 1990, 20.
48 Kristiina Kuisma, "Kuvilla tulkittu teksti." *Aamulehti*, 15.8.1991.
49 Hodgdon 2003, 89.
50 The collection of newspaper clippings in the Finnish National Theatre archives is arranged by stage and year, broken down into individual performances. The placement of the material used can be easily verified. References to direct citations and journal articles from elsewhere than these archival newspaper clippings are separately mentioned.
51 Cf. Niemi 1991, 13, 16.

Section I
Operational frames

2 The Finnish National Theatre and the changing field of theatre

As the 1970s loomed ahead Finnish theatre was fizzing and itching for change as the theatre field readied to transform itself. Necessary reforms had long been sidelined by Finland's more urgent post-war needs and the theatres themselves were keen to adapt to shifting social mores. The pressure to change and reform was felt across the board at Finnish theatres: from the way that they organised themselves, to their funding, their physical spaces, and the way that they trained and managed their professionals. These demands co-existed with the demands placed on their theatrical and artistic output and their content. Reform discussions were conducted among various individuals and groups, both officially and unofficially and these discussions eventually led to tangible outcomes and changes at the Finnish National Theatre.

The Finnish National Theatre had largely kept apart from the social and political agitation that characterised the late 1960s, and as political views became more entrenched, the National Theatre became a type of adversary for more radical elements of society. The Theatre's position as the 'national' theatre was under attack from multiple different flanks and for a variety of reasons. During the two decades that followed 1970, the National Theatre did eventually manage to strengthen its position, and by the beginning of the 1990s, it was largely seen as a powerful cultural influence, not an adversary. At the same time, a new generation had sprung up that was pushing the dramatic arts to develop even further, while the surrounding world prepared itself for the disintegration of boundaries and borders that had been long upheld by the Cold War.

New artistic direction(s)

In the turbulent theatre world of 1970s' Finland, theatre directors changed in rapid succession, often as the cause of a falling-out with the theatre's board. At the National Theatre, the position at the top remained unassailable, but an inevitable change in directorship was nevertheless ahead. Arvi Kivimaa, a central figure on the Finnish cultural political scene and the man who had successfully been at the helm of the Finnish National Theatre for over twenty years, was due to retire. Perhaps one of the best indicators of change in the air was the fact that Kivimaa's views on his successor were ignored, and it is speculated that the final choice might even have gone against his express wishes. The top job at the National Theatre would be given to someone from the outside. Many of Finland's city theatres had recently been re-housed in new buildings and had expanded their repertoire, and at that specific point in time there was actually more demand for theatre director posts than experienced candidates to fill them.

When the board of the National Theatre decided to appoint the current Theatre Director of Tampere's Työväen Teatteri (Tampere Workers' Theatre, TTT), Kai Savola, to the top job at the National Theatre, there was a general sense of surprise. Despite the slightly unforeseen nature of his appointment, Savola's credentials were not generally questioned. At the time Ralf Långbacka was probably the biggest name among experienced theatrical directors, but as he had recently started a joint directorship with Kalle Holmberg at Turku's City Theatre, Långbacka was patently not available. The selection process had been increasingly marked by politics: many candidates had been taken out of the race, owing to their (suspected) left-wing tendencies. Tampere's two theatres, the TTT that represented the traditions of workers' theatres and the more 'bourgeois' Tampere Theatre, were both led by respected directors who had kept apart from the political debates. And so it happened that TTT's Theatre Director Savola ended up with the top job at the National Theatre.

The generational shift taking place at the National Theatre at the time was also significant. Kivimaa, who was leaving the top Theatre Director post to enjoy his retirement, had first risen to fame in the 1920s as a prolific writer, journalist, and

Figure 2.1 New Theatre Director Kai Savola, 1973
Photograph by Kari Hakli, Theatre Museum Archives

Finnish cultural figure. He had become a theatre director in 1937 and had been selected as the Theatre Director of the National Theatre in 1950. Kivimaa had impressive networks, both abroad and at home. In the 1920s he had been part of the young group of artists 'opening the windows to Europe', and his post-war work shows a strong affinity with Western Europe and America.

Savola was almost 30 years younger than his predecessor: his road to the theatre was shorter, and his network of contacts was very different to Kivimaa's. He began his theatrical career in 1955 by joining Helsinki University's Student Theatre, where he spent the following years actively participating in the theatre's artistic direction and the refurbishment of its performance spaces. The theatrical tastes of the day ran to experimenting with the dramatic arts in small performance spaces; this style of intimate dramatic exploration was something Savola extensively witnessed during his travels in post-war Europe. The University Theatre was the first Finnish theatre to visit Moscow and Tallinn, Estonia (part of the Soviet Union from World War II until Estonia won back its independence in 1991).

In 1962 Savola took up the directorship of the Union of Workers' Stages (Työväen Näyttämöiden Liitto, TNL) and was particularly praised for his efforts in developing the ways in which play scripts were distributed and for strengthening the organisation's international connections. Savola made the TNL into a modern theatrical agency and expanded the TNL's network into territories that had been previously less explored such as South America, Australia, Spain, and Africa. Scripts from places like Poland and Czechoslovakia came to Finland via the TNL and even some Finnish dramatists gave distribution rights to TNL. The Finnish National Theatre was a member of an equivalent union and theatre agency originally set up to serve Finland's more 'bourgeois' theatres: Suomen Teatteriliitto (Finland's Theatre Union). TNL was their main competition when it came to distributing the texts of plays.[1]

When working as a dramaturge at the Helsinki City Theatre in 1965–1968 Savola deepened his knowledge of drama and continued to network both in Finland and abroad. His rise to the directorship of the TTT in Tampere in 1968 was a bit of a surprise; even the selection panel had only become aware of his credentials and been convinced of his suitability for the task during the selection process itself. Even though the TTT was traditionally a workers' theatre, Savola's inaugural speech emphasised humanist values and the value of people's theatre as an art form for the general public, steering away from political theatre. He built exceptionally interesting theatre programming and was known to take care of his staff. In the early 1970s under his directorship the TTT was deemed to belong to some of the top theatres in Finland, if not the top spot itself.[2] The move from Tampere to Helsinki meant entering a new cultural milieu. Savola would have to navigate his new position in a new cultural environment, negotiating all the tensions that this would inevitably elicit.

The choice of Savola as the new Theatre Director of the Finnish National Theatre was accepted in a spirit of healthy anticipation. The left-leaning press saw Savola as a progressive choice, but as an individual he was not very well-known. The eminent grey Theatrical Director with staunch cultural influence was now being replaced by a theatre practitioner who tended to stay in the background in times of crises, but was nonetheless clear about his artistic objectives. Everyone felt sure that the National Theatre's artistic direction was bound to change. By choosing Savola, it was clear that the National Theatre was not only distancing itself from the Kivimaa generation, but also from the more radicalised elements of the 1960s generation and their ideologies.[3]

During his time as the Theatre Director of the Finnish National Theatre the picture of Savola became slightly more into focus, but it did not really alter from these initial impressions. Savola did not seem to have had any big disagreements with the other stakeholders at the Theatre during his time there. The Theatre was run by a benevolent dictator, as a young actor who joined the theatre company in the mid-1980s put it.[4] The National Theatre's staff advisory boards encouraged staff involvement and employees had a chance to get their opinions heard (albeit sometimes somewhat slowly), and serious disagreements with management were the exception to the rule. Compared to its internal politics, the National Theatre's public image and its relationship with publicity were much more disjointed, undergoing a lot of change over the decades.

Private, national, and societal pressures

The Finnish National Theatre was at the heart of contemporary cultural political debates, unlike other theatres such as the (also) privately owned TTT that had been previously run by Savola.[5] Influenced by the social changes of the 1970s and the ensuing political activism and the general lean towards the left, 1970s theatrical commentators tended to see state intervention and public ownership of cultural institutions as viable solutions to current problems. When it came to contemporary debates about the Finnish theatrical scene, the Finnish National Theatre and its ownership structure were deemed to be open season in the spirit of the Theatre being a "national institution" that everybody was entitled to comment on. In the ensuing scrutiny a multitude of ideological viewpoints converged on the National Theatre, with suggestions touching on virtually everything, from the institution itself to the way in which it operated. Over two decades though the institutional structure of the Theatre changed little, its public standing and the scope of its activities changed considerably.

The private ownership of the Theatre meant that a large part of its shares were owned by the Finnish National Theatre Foundation. The decisions of the Foundation were made by a board whose members were invited to take up their positions: members were typically made up of socially influential people of a relatively advanced age. Board members were appointed for life and were only replaced when they died. The board of governors running the Finnish National Theatre's limited company was chosen by the Foundation, and though the limited company board members tended to change more frequently, newcomers usually had the same background as their predecessors.

The Finnish National Theatre's ownership structure and form of governance represented tradition and continuity, and many Foundation members were part of the founding families of the Theatre. Belonging to the Finnish National Theatre circles had often been both a cultural duty and a privilege for the educated Finnish-speaking cultural elite of the time. The Theatre's privileged position was further cemented by a 1920s legislative decision that stipulated that the National Theatre would receive financial support from the state in the form of a fixed percentage of the government's cultural income from national lottery profits, further reinforcing the image of a "state theatre".[6] The National Theatre's private ownership did not represent 1970s ideals of democratic art that demanded that people, the "nation", actively participate in artistic activities and define art for themselves.

Owing to the advanced age of many of the Foundation's board members, the board inevitably went through some demographic changes. As cultural-political tensions mounted, the Foundation increasingly brought in influential people from a wider social sphere to take up key positions on the Company board. The most significant change happened in 1983 when the National Theatre decided to change its rules about state representation inside the Theatre. In 1983 the National Theatre's Board welcomed one member chosen by the Ministry of Education, and the board of governors also received two members from the Ministry. The Theatre had previously had political and state representatives in key positions, but they had never officially represented the state or the government, and the choice on who to appoint had been made inside the Theatre. By welcoming representatives of the Finnish state the pool of people making key leadership decisions at the National Theatre widened, but the ultimate decision-making power still remained with the traditional cultural elite.

The Finnish National Theatre was under mounting political pressure in the 1970s, when prevailing values of cultural democracy and the Theatre's private ownership were particularly unaligned. During that time many cultural investigations and reports were compiled in preparation for potential legislative changes, and the National Theatre's position was frequently brought into question in these memos. The most controversial memo was the government's *Teatterikomitea 1972* (Theatre Committee 1972) published in the autumn of 1973. If put into practice, the procedures outlined in the memo would have significantly curbed the National Theatre's independence. The Theatre staunchly objected to its sovereignty being handed to the state. Even though the fiercest debates surrounding *Teatterikomitea 1972* took place in the last years of Kivimaa's directorship and the suggestions about the Theatre's state ownership were quickly rejected, final decisions about continued state funding were not made until the beginning of the 1990s and the very fabric of the theatre industry was under continuous debate for over ten years.

The Finnish National Theatre's cause was helped by the fact that the findings of the *Teatterikomitea 1972* focused on education reforms and regional theatre legislation, issues which only tangentially affected the National Theatre. In fact,

Finland's national network of regional theatres was more affected by the expansion of the country's city theatres, rather than any centralised national project. Some of these repertoire theatres were given more funding to help them hire more staff and take their productions to the rest of the county or organise group transports to the theatre.[7] When it came to theatrical education, the Finnish Theatre School, later the Theatre Academy, enjoyed years of significant development and expansion. The views of the more extreme political left were influential in the Academy in the early 1970s. A sister acting school was founded in Tampere University and over the years these two centres of education increasingly represented competing ideologies.[8]

Extending beyond the National Theatre, the Finnish theatrical system developed in the spirit of the German ideology that emphasised the importance of culture and the tenets of a communal people's theatre. The city theatres functioned under various forms of governance, but representatives of the local political parties tended to influence theatre boards and decision-making frequently became politicised. As theatre professionals became more vocal, the strengthening of the overall position of theatre directors demanded that power and agency shift from the board to the artists themselves. It was an atmosphere rife with theatrical crises.[9] The new independent group theatres were in charge of themselves, but their financial footing was unstable. When compared to group theatres, the National Theatre finances were well-managed and the Theatre was spared from the overt and covert political crises plaguing urban theatres. The biggest challenge for the National Theatre was the fact that criticism about its ownership and economics spilled over into opinions on its artistic output and its public reputation.

The theatre field in the 1970s was influenced by the widespread left-wing leanings of the 1960s generation, theatrical education reforms, the foundation of new theatre groups led by the actors themselves, and regional activities inspired by the idea of equality in arts. The number of actors and theatre audiences grew, new playhouses were built, and theatre professions became diversified. The position of the stage director was emphasised. Generational fault lines were not set in stone and many issues tied different generations together. Theatres were places where different generations worked side-by-side, seeing things from their own respective viewpoints. People working in the Finnish theatre were unionised to a great extent. Research carried out in the 1970s shows that both the radical left and the conservative right saw theatre as an essential building block of a national identity, and these national identities as collective role models.[10] The gap between the young and the National Theatre was widened from both ends, and though it took a while to eradicate prejudices, there were plenty of points of intersection too.

The politicisation of belonging and the idea that political party ideologies should inform the arts started to receive considerable backlash in the 1980s. The focus was becoming more and more centred on the art itself, its content and its form, not its ideology. Similarly, prevailing performing arts methods shifted and a more physical dramatic education trumped an ideological one.[11]

Performance art and urban culture became increasingly serious forms of art. The National Theatre found easier to meet some of these new artistic priorities without compromising its own sense of tradition or its abstention from party politics. The reign of physical theatre in theatrical education was also easily absorbed into the National Theatre's own long-standing tradition of elevated artistic standards.

The National Theatre's institutional authority was based on its independent form of governance married with deep respect for traditionally held cultural conventions and mores. The criticism levied at the Theatre's forms of ownership and governance was almost a confirmation, not a denigration, of its unique status as a nationally important cultural institution. When it came to politics of cultural power the National Theatre had significant resources, but as times changed the relevance and legitimacy of its cultural capital shifted.

The National Theatre and its national operations

The Theatre Director of the National Theatre held all operative power, and the influential post of Director was secure for as long as he or she enjoyed the trust of their own board. This trust was based on the Theatre's financial position, the success of its productions, the Director's cultural and political views, and to some extent, a lack of alternatives. Despite its private ownership, the National Theatre was very much tied to the wider Finnish cultural scene and public opinion of theatres and their position in society. The Theatre had to both differentiate itself and fulfil public expectations.

Savola had a solid idea of what he thought good dramatic theatre was, but he preferred to express himself through dramatic activity rather than general pronouncements. Savola was a whole generation younger than his predecessor Kivimaa and his views about society and the theatre were in many ways representative of this new age. However, his activities did not undermine the Theatre's considerable cultural legacy or challenge the venerable board members who represented tradition. Based on writings of the time, Savola's ideological aims seemed to have stayed on a conceptual level, separate from the 1970s politics that were rapidly becoming dogmatic.

In the press, the new Director's debut was largely seen as promising. Helsinki was able to compete with cities like Tampere and Turku and their strong metropolitan theatres, especially now that the Helsinki City Theatre also boasted new leadership: Paavo Liski and Jouko Turkka's joint directorship started in 1975 and provided a viable counterbalance to the National Theatre's programming. Outside of Helsinki the TTT in Tampere, Oulu's City Theatre, and Tampere's Theatre were also enjoying a boost in audience numbers. The success of the Theatre in Oulu was precipitated by the completion of a new playhouse. Positively impacting Turku's City Theatre's reputation was the artistic direction taken by the new management: the season by Långbacka and Kalle Holmberg was fast becoming one of the success stories of Finnish theatrical history.[12]

In the 1970s the leaders of Turku and Helsinki City Theatres became known as especially strong stage directors. The National Theatre's forte, the strength of its programming, was not at the top of the list when it came to attributes the theatrical elite appreciated.

A closer analysis of those years shows that the National Theatre also received some praise, though none of it without qualification, and that its public image was slowly strengthened, solidifying the position of its leaders. During the 1980s the choice of plays put on at the Theatre was still the major expression of Savola's artistic direction. This was evidenced by his response to dramaturge Outi Nyytäjä's question about the National Theatre's aesthetic: he answered by outlining the Theatre's programming.[13]

The atmosphere in the Finnish repertoire theatres was slowly transforming by the end of the 1970s. A major turning point was the 1978 production of *Pete Q* [14] put on by young theatre students from the Finnish Theatre School. Directed by Arto af Hällström, the production was praised by the experienced theatre critic Maija Savutie from *Kansan Uutiset* saying that the young are now ready to explore 'people as themselves'. The production broke tradition with the social realism and Brechtian style favoured in contemporary theatrical circles, and the production sought to free itself from conventions and reigning boundaries.[15] The production was influenced by the methods of a renegade director who had shaken up the theatrical world of his day, Turkka, but this production was marked by its ambiguity, mysticism, cultural specificity, and the centrality of the artist.[16] Turning towards the human and looking at 'people as themselves' as Savutie described it, did not require a formal change of agenda from the Finnish National Theatre.

When Savola was awarded the honorific title of Professor in 1982, he spoke about his personal feelings about the preceding years as ones full of conflict. Savola felt that Finnish theatre was going through a process of change and fermentation where the old and the new struggled to find each other. Savola had seen the same thing happen before during his youth. 'I had invariably been part of the new generation at one time, but now it's our turn as the older ones to listen to the young, without forgetting what became before us'.[17] The statement bypassed the 1960s generation who did not ever achieve real political power at the Finnish National Theatre. Having said that, the more radical faction of the 1960s generation had also learned to compromise, and some of the faction's original aims had now become universally accepted.

By the 1990s the publicity around the National Theatre had evened out and negative prejudices were rarer by the start of the decade. The Theatre Director was seen out in public more and more, though Savola could hardly be named an active participant in the theatrical debates of the day. One major factor in the Theatre being more publicly accepted was the freer atmosphere of the contemporary theatrical scene and Finnish society as a whole.

Especially significant were the youthful new actors and the beginning of the National Theatre's collaboration with the Theatre Academy. The Theatre Academy had undergone its own turbulent years during the 1980s, but rather than the political, the controversy concerned Professor and stage director Turkka's methods. His radical physicality and the internal power struggles that swirled around his teaching methods caused a bit of a scandal. From the National Theatre's perspective a significant aspect was the concurrent development of dramaturgical training that placed writing in a more central role. Even physicality was more readily accepted than the 1970s left-wing politics at the National Theatre. The National Theatre managed to attract the stage director Arto af Hällström to take up a residency at the end of the 1980s, and change was also afoot in the decision to invite Turkka himself to the Theatre as a visiting director.[18]

The National Theatre's vision was increasingly characterised by its occupation of multiple stages. Until 1977 shows were staged on two stages whose characters barely differed. The Main Stage had to occasionally put aside scruples of great art in order to court audiences, something which the critics did not always approve of. The size of the Small Stage and its relationship with its audiences was commensurate with a good drama theatre. When the Willensauna stage was completed in 1976, it took some of the experimental pressure off the Small Stage by catering to smaller, specialist audiences, though no stage could ever be said to be completely outside experimentation. The completion of the smallest stage in 1987, the Omapohja studio, further expanded the potential for experimentation and was instrumental in finally turning the public attitude towards the Finnish National Theatre into a positive one.

Caught between East and West

Situated to the West of the Iron Curtain, caught between the two power blocs of East and West, Finland's cultural affinity with the West was evident in the country's theatre programming. During the latter decades of the Cold War, before the lines of Europe were re-drawn, being outside of alliances could evidently be useful. Programming was also the basis for the Finnish National Theatre's relations with the East.

However, East and West cannot always be clearly delineated as Katalin Miklossý states in her studies into the Soviet sphere of influence in the countries caught on the Eastern side of the Iron Curtain Miklossý termed 'an in-between space'. Even inside the U.S.S.R. the position of countries was unequal and countries like the Baltics had recent experiences of independence during the interbellum period. Political boundaries were unable to stop cultural collaboration and 'the in-between' countries also benefited from the meeting of different cultural, economic, and political forces.[19] Finland had its own special position as a place where Western, 'in-betweenness', and Eastern tides converged.

The Finnish position became more tangible when the Conference on Security and Cooperation in Europe was arranged in Helsinki in 1975. Alongside other European powers the summit was attended by the United States and Canada, and though the attending countries all had different aims, the leaders did eventually sign a joint treaty. It included an agreement on free movement and over the next decade it became a significant rationale for Eastern European countries demanding the unravelling of restrictions and democratisation. The National Theatre lived out its connection with Eastern Europe in the spirit of that agreement at a time when Finland's official party line was to stay clear of the internal affairs of other countries, especially those of the Soviet Union.

Theatrical visits to and from the National Theatre had taken on a more definitive shape, evincing a new era of international cooperation that broke with the past and differed from other contemporary theatres. Visiting directors were frequent and they were often from Eastern European countries. Soviet companies put on productions that had received international acclaim, Far East theatrical modes were frequently represented, and English theatre companies also visited on a regular basis. Connections to Estonia were activated in the mid-1980s and from then on continued regularly. There was a single visit from Stockholm City Theatre and a few German visits. The National Theatre's German-language connections seem to have especially focused on Austria. Even though the National Theatre also cast its net into Eastern Europe, its Eastern connections differed in their political nature to the bonds formed by left-wing theatre practitioners. And though ties with the Soviet Union were significant, visiting Soviet directors were often post-Stanislavskian innovators, people operating slightly outside the official tenets of what was considered Soviet art.[20]

Finnish theatre organisations actively participated in other international organisations and their activities, and the International Theatre Institute and the Nordisk Teaterunion (Nordic Theatre Union) who worked alongside professional unions formed an active link with other countries. During the directorship of Savola, the Theatre's management did not actively participate in the activities of these organisations, even though individual National Theatre staff members might have been represented through their professional unions. The National Theatre's international connections were "private" and founded on the contacts of its management, reinforcing the idea of the Theatre's distinctiveness. The National Theatre had always supplied teachers to the Finnish Theatre School, continuing when it became the Theatre Academy, but the societal and political agenda of that institution was pretty alien to that of the National Theatre and its practitioners on the whole.

Notes

1 Seppälä 2020, 187, 211–215. These unions had been originally founded in the first decades of the 1900s to serve the politically divided theatres in Finnish urban centres. However, during the 1930s when theatres in Finland started to become more consolidated and were often amalgamated across the political divide, city theatres tended to end up as members of both agencies. Regardless, Tampere's TTT was only a member of the TNL, and the Finnish National Theatre only belonged to the Suomen Teatteriliitto. Both unions functioned as theatre agencies and brokered playtexts. Alongside these two main agencies, there was the Suomen

Näytelmäkirjailijaliitto (Finnish Dramatists' Union) that distributed its members' works. The Swedish-language theatres had their own central agencies.
2 Rajala 2001, 214, 230.
3 Koski 2019, 36.
4 Koski 2019, 179.
5 The TTT received financial support from the Finnish state and the city of Tampere, but its management was in the hands of the Tampere Työväenyhdistys (Tampere Workers' Association).
6 Seppälä and Tanskanen 2010, 160; Koski 2019, 25: In 1926 new Finnish legislation regarding Finnish art and science institutions gave the Finnish National Theatre and the Finnish Opera the right to a license to organise lotteries. The right would be renewed every few years. The Ministry of Education would decide whether they warranted additional funding beyond the percentage of proceeds they were already allocated.
7 Koski 2019. Cf. Holdsworth 2010, 36. These changes can be seen as the building of a 'national theater network' as Holsworth states when using Finland as an example of a nationally decentralised national theatre system only if the entire Finnish theatre system is viewed as 'national'. However, in a way it is possible to do so, as most Finnish theatres had their roots in organisations representing different social classes. It is the case of 'national popular theatre' as defined by Loren Kruger within the system of city theatres in urban centres. However, in Finland, regional theatres were not considered national theatres.
8 Kallinen 2004, 12–34.
9 See also: Seppälä and Tanskanen 2010, 316–319.
10 Paavolainen 1992, 6–7; Kallinen 2004, 13; Suutela 2005, 203; Koski 2013, 432, 439–220; Seppälä and Tanskanen 2010, 370–379.
11 Ibid.
12 E.g. see. Maarit Tyrkkö, *Suomen kuvalehti*, 13/1975, 45.
13 Outi Nyytäjä, *Teatteri*, 5/1984, 4–5.
14 *Nuorallatanssijan kuolema eli miten Pete Q sai siivet* (*The Death of a Tight-rope Walker or How Pete Q Got his Wings*).
15 Maija Savutie, *Kansan Uutiset*, 13.7.1978.
16 Kyrö 1984, 48.
17 Board memo, Finnish National Theatre. 11.1.1984. Appendix.
18 The influence and position of Jouko Turkka was significant, and discussions about him directing emotional violence towards some of his actors did not surface until later. Another Turkka moment that has gone down in history is the moment when three internationally renowned researchers left a production directed by Turkka at an international congress as a protest against the show's misogynist portrayal of women.
19 Miklossý 2018, 32.
20 Kallinen 2001, 234, 244; Koski 2013, 512, 519.

3 Experiencing, conveying, and interpreting

Thanks to the Finnish National Theatre's protected position, people wanting to influence the Theatre and have a say in how it was run were mainly limited to using public appeals, and the press was also an important institution when it came to decoding and interpreting theatrical art. Finnish theatre critics were not shy when it came to asserting their territory in evaluating dramatic output. The importance of such things as characterisation, interpretation, and ideology fluctuated and shifted depending on the times or the theatre critic.

When observing people who regularly go to the theatre in Finland, Outi Lahtinen writes that even though the theatre critics were "the experts", among theatre audiences there were audience members who surpassed professional critics in their knowledge and ability. Lahtinen argues that the main distinction between an audience member and a critic is the fact that a critic must shape their experience into a public opinion.[1] Irmeli Niemi's conclusions from her early 1980s study on regional theatre showed no strong correlation between reviews and audience members; her study also showed that experienced audience members would often appreciate unconventional elements in performance *more* readily than theatre critics.[2]

Helen Freshwater writes about the diversity of audiences, the significance of experiencing performance together and alone, and the effect interpretative strategies have on theatrical reviews. As theatre is a social event, audience reactions can both impact the performance itself and the experience of other people in the audience.[3] However, for a historical researcher, newspaper clippings are often the only form of available primary source material to help us get back to the performance event. Despite their importance as historical source material, they are nonetheless individual pieces of recorded history. Nevertheless, first-hand accounts of productions lift the lid on audience experiences and demographics, and combining these texts with audience statistics unveils contemporary theatrical conventions and expectations.

DOI: 10.4324/9781003047667-4

The Finnish National Theatre and the Finnish press

In the 1970s conversations that centred on the ownership of theatres and their public funding were critical about the private ownership of the Theatre, but overall, the articles written about the Theatre covered a wide array of issues, with the vast majority being play reviews of specific productions. Despite the positive reviews, the overall view of the Theatre remained cautiously negative for a significant period of time and the press now and then even slipped into vitriol. In balance, most of the criticism was free from overt party politics of the time and the writers themselves were not consistently negative. The change in general attitudes was slow, and a realisation in the early 1980s that the Theatre's programming was actually as radical and forward-thinking as it was, surprised even the critics themselves. By the end of the decade, the National Theatre had become popular. The National Theatre changed, but it was also the critics themselves who softened their attitudes.[4]

Just like theatre audiences themselves, Finnish theatre critics were not a homogenous group of people; the majority was not dominated by a male and closed-off critical community unlike in some other countries.[5] Traditionally the Finnish press is diverse and powerful, and thanks to Finland's multi-party political system, both political and unaffiliated national newspapers were commonplace even up until the 1990s. In a similar way, all cultural departments at newspapers operated relatively independently and tended to function in a similar way to unaffiliated papers. Within this broader theatrical and critical field, op-eds aimed at the National Theatre were also written. Debates were undertaken on who had the right to make an artistic choice, what choices that should be made, and how these choices should be executed. In a small country institutional lines were inevitably breached from time to time: the critic who was meant to act as a type of "filter" for the Theatre's activity, can be found in another context on a production team or working high up in the institution itself.

Between 1974 and 1991 there were over 200 premieres at the National Theatre, and each one of them attracted at least eight to ten newspaper reviews. The main Helsinki newspapers of various affiliations and the biggest regional papers followed productions in an ongoing fashion, whereas smaller papers would be more sporadic in their analysis. The sheer abundance of print material and the longevity of certain theatre critics make newspaper reviews interesting source material, despite their obvious shortcomings. About half-way through the time period in question there was a big generational shift in the theatre critics at the top Finnish papers. This gives us the unique opportunity to see the critical material pertaining to the Finnish National Theatre as part of the generational politics of the time.

During the time period in question the papers with the biggest circulations were the politically unaffiliated *Helsingin Sanomat* and the right-leaning *Uusi Suomi* newspaper, their long-standing respective main critics Sole Uexküll and Katri Veltheim both retired during the 1970s. After their retirement *Helsingin Sanomat* had two permanent critics, Jukka Kajava and Kirsikka Siikala/Moring, and in the case of *Uusi Suomi*, the critics at the paper changed multiple times over a ten year period. The centre-left was represented by the *Suomen Sosialidemokraatti* paper (later *Demari*), but their experienced critic Aarne Laurila wrote less and less theatrical reviews. The paper did not have a head critic per say, but Hilkka Eklund who wrote for the paper was a full-time theatre critic who also freelanced for other publications from time to time. Experienced *Kansan Uutiset* critic Maija Savutie also retired during Savola's directorship. Catering to an extremist leftist position, *Tiedonantaja* only attracted a modest readership despite its national status. Among the regional papers National Theatre productions were covered most frequently in *Turun Sanomat* from Turku, *Aamulehti* from Tampere and *Etelä-Suomen Sanomat* from Lahti.

Theatrical opinions among experienced critics differed surprisingly little, and critics often cannot even be distinguished from one another using a political lens. The exception to the rule was the influential Olavi Veistäjä from Tampere's *Aamulehti* who worked there until the 1990s; his strong opinions belied not only his vast expertise, but also a consistent desire to resist the views held by what he saw as the new generation and the 'new left'.

Rather than be characterised by the political leanings of each paper, each individual critic is recognisable in certain personal preferences, "taste", and in some ways their own "party line". Rather than the paper's stance, the critics' opinions can be categorised by differences in age and their relationships with the theatrical world. When older critics retired, attitudes became more radical. The generational shift was reflective of a wider societal shift and the increasingly volatile public debates. This was especially true when it came to the two main publications, *Helsingin Sanomat* and *Uusi Suomi*, as well as *Sosialidemokraatti*. Heated debates were also common within the institution of criticism itself.

At the beginning of the 1980s, Veistäjä wrote a recurring causerie under his pseudonym Parras called *Parraksen pakinat* for *Aamulehti* which in itself was a prime example of the generational gap inside theatre criticism. In his causerie, Veistäjä set up the younger critics from *Helsingin Sanomat*, Kajava and Siikala (later Moring) against the experienced Veltheim from *Uusi Suomi*. He judged Siikala to be a stakeholder for group theatres and Kajava, who had recently been criticised by the left, as an independent agent. He felt that only Veltheim had the courage to actually say when the group theatres performed badly. Veistäjä felt that the National Theatre didn't get any mercy from the young: 'Whatever the National Theatre put on, and however it did it, nothing was ever good enough'.[6] In the context of the theatre criticism of his day, Veistäjä comes across as just as biased as the subjects he accuses of bias. The focus was on the way that criticism was written, rather than what was being reviewed, something that Maria Linko's reception study calls *productive reception*.[7]

When analysing Finnish theatre criticism and its diversity, Lahtinen draws parallels between Finland and New York and their distinct lack of heterogeneous critical voices, though her specific analysis draws on the 1990s post-recession press that was consolidated, owing to the recession.[8] Finnish historians working on the 1970s and 1980s have access to much more varied material.

Finnish theatrical culture tended to downplay the differences between an audience member and a theatre critic and the frequency of theatre-going proves that the theatres had many regular audience members. In a country where almost all theatres got public funding, the price of tickets did not exclude people from participating in theatre in the same way that it did in some other countries. Going to the theatre was not an elitist activity, and active theatre-goers could be found in different social groups.[9]

Owned by a group of theatrical arts associations, the aptly-named *Teatteri* (Theatre) magazine was a significant player: its diverse ownership guaranteed a heterogeneous editorial stance and its magazine format encouraged lengthy analysis and editorials. The articles brought different opinions to the fore. E.g. the magazine's Editor, Pekka Kyrö, used his editorials to task the country's critics to develop more expertise and knowledge, but he also wanted critics to increase their scope of movement. He did not encourage using reviews as a place to tease out theatrical politics. The review was meant to "open up" the play to the reader, not be a vehicle for communicating the critic's own views about theatre. The theatre critic was also not a servant of the theatre, and theatres themselves should not try to influence a critic at work.[10] According to the magazine, noted attempts by theatres to influence critics and reviews did crop up from time to time, and Director Savola was one of the named examples. 'Often they were known personages who you would think were above nitpicking' writes Hannu Harju.[11]

Writing in the *Teatteri* magazine in 1990, Hannu Harju looked back at the preceding decade in Finnish theatre and felt that the theatrical scene was changing: the years of rebellion were over and the young were 'increasingly becoming part of the masses'.[12] 'Before you were almost *obliged* to criticise the National Theatre. But now I think we can all set old prejudices aside. [- -] The National Theatre has become Finland's most versatile playhouse' wrote Seppo Roth from Tampere in Spring 1990.[13] The Director of Tampere's Theatre Rauli Lehtonen praised the National Theatre for its versatility and encouraged other theatres looking to court audiences to do the same.[14] Heikki Eteläpää from *Uusi Suomi* wrote in 1991 that the 'chorus of critics' had to their surprise found out that the National Theatre had become Finland's leading avant-garde theatre.[15] Popular repertoire theatre no longer posed a particular threat. By building different stages and performance spaces the National Theatre embraced versatility. As different forms of theatre became more widely accepted over the years, the Finnish National Theatre was able to benefit from this diversity.

The National Theatre and the general public

In order to commemorate 100 years of Finnish theatre in 1972, the Finnish National Theatre sought to find out who its audiences actually were. At the Finnish National Theatre only a quarter of audience members were men. The middle classes formed 68 percent of the audiences. There were no huge differences between generations and the regional makeup of the audience members represented the Theatre's national character, the vast majority of people came from Helsinki and its surrounding counties, but up to a quarter of people came from elsewhere.[16] Based on survey data the Finnish National Theatre was an artistic institution frequented by the middle classes, and a considerable proportion of its audience came from outside its city and its county.

Surveys into audience make-up and their experiences were not conducted after 1973, but the number of audience members and shows at different times and on various stages is well-documented in the Theatre's annual reports, and the national statistics for the country's professional theatres include the Finnish National Theatre.[17]

The results were commensurate with similar audience studies done across the country that concluded that the most faithful theatre-goers were educated middle-class women.[18] A similar audience survey conducted in the early 1990s also showed that education levels were a likely factor when it came to predicting audience interest. The academic theatre-goer was interested in a wide range of theatre, whereas someone with a more occupational educational background favoured domestic and "light entertainment" productions.[19] In practice, few audience surveys were conducted and what they can tell us about theatre history will inevitably be generalised. However, based on the records of audience hits and failures it is possible to deduce some general trends.

According to the records, the Finnish National Theatre attracted the second largest audiences in the country. The Helsinki City Theatre had surpassed the National Theatre in audience numbers as soon as their new building opened in 1968. Turku's City Theatre also saw a steep increase in audience numbers once their leadership changed in the early 1970s, but they did not reach the Finnish National Theatre levels.[20] The competition for audiences was played out among theatres of similar sizes. Most larger theatres had at least two different sized stages by the early 1970s, where the popularity of the bigger stage often dictated sales and the theatre's financial position.

The National Theatre's annual reports show that audience numbers were steadily climbing in the 1970s. From the end of the decade to the mid-1980s the annual audience numbers were over 300,000 a year. When compared with the population of Helsinki (about 484,000) and Finland overall (some 4.8 million), the numbers are especially significant. After a few difficult years, the Theatre went back to these higher audience numbers again in 1988 and 1989. In the early 1990s there was a big crash and audience numbers dropped down to lower than they had been in the early 1970s. The peaks correlated with the opening of the new stages and the extensive press coverage this entailed: first the Willensauna stage, then the Omapohja studio. The last dip in numbers can be explained by the rapid deterioration of the country's economic position and the tailing off of group bookings for the Main Stage caused by the recession. The importance of the Main Stage for the Theatre's finances becomes obvious when we consider that its audience capacity (1,083) alone was more than the Small Stage (311), Willensauna (154), and Omapohja (50–70) combined.

Experiencing, conveying, and interpreting 35

Figure 3.1 The Main Stage audience from the stage

The differences between the stages were significant. The Main Stage reflected the national average when it came to filling up seats. During its best years its seats were often over 80 percent full, which fell over the years and was as low as 61.2 percent in 1991. The Small Stage always filled its seats at over 80 percent occupancy and at its best the auditorium was over 90 percent full. At Willensauna, except for a few exceptions, the lowest threshold was 90 percent audience capacity, and in 1989 it even reached 97.5 percent. Over the years, the Omapohja studio was practically always sold out.

The Main Stage was more susceptible to economic changes than the other stages and its audience was more heterogeneous. From analysing audience numbers and reviews it can be concluded that critics and the general public seem to have placed value on slightly different things. To fill the auditorium of the Main Stage, the Theatre needed to also attract people outside the traditional theatre demographic highlighted by its surveys. The success of the other stages seems to have been more in sync with critical reception. "The people" as imagined by the National Theatre was made up of different groups and the assumptions about the Main Stage audience set it apart from the others.

People who went to the theatre also sometimes published their observations. Pentti Paavolainen had spent time studying the relationship between the Finnish National Theatre and its closest competitor, the Helsinki City Theatre, and he wrote in the *Teatteri* magazine in 1990 that the National Theatre was edging past its competition. It had a clear direction and young people and the middle-aged had their own distinct programming. Middle-aged programming at the Theatre was 'One of a kind and dignified - and sparky'. The Helsinki City Theatre was also a theatre for the middle-aged, but it tried to look younger and the effect was not achieved. Paavolainen said that even the young felt able to go to the Finnish National Theatre, and the Theatre itself had started to take on ex-radicals as visiting and resident directors as they matured into visionaries of the human condition. The National Theatre had always been canny about maximising the pull of its biggest stars and the actors themselves were getting younger.[21]

The National Theatre also had actively conservative audience members who insisted on continuity over relevance and wanted to see the values they saw as essentially national ones upheld. For example, the way in which stage director Jotaarkka Pennanen ended *King Lear* by bringing previously dead characters back on stage in civilian dress was met with approbation from one audience member who felt that the whole work was nullified, and some people felt that *In The Night of Gehenna* by Ilpo Tuomarila mocked the memory of the national poet and dramatist Aleksis Kivi.[22]

A more exact analysis of how the audience reacted to the National Theatre's interpretation of national theatre can only be unearthed by looking at individual productions and the reactions they elicited. The statistics already tell us that there was no coherent single national audience and that the Theatre's development and programming also reflected that fact.

Notes

1 Lahtinen 2012, 113–114.
2 Niemi 1983, 71–72.
3 Freshwater 2009, 6–9, 13, 15.
4 My own critical reviews from Kai Savola's time did not enter into the debates about the Finnish National Theatre's status. My reviews tended to be relatively neutral, a little academic in their tone when it came to exploring the plays' backgrounds, and in parts slightly moralistic (evident in comments about the production's relevance, or lack thereof).
5 Cf. Freshwater 2009, 34.
6 Parras [Olavi Veistäjä], *Aamulehti*, 12.1.1980.
7 Linko 1990, 20.
8 Lahtinen 2012, 114. Lahtinen is referring to Kalina Stefanova's analysis of theatre critics in New York and London.
9 Cf. Freshwater 2009, 35.
10 Pekka Kyrö, *Teatteri*, 9/1985, 4–6.
11 Hannu Harju, *Teatteri*, 5/1988, 26.
12 Hannu Harju, *Teatteri*, 5/1990, 2.
13 Seppo Roth, *Aamulehti*, 13.3.1990.
14 Rauli Lehtonen, *Aamulehti*, 17.3.1990.
15 Heikki Eteläpää, *Uusi Suomi*, 30.9.1991.
16 Audience survey of the National Theatre 1973. (Statistical profile of audience members of the National Theatre.) Handout, Finnish National Theatre Archives; 'Finland's largest audience survey conducted at the National Theatre.' *Ramppi*, 3/1973, 8–9. In March-April 1973, 9,400 questionnaires were distributed to audience

members and 7502 (80%) responses were received. Forms were not distributed in any children's or school productions, and for these age groups (13% of all viewers), audience data must be sought from other sources.
17 *Teatteritilastot*. Published by the Central Association of Finnish Theatre Organisations.
18 Compare e.g. Niemi and Lotti 1977.
19 Mäkelä-Eskola 2001, 30–31.
20 Compare. Maarit Tyrkkö, *Suomen Kuvalehti*, 13/1975, 43–45; *Teatteritilastot*. Published by the Central Association of Finnish Theatre Organisations.
21 Pentti Paavolainen, *Teatteri*, 7/1990, 6–7.
22 Koski 2019, 235.

4 The creators of artistic direction

The Finnish National Theatre's artistic team in the 1970s did not include many representatives from the baby boomer generation, or indeed any young actors. Even the new resident stage directors were born back in the 1920s or 1930s. When the artistic team went through a major demographic shift at the end of the next decade, becoming considerably younger, the newcomers represented the generation that came after the radical 1960s generation; the time for great social and political shifts was over.

In the beginning of the 1970s, professions and professional expectations in Finland's theatres underwent a shift, renegotiating their scope and responsibilities. Dramatic training diversified, the building of large playhouses changed professional expectations, and the new group theatres founded by young theatre professionals changed their ways of working and attitudes. Theatre professionals were moving in different directions and radicalisation caused tensions in the theatrical workplace.

The National Theatre did not want a strong left-wing community inside its institution. There was an atmosphere of mutual distrust between the politicised faction of the 1960s generation and the leadership at the National Theatre. However, the exalted position of the Theatre and the traditional respect accorded to its artists often weighed more than ideology. Among artists political prejudices were easily put aside. Over the next two decades the National Theatre and the surrounding theatrical world changed, and these changes brought about a softening of attitudes towards the Theatre. Its popularity was further increased by its international connections and the Theatre's policy of securing big name European stage directors to direct its productions.

The actors' theatre

The actors were the single biggest group of staff at the National Theatre, and they played a significant role when it came to wetting audience appetites. One of the Theatre's most acclaimed actors, Pentti Siimes, praised Theatre Director Kai Savola for his actor-led approach to artistic programming.[1] And though it seems that performers were largely hired in function of upcoming theatrical programming rather than the other way round, the two nevertheless functioned in harmony.

DOI: 10.4324/9781003047667-5

In Finnish theatres, artistic personnel, especially actors, were often attached to theatres on a relatively permanent basis until the recession of the 1990s. The contracts between theatres and actors usually lasted two years and in practice were often permanent.[2] Project-led contracts did not become prevalent until the 1990s. In the early 1970s, the National Theatre company had 42 actors, of whom 16 were women, and 26 were men.[3] Different age groups were pretty evenly represented throughout the company, though some roles did require a slight adjustment in age as even the youngest actors were approaching early middle age.

Until the 1960s the National Theatre had been at the top of the list of young actors' career aspirations, and when the Finnish Theatre School operated in the same building, the National Theatre attracted young graduates who had assisted in the Theatre's productions as part of their studies. Even during the turbulent cultural debates of the 1970s the professionalism of its actors was never under question. The actors were mostly older than the industry average, so the vast majority of the Theatre's actors had learned their trade using traditional acting conventions and the Stanislavskian method, further honing their craft by working with renowned directors. The dramaturge Outi Nyytäjä felt that a National Theatre actor mastered many different acting techniques, including comedy. The core group of actors at the Theatre had a strong reputation and tended to challenge stage directors, even those with lots of experience.[4]

Conversely, in the 1970s the ideal scenario after graduation for students of the Finnish Theatre School (soon-to-be the Theatre Academy) was to become attached to a group theatre, preferably one like the renowned and left-wing KOM Theatre. Left-wing ideology had started to take a stronger hold at the Finnish Theatre School from the end of the 1960s. The 2001 book *Näyttämötaiteilijasta teatterityöntekijäksi* (*From Stage Artist to Theatre Worker*) by Timo Kallinen describes this shift in ideology.[5] The National Theatre primarily saw its actors as artists and the Theatre's leadership was unenthusiastic about the politicisation of their craft. The Theatre's close relationship with the Finnish Theatre School (soon-to-be Theatre Academy) drifted as their ideologies moved further apart. However, the connection was never completely severed, and the Academy's teaching staff itself was diverse and always included actors from the National Theatre. In the 1980s young actors were being attached to the Finnish National Theatre in increasing numbers, and the average age of its acting cast dropped considerably.

Tampere University started its actor training programme in 1967, and theatres outside Helsinki exerted their own pull among its graduates. During the 1970s and 1980s attitudes towards traditional professional theatres started to shift and soften more generally, partly thanks to the successes of the *masters*[6] of the 1960s generation, such as Ralf Långbacka and Kalle Holmberg and their work at the Turku City Theatre. The theatre directors at the Helsinki City Theatre were also known as solid stage directors and Jouko Turkka who was hired there in 1975 was known as a significant reformer of Finnish theatre. Up until the beginning of the 1980s, a few younger actors did actually jump ship and transfer from the National Theatre to the Helsinki City Theatre.

With actors permanently attached to the National Theatre, programming choices did not provide equal opportunities for men and women. In 1980 the discrepancy between male and female roles became so large that challenging roles for women were only to be found in a few plays.[7] The unequal distribution of roles between men and women was not a problem unique to the Finnish National Theatre, even though things came to head there at the end of the 1970s. According to the 1980 survey conducted by the *Teatteri* magazine, only a few women actors in Finland felt that their career progress had *not* been hampered by their gender. Directors often had conservative views and male unemployment was seen as more tragic than female unemployment. The magazine made a list of the gender imbalance at premieres during two separate two-week periods and ended up with a ratio of 218:153 in favour of the men, meaning that women had 30 percent less roles. In this cataloguing the National Theatre did not come off well, during the weeks in question the ratio at its plays was as high as 16:5 in favour of the men.[8]

The situation was not always that unequal and it shifted with the times. Savola stated that the available roles for male actors simply reflected the gender ratio of the scripts where roles were about two-thirds male.[9] In the Finnish context this seems surprising as many notable Finnish playwrights were women and their plays had challenging roles for female actors. The distinction accepted the unequal distribution of roles between the sexes. It is also worth considering whether the hiring of actors and programming created a type of vicious cycle of gender inequality, and how that cycle could possibly have been disrupted.

Productions consisted of both small and large parts, and there were not always enough great roles to go around. The National Theatre always had spare small-part actors, and a lot of actors who were permanently attached to the Theatre would gradually go without larger roles over the years. In the early 1980s the Theatre changed the principles for permanent actor residencies and hired many experienced actors from up and down the country, and only a few of the newcomers were consistently given leading parts over the coming years. These actors had once belonged to the dramatic elite of their own theatres, but were often sidelined at the Finnish National Theatre with small parts. As Nyytäjä writes, the circumstances created an internal power struggle.[10] Some of the actors ended up leaving the National Theatre and returning to their previous theatres.

As well as their film roles, National Theatre actors had always attracted celebrity through the popular press. Many actors had public personas with considerable star power, often a combination of news coverage of their roles and their private lives. From the 1970s onwards television played an increasingly central role when it came to building an actor's public image. Among thespians, involvement in theatrical organisations and unions was also a route to fame. When it came to the actors at the National Theatre, a central tenet of their public image was usually their position at a prestigious cultural institution.

The 1970s and the 1980s were not particularly significant years in the Finnish film industry, but the National Theatre housed many stars from the industry's halcyon years, with perhaps Eeva-Kaarina Volanen and Leif Wager being the most notable cinematic stars. Other actors such as Jussi Jurkka, Siimes, Hannes Häyrinen, and the eccentric Tarmo Manni made a name for themselves acting in films when they were young. Wager who had moved to the National Theatre from the Swedish-language theatre Svenska Teatern was better known for his film roles than his exploits on stage. The institutions were valued in very different ways: the Finnish film industry was still seen as entertainment, whereas the Finnish National Theatre enjoyed status as a creator of high art.

Television changed the nature of fame and allowed people to harness their public image in an entirely new way. The Helsinki television channels already had their own permanent theatre companies, so for actors financial and celebrity opportunities in television were mainly limited to entertainment shows. Attitudes towards television could be divided into at least two camps. Actors such as Jurkka, Siimes, and Häyrinen who ventured into television had successful careers as stage actors and their on-stage reputations increased the success of their television appearances. When it came to the younger generation, their attachment to a theatre often went unnoticed and television acting was what they were publically known for, something which may have even slowed down their theatrical careers.[11] In all cases fame and celebrity were responsible for building a public persona that had little to do with the private person themselves, or even their role as a stage actor.

Before the 1980s, working in television did not come into the same league as acting in the theatre, and television had little impact on theatrical expression, though slowly the two mediums came closer to each other. When the younger generation took charge of television entertainment in the 1980s, even political television took on more carnivalistic and pluralist tendencies; at the same time the artistic expression and methods of television work finally impacted the stage.

In the early 1990s *Teatteri* magazine listed the 130 biggest names in Finnish theatre. The nature of Finnish fame and the wide networks enjoyed by actors were apparent by some of the choices: Siimes as 'the household name', Tapani Perttu who had transferred to the National Theatre from Tampere, Olli Ikonen who had made a name for himself in the Finnish Actor's Union, and Kyllikki Forssell who had taken charge of challenging parts was described as the 'restrained diva of the bourgeoisie'.[12] Even though the list did include some of the National Theatre's leading board members, its Theatre Director, and a few of its visiting stage directors, as a whole the National Theatre and its practitioners were not seen as big names in contemporary theatrical circles, creating an interesting tension with the Theatre's wider public image. The era of 'star theatres' was over and though the actors and performers of the National Theatre were still highly revered, the decision to hire new experienced actors such as Tiina Rinne, Heikki Nousiainen, and Ismo Kallio, who were invited to join the Theatre company was based on their theatrical successes, and not their impressive public images.

The artistic backgrounds of the productions

In the early 1970s Finnish stage directors still tended to have very different theatrical backgrounds. During the 1960s formal training in theatre directing was being developed at the Draamastudio at Tampere's University and at the Finnish Theatre School whose tertiary education unit was affiliated with Helsinki University for a time. In 1969 the Helsinki arm of stage director training was wholesale moved to the Finnish Theatre School, whereas the stage director training in Tampere was slowly phased out.[13] A new generation of Finnish stage directors were becoming ever more prominent and bolder, especially as the Finnish Theatre School grew and became Theatre Academy.

The changes to how stage directors were trained meant the creation of new ideological fault lines. The first generation of formally trained stage directors were largely influenced by the more radical factions of the 1960s generation. The headmaster of the Finnish Theatre School from 1968–1971, Holmberg, is inarguably one of the most influential theatre figures of the 1960s generation and one of the undisputed *masters* of Matti Virtanen's generational model. Gradually Holmberg played a vital role in creating an ideological faction that successfully bridged the political gap between generations.

However, the lack of a coherent culture of 'Finnish stage directing' was evident, though the social agendas of individual stage directors were often seen as the basis for their creative visions. Even though the education of stage directors in Finland was formalised rather late, Finnish stage directors had always followed theatrical trends and fashions, especially those on the Continent. The acting methods of Stanislavski were already known outside of the Soviet Union; his methods were particularly influential from the 1940s onwards. At the same time the popularity of Brecht was on the rise in both educational and cultural circles, thanks in part to the writings of and productions directed by Långbacka. Other big influences on the Finnish theatre of the time were visits made by British theatres and the Berliner Ensemble, Peter Brook's productions and work, as well as theatrical phenomena influenced by ideas from Artaud and Brecht. Turkka's distinctive combination of Stanislavski, Meyerhold, Tadashi Suzuki, Artaud, Grotowski, and his own idiosyncratic thinking impacted Finnish theatres, eventually bleeding into Finnish theatre education.

Many theatres up and down the country had recently expanded their operations and they required increasingly professionalised stage directors who could handle the demands of large theatrical stages. For a traditional institution like the Finnish National Theatre, this competitive atmosphere posed significant challenges. By the beginning of the 1970s the Theatre's two resident stage directors had been born at the turn of the century and were headed for retirement soon after the new Theatre Director joined in 1974. One of them, Edvin Laine (born in 1905), had had a long career in Finnish theatre, and would continue to visit the Theatre as a visiting director for the next decade or so. His audience-friendly approach was based on a realism that emphasised the

Finnish national story and represented the spirit of Finnish folk theatre. Alongside the Theatre Director, the renowned English-educated Jack Witikka (born in 1916) was both the Theatre's Associate Director and a leading stage director himself. As an aficionado of British culture, Witikka had made a solid reputation for himself over the preceding decades with his impressive international contacts, as well as his post-war productions of new drama that had excited the youth of Savola's generation.[14] However, the 1970s were not significant years in Witikka's artistic career, even though many of his productions were a success. Witikka left the National Theatre in 1980.

When choosing new stage directors to attach to the Theatre, Savola chose candidates from the generation sandwiched between the one that was moving towards retirement and the 1960s generation; in practice this meant stage directors that Savola knew and had previously worked with. Hired in the first year, 1974, Esko Elstelä (born in 1931) was also a Finnish translator, and though he worked at the National Theatre for almost two decades, the number of plays he directed steadily declined, whereas his translation work increased. In the autumn of 1977, he was joined by Eugen Terttula (born in 1926) whose focus was stage direction, though Terttula was also named Associate Director of the Theatre in the 1980s after Witikka's departure. Terttula had worked at Yleisradio (General Radio) and the experimental theatre company Intimiteatteri, as well as enjoying a ten-year stint in Tampere as a teacher, stage director, and Theatre Director. Before joining the National Theatre he had worked as the Associate Director of the Helsinki City Theatre and had also spent a few years as a freelance director. Terttula was known for his Brechtian plays and his epic depictions of the Finnish psyche marked him out as a generational amanuensis. After he died of cancer, in 1977, the Associate Director's post at the National Theatre was taken up by an actor.

The actors often made pointed reference to the fact that there seemed to be a dearth of permanent stage directors attached to the Theatre, and the situation was only slowly remedied over the years. The young Lasse Lindeman (born in 1951) hired as a stage director in 1983 moved on after two years to become a theatre educator and theatre manager at Tampere University, eventually going on to become a theatre director at many city theatres. Following Lindeman, the Oulu City Theatre Director Markus Packalén (born in 1946) was chosen as a stage director. He stayed on until 1994. In 1989 he was joined by Arto af Hällström (born in 1952) whose tenure at the Theatre was culturally and politically significant. Af Hällström was one of the key members of the youthful rebellion movement of the late 1970s who had agitated against the 1960s generation's staid and bureaucratic attitudes. He was also a stage director at Helsinki City Theatre during its 1977–1980 golden season and had gained particular note as a stage director and Artistic Director of Ryhmäteatteri from 1981 onwards. His reputation as a director who gave plenty of space to the actors he worked with made him ideal for the National Theatre and its strong artistic community of performers. His tenure at the Theatre also reflected and precipitated the birth of a considerably more youthful public image for the National Theatre.

The boundary between permanent and visiting stage directors was blurred by visiting directors being occasionally hired to direct more than one production. Lisbeth Landefort who had visited Tampere and its Työväen Teatteri (Tampere Workers' Theatre, TTT) TTT as a stage director during Savola's time there, directed a play at the Finnish National Theatre on an almost annual basis all the way up until 1984, a feat that only one other (permanent) director, Witikka, achieved at this time. Having come to Finland in the 1930s as an Austrian refugee, Landefort was renowned as an innovator in the field of radio plays, and her methodologies tended to greatly differ from accepted Finnish theatrical practices of the late 1970s. As Leena Kulovaara explained in *Teatteri* magazine: 'Landefort had a type of tireless individualism and unquestionable vision, a vitality paired with a curious lack of anxiety'.[15] The primacy of her art's message connected her with Savola since they both saw theatre as a vehicle for defending humanity, not about any specific social or political battles.

Hailing from the TTT theatre company in Tampere and directing two plays at the Finnish National Theatre, Vili Auvinen would have been given a permanent residency at the Theatre, but he did not want to leave Tampere. Stage directors such as Patrick Drake, Jotaarkka Pennanen, and Kurt Nuotio who had successful track records at Finland's other theatres began a whole series of engaging directorial visits to the National Theatre in the beginning of the 1980s that would span the entirety of Savola's era (especially Pennanen and Nuotio). They were all part of the 1960s generation, though none of them belonged to their generation's extreme left-wing faction and its group of core agitators. This was also true of Ritva Siikala who directed two classic texts for the Willensauna stage, but from the end of the 1980s Siikala shifted her focus to leading a group of female artists and performers known as Raivoisat Ruusut (Raging Roses). Directors such as Katariina Lahti, Olli Tola, and Heini Tola also visited the National Theatre as stage directors on multiple occasions. All of their careers had been built at other Finnish theatres; only Lahti worked her entire life as a freelance artist, save a one-year stint at Schauspiel Bonn.

The sheer number of visiting directors tells us that during the years 1982–1987, 25 separate stage directors were responsible for 44 different productions, with five of those directors coming from outside Finland. Most of the sensationalist productions were directed by visiting stage directors. Visiting stage directors were in marked contrast with the National Theatre's and the rest of the country's traditional set-up for artists where most working relationships were permanent. Pekka Kyrö calls the 1980s 'the era of women's awareness', highlighting the prominence of women stage directors in Finland at the time. Statistically, women were less represented in the National Theatre than men, and the names mentioned in Kyrö's writings were completely absent from the National Theatre.[16]

The lack of permanent directors at the National Theatre was an issue that the press picked up on numerous occasions and Nyytäjä in 1984 hailed it as being part of a wider problem: 'How have we found ourselves in a situation where the National Theatre as an institution seems to be avoiding strong writers, strong directors, maybe even new original performers?' She felt that the National Theatre and its actors were capable of rising to bigger challenges. Nyytäjä made specific references to personages like Holmberg and Turkka. 'The National Theatre could probably handle one genius'. She also made reference to the reputation of the Theatre's actors and the fact that they did not easily submit to direction and encouraged them to demand stronger directing a la Peter Stein. 'You people have enough courage and masochism to demand it', writes Nyytäjä.[17] Olavi Veistäjä from *Aamulehti* looked into Tampere Theatre's visiting directors over a ten-year period and came to roughly the same amount of visiting directors as the National Theatre.[18] The phenomenon of visiting stage directors was a general one, and was not unique to the National Theatre, though the National did tend to have a slightly higher proportion of international visitors.

A veteran actor of the Theatre, Häyrinen, expressed himself in his usual straightforward manner when he was asked to give his viewpoints on directors of his time in a newspaper interview in the early 1980s. He gratefully reminisced about the good old days and particularly praised Eino Salmelainen who had a long and successful career as a stage director. According to Häyrinen there were few left who possessed Salmelainen's talents: 'Some of the younger directors do have the special "it" quality, ones like this [Arto af] Hällström, [Kalle] Holmberg and [Kaisa] Korhonen, though of course they are all commies'.[19] In the same breath he may have voiced the real reason why the latter two were never seen at the National Theatre in the 1970s or during the politicised years that followed, despite actors frequently asking for them. Häyrinen's interview also outlines political tensions, but it betrays a short memory; he had glossed over the fact that liberal Salmelainen had also been labelled as left-wing in his time, though perhaps never quite as a 'commie'.

Alongside its directorial choices, the Finnish National Theatre also distinguished itself from the rest of the Finnish theatre scene in who it hired to its audiovisual team. The permanent artistic staff at the Theatre in the 1970s included two set designers, including Rolf Stegars who had started as the main set designer in 1954, and who eventually retired in 1979. Pekka Heiskanen had graduated from the Technical Arts College back in the 1950s and spent his whole career at the National Theatre. He solidified his reputation as an accomplished set designer of modern plays and an innovative reformer of stage and theatrical space.

Savola's hiring choices and decisions in these artistic departments told of a respect for the unique characters of each art form that was not tied to purely theatrical concepts; both permanently tenured scenographers and visiting artists had often learned their craft outside of the world of theatre. Anneli Qveflander who was hired by the Theatre as a costume and set designer was a graphic artist who had started working at theatres alongside her other artistic pursuits by visiting the National Opera in the 1960s. A few of the other visiting scenographers were also visual artists. For example, Oiva Toikka, a visual glass artist with a very distinctive style, designed the sets for many productions, and the set for the play *Mr Puntila and His Man Matti* was designed by Björn Landström who had previously done some very striking book illustrations. And though Heiskanen also had extensive artistic training, he could be distinguished from the others thanks to his focus on the collective artistic atmosphere of the theatrical community. After a small gap, the National Theatre once again had a permanent costume designer in 1978 with the hiring of Marjukka Larsson who had worked as a designer in the fashion and textile industry.

Even though the National Theatre did not favour musicals, music played an important part in many of its productions and the Theatre's permanent staff usually included a conductor who was in charge of background sounds and music. The choice of visiting conductors reflected Savola's knowledge of classical music. The Theatre welcomed many famous composers such as Ilkka Kuusisto, Aulis Sallinen, and Esa-Pekka Salonen who later rose to great international fame as a grand orchestral conductor. As with the visual artists, it was clear that all the different elements that went into a performance were appreciated as their own artistic category.

Especially significant was Terttu Savola's position as a new dramaturge from the year 1973 onwards. Kai and Terttu Savola collaborated extensively over the years, and Terttu's contribution to the building of the Theatre's programming is undeniable; the dramaturge was a central figure when it came to influencing the Theatre's artistic output.

Artistic forays over the border

The increase in the number of visiting directors from abroad helped to fulfil the Theatre's need for experienced stage directors. From 1976 onwards the National Theatre welcomed at least one foreign director a year. They often chose to stage a play that they had previously directed, usually a classic, often arriving with a clear picture of what they wanted the production to look like. On the whole, the visiting stage directors represented an internationally acclaimed standard of stage direction and many of them brought along their own set or costume designer, sometimes even a musician. This gave staff at the National Theatre an opportunity to experience European theatre in a more well-rounded way.

The staging of Aleksandr Ostrovsky's play *Enough Stupidity for Every Wise Man* in the autumn of 1978 signalled the end of a series of visits from veteran director Georgi Tovstonogov. The director described himself as a Stanislavskian practitioner. Tovstonogov felt that stage directors needed to be both talented and in possession of a strong will, both things that he himself possessed in bags according to the actors who worked with him.[20] The theatre critic Veistäjä described Tovstonogov's interpretation of Ostrovsky's play as an exuberant and larger-than-life adaptation of the play. Veistäjä argued that had the play gone to a Finnish contemporary stage director instead, the Finnish director would have no doubt 'bludgeoned it until it became old-fashioned, behind its times, covered in dust'.[21]

Savola's own artistic choices tended to favour the next generation of stage directors, but the National Theatre also welcomed some internationally acclaimed practitioners from older generations. Most of the visitors came from behind the Iron Curtain in the East, and as the 1990s loomed, many of them were labelled as dissident thinkers in their countries of origin. The National Theatre welcomed only a handful of visiting directors from the West.

During this time period, Hungarian László Marton was the National Theatre's first visiting international director. Marton's adaptations tended to make the most of theatrical metaphors that could also be read as social commentaries. He was eventually invited for three residencies in total; in 1976, 1977, and 1979. Radu Penciulescu visited twice, in 1977 and 1982; he was a Romanian director working in Sweden where he had built himself a remarkable career as a stage educator and an expert in theatrical methodologies. Both directors brought their own colleagues with them, including a set designer, a costume designer, and a choreographer.[22]

Czech Vojtěch Jasný who visited the National Theatre in 1980 was known for his cinematic interpretations and his screenwriting. He had won multiple awards in his home country before moving to the West after the 1968 occupation of Czechoslovakia. Jasný worked as a visiting stage director in Germany, France, Yugoslavia, and Israel. He had also worked as a professor and lecturer at Vienna's Film Academy and Salzburg's University. He also won accolades for his films at the film festivals of Cannes, San Sebastian, and Bologna.[23] Jasný directed Dostoevsky's *Idiot* adapted for the theatre by Tovstonogov, and young Finnish critics felt largely the same way about him than they had about Tovstonogov: they felt he was a renowned, but perhaps a slightly too traditional of a director. Out of all the Eastern European directors who visited the Theatre in the 1970s, only Jasný was known to have experienced direct political persecution back home.

During the 1980s it became increasingly clear that Savola's interest in Eastern Europe drama did not reflect Finland's cautious official policy towards Eastern politics at the time. The National Theatre's justification for these cross-cultural partnerships was mainly artistic. But as the visits became more frequent, and many Eastern European artists were increasingly openly or covertly critical of society, their critical attitudes made them increasingly unpopular with the cultural powers back home.

In 1983 Anatoli Efros, one of the most famous Soviet masters of his day, directed Anton Chekhov's *The Cherry Orchard*. Efros was a respected director in his home country; he was happy to respect traditions, but he also felt that blindly following them would lead to the creation of mere artistic copies. The Soviet Union's strict stipulations concerning art came to the fore when the National Theatre tried to take their acclaimed production of *The Cherry Orchard* to Moscow as part of a planned theatrical visit. However, this adaptation of *The Cherry Orchard* did not represent the prevailing Soviet conventions of what a classical interpretation *should* look like, and the Theatre was forced to choose another production to replace it.[24] The Director of Warsaw's National Theatre

48 *Finland's National Theatre 1974–1991*

Figure 4.1 Valeri Levental and Anatoli Efros with the *Cherry Orchard* ensemble, 1983
Photograph by Leena Klemelä

Adam Hanuszkiewicz directed *Cid* by Pierre Corneille in 1986 – a play rarely seen in Finland – and two years later he returned with a production of Woody Allen's play, *Play It Again, Sam*. Hanuszkiewicz was known in Finland thanks to the Warsaw National Theatre's previous visit to Finland and his other visiting directorships at Finland's other theatres.

A visiting British director was a rarity and Declan Donnell differed from the other visiting directors who tended to come from large, grand theatres as he was the Director of an experimental theatre company Cheek by Jowl which had its origins in the academic world.[25] His choice of Shakespeare's *Macbeth* in 1986 was expected because of his nationality, but the director brought his own stripped back interpretation to the play, placing special emphasis on diction. Donnell returned to direct again at the National Theatre again in1988.

As the 1980s came to a close, the pace of visits accelerated. After Efros, the next Soviet director was Lev Dodin in 1987. Dodin had spent a long time working at Leningrad's Malyi Theatre, working as its main stage director since 1983. In Finland he directed a Russian classic, *Bankruptcy*, by A. N. Ostrovsky.

At the turn of the decade two of the most sensationalised Soviet directors of the age visited the National Theatre. Yuri Lyubimov had become a problem for Soviet politicians. Finnish audiences recognised him from his visiting directorships at the Taganka Theatre and from his book *The Memoirs of a*

Figure 4.2 Declan Donnellan
Photograph by Johnny Korkman

Theatrical Man that had been translated into Finnish in 1987, but he had actually not *physically* worked in Finland before his visit to Finland in the autumn of 1991. After losing both his Soviet passport and his position as Theatrical Director at the Taganka Theatre in Moscow, Lyubimov had been living in

50   *Finland's National Theatre 1974–1991*

Israel, but now his nationality had been reinstated and he had even been able to return to the Taganka Theatre in 1989. He adapted his production of Dostoevsky's *Adolescent* specifically for the Finnish National Theatre. As a stage director he was demanding and impatient, but he achieved impressive results. In the autumn of 1992 Yuri Lyubimov returned to the National Theatre to direct his adaptation of a quartet of Ostrovsky's plays he called *Komeljanttarit (Comedians)*.

Robert Sturua was one of the last visiting directors invited to the National Theatre by Savola, but his production of *The Comedy of Errors* did not have its opening night until after the end of his directorship at the Theatre, in the spring of 1992. Sturua was a Georgian who wanted to represent Georgian, rather than Shakespearian traditions. Sturua also rejected stale realism and wanted theatre to look like theatre. He was an open practitioner of political theatre and a spiritual disciple of Brecht and Meyerhold.[26]

At the end of the 1980s, the National Theatre's connections to Estonia became stronger. Estonian director Mati Unt was working abroad for the first time when he directed Rein Saluri's play *Lähtö* in 1988 at the National Theatre. The play depicted the mass deportation of Estonians to Siberia during the early days of the Soviet occupation. Perestroika meant that even in Soviet-Estonia staging a play about the Soviet deportations was now possible, and that the play could even be sent to the West with an Estonian director. Like Unt, actor and director Mikk Mikiver directed another Estonian play for the Finnish stage, Jaan Kross's *Tohtori Karellin vaikea yö*. Mikkiver had first made friends with Finnish actors way back in 1965 during his first visit to Finland.

The reputation of *The Three Sisters* as imagined by Hungarian director Tamás Ascher secured him his position as the promising new theatrical star of the late 1980s. The production had been well-received all over Central Europe, and it had even reached the Finnish National Theatre during its tour. Ascher directed Ödön von Horváth's *Tales From the Vienna Woods* at the National Theatre in 1987. This was his first time directing a play outside Hungary, though later he went on to work all over the world. Ascher was fascinated by the theatrical potential of the absurd and the grotesque. In an interview with Olga Huotari he told her that he felt a special affinity with other directors who broke the mould, and that he was impressed by the work and philosophies of directors such as Brook, Giorgio Strehler, Tadeusz Kantor, Eugenio Barba, Jerzy Grotowski, and Stein — names that were also known and revered in Finland.[27]

Ascher came back to the Finnish National Theatre for the second time during Savola's era in 1989 when he directed Nikolai Erdman's play *The Suicide*. 'We appreciated Ascher's vision. He seemed to know what he was doing. It felt like he was creating theatre that was brought forth from Europe's brutal history', actor Markku Maalismaa reminisced.[28]

By the time he came to direct Arthur Schnitzler's play *The Vast Domain* at the National Theatre, in 1990, Otomar Krejča was already very well known throughout Europe, especially in German-speaking countries and France. In the 1960s Krejča was the most famous and renowned stage director in

Czechoslovakia, but his opinions got him into trouble at the start of the decade, and by the end of the 1960s, he was fired from his post. He was given a travel ban and was not allowed to leave the country, forcing him to cancel his foreign contracts and earn a living by driving a taxi. After the Germans exerted pressure on the government, Krejča was given permission to work abroad and he spent 14 years directing all over Europe. By the time of his visit to the National Theatre he had once again gained control of his old home theatre in Prague and had begun rehearsals for *The Cherry Orchard* there. Like many other visiting foreign directors, Krejča also brought his own set and costume designers to the Theatre. His collaborator, the French Guy-Claude François, was known as the set designer for the Théâtre du Soleil and costume designer Jan Skalicky's relationship with Krejča stretched all the way back to 1970s' Düsseldorf.[29]

When interviewing Krejča, Heikki Eteläpää compared him to Soviet stage director Yuri Lyubimov. When Krejča had re-gained access to his theatre at the end of the 1980s (it had been closed down in 1972), Krejča had dissolved all his theatre's overseas contracts, except his contract with the Finnish National Theatre. Krejča emphasised the fact that his home had always been in Prague. Back when he had accepted the managerial role in Düsseldorf, he had insisted on an official memo documenting his right to return to his home country, as many artists who had left the country had found it impossible to return. Eteläpää described Krejča's final production at his home theatre before it was closed in 1972: 'The last night of *The Seagull* in a theatre that had been closed will go down in the history books as a one-of-a-kind cultural funeral: after the show the applause went on for a full hour as the house and the actors openly cried together as one!'[30]

Most of the international directors invited to the National Theatre were globally renowned, but a few of them were still at the beginning of their international careers. The interviewer who interviewed Savola on his 60th birthday in the autumn of 1991 noted his apparent uncanny ability to spot international directors before their global breakthroughs.[31] Nevertheless, the cavalcade of visiting directors included many international stars, and in their case, it says a lot about the Finnish National Theatre's reputation that they agreed to come and direct a production there. Visiting foreign directors played a significant part in elevating the National Theatre's public image and were an interesting phenomenon for the contemporary cultural and political landscape. Many of the visiting stage directors came from Eastern Europe and were critical of the politics of their native countries. The renewed Finland-Estonia connection was responsible for reviving a sense of Finnish-Baltic tribalism that had reigned at the beginning of the century.

Notes

1 Koski 2013, 451.
2 Koski 2013, 520.
3 The number of permanent artists at Finnish theatres has decreased, but the difference between the sexes has evened out. At the end of the 2000s, the Theatre had 25 actors, of which 12 were women and 13 men.
4 Outi Nyytäjä, *Teatteri*, 1984:5, 7–9.

52 Finland's National Theatre 1974–1991

5 Koski 2013, 510–511; Kallinen 2004, 22–23.
6 Virtanen 2001, 353–355: In Virtanen's generational model in order for a faction to develop there are three groups: the *masters*, the *journeyman*, and the *apprentice*. Långbacka and Holmberg were significant theatrical influencers of the post-war generation.
7 See the Actor's Union's letter to the Finnish National Theatre's board, 8.10.1981 and Finnish National Theatre's board memo, 15.10.1981.
8 "Tilaa naisten luovuudelle", *Teatteri*, 1980:11–12, 12–13.
9 Savola's letter to Pirkko Koski, 30.5.2016.
10 Outi Nyytäjä, *Teatteri*, 1984:5, 7–9.
11 Out of the National Theatre actors Hannes Häyrinen had his own Hanski series and Seppo Laine was in his own series called *Sämpy*. Many actors such as Soila Komi were part of the show *Naapurilähiö*. Jussi Jurkka was known as the guy from Römppä and Siimes was widely known for his various popular television roles. Pertti Pasanen's television shows and films brought celebrity to actor Seppo Laine whose interviews filled the gossip magazines of the 1970s, only briefly mentioning his work at the National Theatre.
12 "Valta. 130 teatterivaikuttajaa". Teatteri, 1992:8, 20–21.
13 Kallinen 2001.
14 E.g. Eteläpää 1986, 204–205; for more detail, see Nevala 2018.
15 Leena Kulovaara, *Teatteri*, 1979:4, 7, 9.
16 Kyrö 1984, 50.
17 Outi Nyytäjä, *Teatteri*, 1984:5, 7–9.
18 Parras [Olavi Veistäjä], *Aamulehti*, 1.11.1986.
19 Katri Wanner, *Ilta-Sanomat*, 25.2.1981.
20 *Kansan Uutiset*, 9.5.1978; Katri Veltheim, *Uusi Suomi*, 9.5.1978 and 9.9.1978.
21 [Olavi Veistäjä], *Aamulehti*, 19.11.1979.
22 Koski 2019, 55.
23 https://en.wikipedia.org/wiki/Vojt%C4%9Bch_Jasn%C3%BD. Last visited 3.1.2016; *The Idiot* [programme] 1980, The Finnish National Theatre Archives.
24 Riitta Wikström, *Etelä-Suomen Sanomat*, 9.2.1992.
25 www.cheekbyjowl.com, 7.5.2017.
26 Liisa Byckling, *Teatteri*, 5/1989, 24.
27 Olga Huotari, *Suomi – Unkari*, 4/1987; Olga Huotari, *Teatteri*, 3/1988, 18–19.
28 Markku Maalismaa's email to Pirkko Koski, 3.1.2017.
29 *Arthur Schnitzler: The Vast Domain*, [programme 5–6], The Finnish National Theatre Archives.
30 Heikki Eteläpää, *Uusi Suomi*, 27.5.1990.
31 Mikael Kosk, *Hufvudstadsbladet*, 30.9.1991.

5 A national landmark renewed and replenished

Situated in Helsinki, the Finnish National Theatre is characterised by its centrally-located main building that was completed in 1902. The building itself is an architectural example of early Finnish national romanticism. As well as conveying a sense of heritage and prestige, the building physically dominates the city landscape, luxuriating in its prime position. In 1954 the Finnish National Theatre expanded its main building with a prime example of post-war modernist architecture: its new parkside extension. This new annex to the Theatre was known as the Small Stage building. As well as housing the new Small Stage performance space, the building complex also housed the Finnish Theatre School (later the Theatre Academy) and a restaurant that traded until the 1970s. Later, the National Theatre added two further performance spaces to its portfolio, the Willensauna stage and the Omapohja studio space. From an architectural point of view, both of these new stages blended in seamlessly with the existing space and the surrounding city. They did not permanently alter or change the Finnish National Theatre's architectural framework.

The building that houses the Finnish National Theatre emphasises the National Theatre's enduring cultural role during times of social change and upheaval. The Finnish National Theatre's continuity as a building intersects with Marvin Carlson's theories on how a theatrical building adapts even when the surrounding city changes and what happens to our relationship with a building as it intersects (referencing to Kevin Lynch's classification of space) with the mental 'image' of a city: with our daily learned routes known as *paths,* at 'relatively large areas with some common characteristics' termed *districts,* that is, places of note; at *nodes* that reside at the intersections of two or more paths; *edges* 'which act as barriers to paths and as boundaries to districts'; as well as *landmarks.* [1]

Loren Kruger highlights the importance of national theatre buildings in the context of late 19th century transnationalism and the production of the cultural industry, national theatres being part of a project of cultural legitimation. Legitimising a national theatre's position as the nation's premier theatre was wrapped up with its impressive building. Even though national theatres were forced to constantly compete with large scale cultural productions staged elsewhere, they were literally buoyed by the strength of their permanent theatrical homes. Kruger asks: 'when and why do arguments about the building or, more

DOI: 10.4324/9781003047667-6

broadly, in its naturalized form as the *national house*, take precedence – or not – over questions of language and cultural affiliation?'[2] Her questioning of the status of the building and its cultural affiliations are relevant to my study. Throughout its lifetime, the National Theatre was wedded to a building that formed the basis of its legitimate position as a national institution, but this spatial continuity also created tensions as performances and productions struggled to keep up with the times. In order to rise to these challenges, the Finnish National Theatre decided to transform its performance spaces. By emphasising national motifs in the Main Stage foyer and by creating newer and more experimental performance spaces in and around the Theatre's main building, the Finnish National Theatre used space to transform its own public image.

National Main Stage

The main building of the Finnish National Theatre, housing the Main Stage, was erected in a central location in Helsinki. Despite its centrality, it stood slightly apart from the traditional seat(s) of power (e.g. University, Church, government, municipal offices). However, the building was situated adjacent to the central railway station (the city's main transportation hub) whose architecturally significant main building was completed in 1910. Directly opposite the Theatre across the square stood another national cultural institution: the National Art Gallery, Ateneum. The plot now occupied by the National Theatre had originally been earmarked for another cultural institution: a historical museum. It seems clear from these developmental plans that the area had been designated as a zone for cultural buildings and institutions. Once the theatre building was completed in 1902, the Finnish Theatre occupied the space, eventually becoming known as the Finnish National Theatre without an official decree for the name-change. Luckily for the Theatre, Helsinki expanded considerably during the 20th century and the building that used to be slightly on the outskirts of the core city centre slowly "moved" to its nucleus. By the beginning of the 1970s, the National Theatre was situated at the centre of important business and social routes, a massive national landmark looming at the end of the square. The Theatre's national romantic façade stood for tradition and history, and an impressive stage tower highlighted the building's dramatic function. Fittingly, a statue of the national poet and dramatist Aleksis Kivi was erected in the foreground of the Theatre.

When it was first completed, the building housing the Main Stage represented a new type of theatrical building in Finland, creatively blending stylistic influences from abroad. The stair towers were modelled after urban theatres in Germany and the 1083-seat theatre auditorium comprising stalls and two galleries was influenced by both German and Austrian theatre design. Some unique features such as surplus areas to the side of the stage for things such as extra scenery and the routes inside the Theatre have helped ensure the Theatre's continued success as a performance space. The Theatre's facade designed by architect Onni Tarjanne did not follow the conventions of traditional

European theatre design. It differed from a more conventional style of architecture represented by Ateneum over the other side of the square, and it also differed from other Nordic theatres of the time. Timo Koho, a researcher who has delved into the architecture of the National Theatre in more detail has unearthed some striking similarities with American architecture of the 1870s and 1880s, especially Henry Robson Richardson and the new romantic style he adopted for urban public buildings.[3] The Main Stage presented both technical and aesthetic challenges for dramatic expression. In accordance with theatrical conventions of the early 1900s, audience members were split across a pit and two galleries, interfering with natural lines of sight. This posed a particular challenge for theatre practitioners and those in charge of artistic programming.

The National Theatre re-emphasised its nationalist mission on the inside: decorative elements with nationally important motifs were interspersed with more traditional classical scenes and figures. In fact, Finnish art was dotted throughout the building, though the foyer for the first gallery and the walking galleries were adorned à la Comedie Française.[4] Overall, the Theatre's interior incorporated a mixture of local and foreign designs, though the building itself has maintained a strong nationalist identity over the decades. Each era had its own vision when it came to the National Theatre's building and design. Some of the most radical changes to the building took place in the early 1960s when Kaija and Heikki Siren modernised the foyer and other audience areas, stripping back some of the colour and ornamentation in favour of a more abstract and "clean" style. The changes at the Finnish National Theatre were in sync with the onward march of Modernism in Finnish building and design at the time.[5]

The National Theatre's traditional building embodies the sediments of its history. But as a building, it could suitably impress the younger generations too, as dramaturg Outi Nyytäjä's 1984 description belies: 'I had almost forgotten what a powerful impression the National Theatre makes as simply a building, a space, an environment. The dark wooden surfaces, the old thespian red, countless aesthetic details, the curve of the balustrades, and the unusual windows'. Nyytäjä felt that the building was almost mysterious: 'As a child, it would have been a dream to play in. Even now it feels like there is a surprise waiting behind those doors'. The Theatre wrapped itself around you, enveloping you in a warm and safe blanket that weighed you down, making it challenging to connect with the outside (real) world once you were inside the Theatre.[6] This insularity was a challenge for the Theatre, as well as the fact that younger theatrical types did not necessarily even make it far enough in order to step through the Theatre's doors and feel the extraordinary pull and charisma of its building.

The theatrical conventions of the 1970s did not yet include ideas on how to adequately leverage historical layers and sediments in performance. In general, the aesthetics of the Main Stage were seen as a problem, not a potential. During the following decade when theatre practitioners finally started exploring the meaning of historical context and space in performance, these spatial experimentations were almost always done in the context of "discovered performance spaces" outside of traditional theatrical buildings.[7]

From modern architecture to spatial exploration

The modern building designed by Kaija and Heikki Siren that housed the Small Stage represented post-war architectural mores and its interpretation of theatrical space. The building's location at the edge of a park behind the National Theatre's main building never obtained a real significance in the city's landscape, despite the building itself being one of the gems of Finland's theatrical architecture. Directly in front of the Small Stage lies a park that was eventually graced with a water feature and a statue of Finnish national icon and actress, Ida Aalberg, to commemorate the National Theatre. However, the reality is that the area feels like somewhere you pass on your way to your final destination, rather than a place of contemplation or relaxation. According to Lynch's classification, the Small Stage was situated on the 'edge' which mirrored its position in the national hierarchy of tradition as well. It was the Main Stage that regulated the Theatre's public image, not the Small Stage. It was the Main Stage that reflected the attitudes and expectations wrapped up in the Theatre's status as "the" National Theatre. Conversely, the Small Stage did not embody Finnish national culture and its values, but rather limited itself to the specific values of post-war Finland. The Small Stage was built to foster artistic reform and training, to develop a more intimate form of expression, and to support the development of native Finnish drama. As Hanna Korsberg highlights, it also became the preferred place for staging international dramatic debuts.[8]

Figure 5.2 The Small Stage of the Finnish National Theatre

Though pre-war Finland already boasted numerous permanent and publicly funded theatres up and down the country, the building of new theatres had been slowed down by the economic depression of the 1930s. And during the national urgent post-war rebuilding project, other buildings had naturally taken precedence. The National Theatre's Small Stage was the first new theatrical building in Finland to be built in decades. It was not until the 1960s that a real theatrical building boom started up in Finland again. Koho, researcher of theatrical buildings, explains how Kaija and Heikki Siren's vision helped create a new type of Finnish theatrical architecture that incorporated post-war equality and ideas of social progress. On the Small Stage the auditorium was roughly the same breadth as the stage and the view to the stage was unimpeded all-over. The egalitarian principles of the architects framed the design of the Small Stage and those same principles found themselves into equivalent theatrical spaces springing up and down the country.[9]

However, though building the Small Stage fed into the increasingly popular concurrent stage model seen in professional theatres, its 311-seater capacity no longer really represented what would have been deemed an intimate or studio performance space in the 1970s. By then, the expectations placed on the theatres themselves had also changed. Simply modifying the National Theatre's existing performance space was not going to solve the Theatre's central artistic conundrum: it did not own a contemporary-style studio stage and it was also lacking in sufficient rehearsal space. To lend support to the Theatre's Director Kai Savola, Heikki and Kaija Siren were drafted in to help solve the Theatre's spatial challenges. The Sirens had moved on from their ideas of monumental construction and were now primarily interested in creating intimate spaces and how they could make these new spaces appeal to new types of audiences.[10] In 1976 the 151-seater Willensauna stage inside the Small Stage building was completed, and in 1987 the even smaller basement Omapohja studio space opened on a side alley backing onto the Theatre. When it came to battle to be the country's main stage and to win the hearts of Finnish audiences, these new stages were instrumental to the National Theatre's strategy. Building these new performance spaces was also a solution to the increasingly fragmented Theatre audiences that had been breaking up into ever more stratified segments during the past decade, leading to artistic challenges.[11]

The Willensauna stage was built into the Small Stage building in the space previously occupied by the restaurant Teatteri-Grilli (Theatre-Grill). The restaurant itself had been a type of performance space and in the mid-1960s it was referred to as a stage. The idea of the National Theatre having a studio performance space was not a novel one. Previously, National Theatre associate director Jack Witikka had presented plans for a new studio space. He had been influenced by other European theatre schools and small stages; Witikka modelled his ideas on the Royal Shakespeare Company's dramatic workshops and creative group work. The Theatre's board was not enamoured by Witikka's plan to make the studio space into a more permanent arrangement and the studio experimentation came to an end in 1968.[12] Similarly, the

National Theatre's new Director, Savola, had personal experiences of a studio performance space in Tampere at the Kellariteatteri (Basement Theatre) of the Työväen Teatteri (Tampere Workers' Theatre, TTT). Tampere's studio theatre space had been opened in 1965 with an audience capacity of 123 people and a front row that was completely level with the stage. The principles and goals for the TTT's Kellariteatteri were outlined in much the same way that the National Theatre's aims were: a need to experiment and dedicate more rehearsal time in order to deepen artistic expression.[13]

In the beginning there had been talks of creating a third stage somewhere inside the building, perhaps in the attic in the style of Stockholm's Dramaten's Målarsalen stage or somewhere else in the upper storeys of the building. At first, the Willensauna stage was not envisioned as a permanent third stage, but rather an additional auxiliary stage, possibly as a space for children's theatre.[14] The eventual decision to make the Willensauna stage a permanent fixture and the Theatre's third stage was influenced by the fact that the Finnish Theatre School had moved on, freeing up rehearsal space in the Small Stage building. In the end, other alternatives were not feasible, owing to technical or financial difficulties.[15]

The artistic programming for the Willensauna stage was integrated with the Theatre's wider artistic vision. The Willensauna stage did not represent the national romanticism embodied by the impressive public building of the Main

Figure 5.3 The Willensauna Stage of the National Theatre
Photograph by Johnny Korkman

Stage, but it was also not a disciple of the Modernism embodied by the Small Stage and its modernist building. By situating itself behind the frontispiece of an existing performance space, the new Willensauna stage brought a breath of fresh air to the theatre's public image: a sense of reform and experimentation that would match the spirit of the times. What Carlson calls the concept of 'the jewel in the casket' can be figuratively, even ironically, applied to this new performance space. Carlson uses the term to describe the concealed performance spaces that characterised the private theatricals of Renaissance courts.[16] In this context, Willensauna is a theatre within a theatre – an exceptional space that drew people in with its progressive programming, not because of its visibility in the cityscape.

Unlike previous one-off experimentations that had failed to shake off the Theatre's reputation for being a staid institution, the founding of the Willensauna stage finally disrupted the narrative that the Finnish National Theatre was rigid and unwilling to reform. The stage's name, Willensauna, was unveiled during its opening year. Through its name this third stage established its own link with history by inheriting the name of the hotel and spa that had stood on that very spot; the hotel itself had been popular with the movers and shakers of the time.[17] The relationship between the institution of the National Theatre and this new, small performance space was mutually beneficial. The former proved itself to be in tune with the times, the latter was able to benefit from the institutional structures of the Theatre as well as being exempt from having to build up its own independent public profile.

Willensauna productions quickly became a popular fixture in the Theatre's overall programme. To enable further dramatic experimentation, it was deemed that a new, even smaller performance space was needed. The fourth National Theatre stage was opened in a building adjacent to the Theatre. This new studio space placed the audience and actors in even closer contact. The Omapohja guest house that operated out of the same building gave the new studio performance space its name.

Depending on where you placed the audience, the performance space catered for between 50 and 80 audience members; the idea was that each production would rebuild the performance space for their run. Thus, staging decisions and decisions on where and how to house the audience were independently controlled and not wedded to the Theatre's overall schedule. Koho felt that Heikki Siren's architectural goals were specifically aimed at the young. The slightly "unofficial" feel of the space helped people cross its threshold with less prejudice making it into a more accessible space. The Omapohja studio fostered cultural experimentation and new social contacts. The foyer was small and during the intermission people would spill out onto the streets in the European fashion.[18]

For the National Theatre's Director, Savola, the goal of the new studio space was to be the 'fulcrum of artistic experimentation and the renewal of performance arts'.[19] The goal was to 'explore things and learn how to make theatre'; a production would be shown only to an audience if the work actually made it to that stage. The point of departure was Poor Theatre and the actor's performance was paramount.[20] The space was the fulfilment of the Theatre Director's wishes, but the National Theatre's Actors' Association also felt that the new studio space was highly justified. Competition between the National Theatre and the National Opera that had recently relocated into a new building and the Theatre's traditional adversary the Helsinki City Theatre was ramping up.[21]

Spatially, the Omapohja studio left no mark on the city around it. Even though the studio had its own position in the cityscape, using Lynch's classification the space was along a 'path', the main building was definitely a 'landmark', and operative ties to it were strong. However, the internal architecture of the Omapohja studio worked to underline its experimental nature and independence: the entrance hall was a mixed-use space used by the building's other occupants, the performance space and the foyers for actors and the audience were on other sides of the corridor, the performance space was reached by descending downwards, and the performances were done below street level. In the early days of Omapohja the studio space bore clear hallmarks of being a cellar.[22] Very soon it became apparent that opening nights at Omapohja attracted particular public attention and the envisioned scenario of exploring plays without ever putting them on did not come to pass. The Omapohja studio did not put on unfinished texts. As a performance space, the Omapohja studio had an even stronger sense of its own uniqueness than the Willensauna stage. The space prioritised actors' performances, over everything else, stripping back all other features.

Figure 5.4 The Omapohja Stage of the National Theatre
Photograph by Mauri Helenius

A functioning family

The spatial experimentation at the Finnish National Theatre turned out to be very successful. The Theatre's various stages attracted audiences in inverse proportion to the size of their auditoriums, and the smaller stages were often sold out. At the end of the 1980s the Theatre started considering the possibility of investing in a new playhouse. The new playhouse was envisioned for the new millennium or then the centenary year of Finnish independence, 2017.[23] Before the eventual shelving and abandonment of the new playhouse project the idea went through numerous stages, but by the time the time to make the final decision came round, the economy had taken a downturn and the idea was swiftly buried. By the centenary year, the whole idea had been completely forgotten.

By the early 1990s the National Theatre had four different kinds of performance spaces, though the Theatre's architectural legacy in the city was effectively still composed of the Main Stage and Small Stage buildings. The Willensauna stage existed inside the theatrical landmark and the Omapohja studio space melted into the surrounding urban environment. When it came to the performances themselves, the Main Stage posed its own challenges – making it a challenging space for performers and marketers alike. The Main Stage audience was far away and the pit was low when considered from the stage. Quieter speech or hushed tones could only be conveyed when standing on a ramp. The intimacy of the Omapohja studio was freeing; every little sound and sigh was transferred to the audience, everything was visible, and actors were not required to stand diagonally. The Willensauna stage was wide and squat. The Small Stage was well-proportioned, its audience was raised to the ideal height and the acoustics were great.[24]

The stages of the National Theatre became hybrid spaces – they reacted to the constant changes around them and enabled a national institution to successfully stay abreast with a changing dramatic landscape. The National Theatre succeeded in winning over its critics by forging a new path for itself that relied on its traditional building. While the cultural capital tied up in the National Theatre's building guaranteed its position as a national treasure, it also freed the Theatre to look at its programming from a dramatic perspective; and paradoxically freed it from having to promote an overtly nationalist programming agenda.

Notes

1 Carlson 1989, 7, 10–12.
2 Kruger 2008, 46–47.
3 Koho 2003, 27–32.
4 Koho 2003, 32–40.
5 Schulman 2003, 132–133.
6 Nyytäjä, *Teatteri*, 5/1984, 7.
7 Koski 2013, 526, 534. Notable productions included performances in buildings that were being torn down, a rope factory, and the ballroom of an artist residence.
8 Korsberg 2014, 32, 37.
9 Koho 1991, 15, 17.

10 Koho 1991, 16–17.
11 Heiskanen and Nevala 2006, 3.
12 Nevala 2018, 171–185.
13 Lehtinen 2006, 15, 24.
14 This topic was covered more widely in *Helsingin Sanomat*, 29.4.1976 and *Uusi Suomi*, 29.4.1976.
15 The memo and appendix from the Finnish National Theatre's board meeting, 27.8.1979. At first the Finnish Theatre School operated out of an old school building and other temporary building arrangements until it received its own permanent building in the 1990s.
16 Carlson 1989, 38.
17 The splintering of history is evident in the fact that Willensauna (Wilhelmsbad) was featured in a KOM theatre company comedy in the spring of 2019 that told the story of the rehearsals for Finland's first professional theatre production of Kivi's *Lea* in 1869.
18 Koho 1991, 48.
19 Kirsikka Moring, *Helsingin Sanomat*, 6.9.1987.
20 Arja Piispa, *Suomen kuvalehti*, 4/1987, 26–29.
21 A letter from the Finnish National Theatre's Actors' Union to the board's artistic leadership, 29.4.1986, Finnish National Theatre Archives.
22 Simopekka Virkkula, *Aamulehti*, 6.9.1987.
23 Press reports in the popular papers, 31.8.1984.
24 Markku Maalismaa's email to Pirkko Koski, 3.1.2017.

Section II
Programming, performances, and the national agenda

6 The national mission driving the National Theatre's programming

The Finnish National Theatre's policy had always consisted of putting on both classic and contemporary drama by domestic and international playwrights. This cultural mandate is evident in the Theatre's artistic programme throughout its history. The traditional mandate did not actually specify genre or geography. Broadly speaking, these same objectives were ones that other mainstream Finnish theatres also shared, so in order to differentiate itself and justify its 'national' status, it was essential that the National Theatre kept re-emphasising its policy. As the Theatre's leadership changed in 1974, the superstructure of the programming remained the same, but especially when it came to contemporary drama, there was a wide scope to play with.

It was really through its programming that the Finnish National Theatre was able to legitimate its national status. The programming choices made by the National Theatre were in dialogue with wider theatrical traditions and methodologies and the changes happening in theatre and wider society at the time.[1] A "national" theatre programme was also open to influences that transcended national borders. This was evidenced by both the geographic diversity of the plays selected for production and the international connections of the Finnish plays themselves. Over the two decades in question the form and the content of the Finnish National Theatre's dramatic choices varied greatly.

Chasing diversity and artistic merit

'A repertoire "find" is a concept associated with Kai Savola. The secret behind Savola's ability to consistently find dramatic gems stems from the fact that Savola's tastes are so different to the average Joe's. He appreciates details that at first others tend to ignore, but those same details end up being essential to everyone' the *Teatteri* magazine opined in the mid-1970s.[2]

In the inaugural speech of his directorship at the Finnish National Theatre Savola described the Theatre as a 'forum for human connections' whose power predicated mutual respect in an age where rudeness and tactlessness had crept in, leading to an insidious complacency even when faced with blatant cruelty. Over the next few years he highlighted the importance of free thinking and accountability, as well as the ability of classics to unlock the secrets of the

DOI: 10.4324/9781003047667-8

human condition. The opening of the new Willensauna stage inspired Savola to talk about the importance of artistic exploration, experimentation, and the ability to tolerate failure. Savola also emphasised the need to protect culture and the creative freedom of the artist. When the general atmosphere in Finland in the late 1970s started to suffer, owing to economic hardships caused by the oil crisis and the population exodus to Sweden, Savola questioned whether spiritual malnourishment had pushed the Finns to leave their homes and travel abroad.[3] The rest of the country tended to question the economic reasons behind the exodus. For Savola, the Finnish National Theatre programming was more about believing in people rather than solving the pressing political problems of the day.

A commentator in the *Teatteri* magazine in the mid-1970s was sceptical about how Savola's previously attention-grabbing repertoire choices from his time in Tampere would fare in Helsinki. Despite these misgivings, the National Theatre's programme was actually largely commensurate with Savola's vision from his time at Tampere's Työväen Teatteri (Tampere Workers' Theatre, TTT). The continuity was especially evident in Savola's avoidance of direct politics (despite politics being a hallmark of contemporary drama at the time) and Savola's successful popularisation of previously unknown or new plays. Both theatres enjoyed a unique national standing, as the TTT in Tampere was the most important representative of the historically significant Finnish workers' theatre movement. Both theatres had to tease out their relationship to the Finnish nation. When it came to the National Theatre, the relationship was defined by a cultural elite, whereas the TTT's political background inevitably shifted its concept of the nation towards the man on the street. Despite this historic distinction, these definitions actually made very little difference to the theatres' aesthetic or ideological dramatic choices. By the 1970s the TTT's political label had become largely historical and was consigned to the early 1900s. However, in the context of the Finnish National Theatre and its heritage, choosing Savola to be its Theatre Director did signal a shift in its national programming.

By favouring premieres of new domestic and international dramas alongside previously unknown or rarely staged plays from known dramatists, the Finnish National Theatre aimed to diversify audience tastes. However, many of the new plays were essentially one-off productions that left no lasting impact Finnish theatres' repertoires. The National Theatre's theatrical programming did not make it a forerunner of the dramatic world.

During the time period under analysis, the world fundamentally changed in Finland, in Europe, and across the entire globe. The Second World War had already passed into "history", but wars were still close and the Cold War borders were real enough. Economic vagaries and political tensions had an impact on contemporary art and culture. The need to understand this new world (order) is illustrated by the ideology behind the Theatre's programming. The National Theatre preferred to stage a diverse range of productions that depicted events and scenarios from around the world with a human, rather than a political, emphasis.

Overall, Finnish repertoire theatres had received a lot of backlash in the late 1960s, owing largely to the fact that theatres were 'obliged to include all sorts of productions in their repertoire', as Pentti Paavolainen described the emerging theatrical landscape. The radicalised factions of the theatre field wanted to act in accordance with their convictions, whereas traditional theatres also performed comedies and other more ideologically ambiguous works.[4] Despite having diverse repertoires and interesting conceptual themes behind their productions, the diversity and artistic merit of Finnish repertoire theatres were often ignored and pushed aside with resounding accusations of a 'smörgåsbord' approach to theatre programming. As critical opinions became entrenched in the 1970s, this attitude towards repertoire theatres became 'the norm'.

The National Theatre's lack of an easily discernible political agenda elicited criticism, especially in the late 1970s when the radical faction of the 1960s generation held sway in public discourse. As the new decade loomed, the National Theatre's diverse programming choices received more widespread approval. And though international premieres still featured, alongside texts from famous playwrights, more and more of the plays were dramatic classics, part of the theatrical canon.

The Finnish National Theatre's repertoire offered 'an endlessly rich selection of a wide range of plays', as Panu Rajala stated in his *Teatteri* magazine roundup in 1980. Still, he did pick up on a few distinctive themes: the staging of Russian dramatic classics with a new twist, the favouring of texts by nonconformists, the dramatic exploration of personal problems, and the distinct scarcity of Finnish plays.[5] The list of nonconformist drama included two Shakespeare plays *Measure for Measure* and *King John* that were rare in Finland, as well as plays from Czechoslovakia, Austria, and Hungary. This dissident angle was not one that many critics picked up on, probably because the programming choices did not immediately convey a desire to explore contemporary social realities on stage.

In a newspaper interview in 1985 Savola himself opined that television filled the need for domestic entertainment programming. He felt that the Theatre had staged most of the new Finnish drama that came out and had always championed folk theatre. Farcical folk theatre and musicals had traditionally been a gateway for people to enter into the world of drama. Classics had to be re-staged for every generation, and though the playwright and the text should be respected, drama should also adapt to contemporary realities. Classical Greek and Roman drama should also be staged, but at longer intervals. Savola said that he avoided theatrical politics and its 'rigidity, classifications, labels, and cheap theorising'. A point of comparison was Central European theatre: all genres were available as a dramatic possibility, but you always had to insist on quality.[6]

The National Theatre's Director had a stable artistic vision and mission, but public opinions about the Theatre did not become largely positive until the beginning of the 1980s. According to dramaturge Outi Nyytäjä in *Teatteri* magazine's analysis of the National Theatre's 1983–1984 season, the programming was ethically sound. 'And even though I would concur that the Theatre does not attack its subjects particularly radically, I appreciate its silent bravery', writes Nyytäjä.[7] Pekka Kyrö felt that the National Theatre had an unparalleled position and its own unique agenda. The Theatre was a sophisticated conduit of drama from around the world and it had earned its reputation as a champion of international drama.[8] In the spring of 1985 the new critic from *Kansan Uutiset*, Anneli Kanto, felt that new domestic drama and international masterpieces justified the Theatre's status as a national theatre.[9] In 1985 the *Teatteri* magazine reported on the state of Finnish theatres, and towards the end Juha-Pekka Hotinen explained how the National Theatre differed from other theatres at the time in a surprising way: 'The National Theatre upheld a clear artistic vision throughout our study: resisting petty bourgeois prejudices and fighting against narrow-mindedness and bigotry'.[10] The National Theatre's repertoire was praised for its ethics, its artistic merits, its international flavour, its inclusion of landmark texts, and now also for its championing of domestic Finnish drama.

The Finnish National Theatre's repertoire was eventually acknowledged for its quality in the last year of the 1980s. 'Smörgåsbord' and repertoire theatre were no longer banned or frowned upon. According to Hannu Harju in the autumn 1990 edition of *Teatteri* magazine, the Finnish National Theatre's current season's programming was one of the most interesting ones in the country. He felt that the Theatre had probably been working on shaking off its staid reputation a lot earlier, but that the subtle changes made to its programming had gone undetected by the general public and critics alike.[11]

Debates about the development of domestic Finnish drama

Discussions about the ratio of Finnish domestic drama being staged in Finnish theatres was a discussion that kept resurfacing in the public arena, but only part of that criticism was levied at the Finnish National Theatre. However, championing Finnish drama was seen as intrinsically part of the National Theatre's policy. In a committee report on the topic in the early 1970s a central tenet for the Theatre was the 'preservation of Finnish dramatic arts and the development of the Finnish language'.[12]

Throughout the 1970s about half of all the shows put on at professional Finnish theatres were Finnish plays; ten years on, the proportion was still at 43 percent.[13] At the National Theatre, new Finnish drama took up a smaller-than-average proportion of programming, and things were only improving slowly. It was evidently challenging to meet the expectations heaped on the National Theatre. A relatively small corpus of Finnish dramatic classics were already being staged up and down the country, and the National's rival theatre's, Helsinki City Theatre's, management were known for championing and directing new Finnish drama.

The lack of native Finnish drama was a topic that generated intense debates in the press from time to time. In the autumn of 1975 the debate had been started by the writers themselves and it became particularly heated. In the early

1970s financial negotiations between Finnish playwrights and the theatres had broken down and the theatres were threatened with a playwright-induced shutdown. Because of its lack of domestic dramatic programming and its unique national position, the National Theatre was a frontline respondent in the case.

According to a letter written by the Finnish Dramatists' Union (today Writers' Guild of Finland) and sent to the National Theatre, the Theatre ought to reserve about a half of its programming for Finnish drama in order to maintain its "national" status.[14] The criterion was the *number* of Finnish plays staged, not their national or thematic contents, and not even the playwrights themselves demanded a *majority* of Finnish drama. The Finnish National Theatre answered the letter through a press conference where it promised a 'spring of national domestic drama'.[15] The spring's national programming did not quite go ahead as planned, but the Theatre was not (solely) to blame for this.

The *Teatteri* magazine also weighed in on the issue in its main editorial. The magazine felt that national drama had now spread across Finland, and that the repertoires at Helsinki City Theatre and Turku City Theatre were also doing a good job of fulfilling the role of Finland's national stage. The article opined that the new Director at the National Theatre was wary of 'tradition becoming patriotism and patriotism becoming indistinguishable from smug nationalism'. The Theatre's Director and lead dramaturge saw Finnish drama as essential and necessary, but the magazine also demanded more concrete evidence of this interest.[16] The article juxtaposed the traditions of cultural nationalism with the modernity that had prevailed in the theatrical milieu of Savola's youth, and sided with the latter.

The sensation wrought by the Finnish Dramatists' Union spread out into a discussion on a TV chat shows, where the *Helsingin Sanomat* critic, Jukka Kajava, stated that 'writers were speaking about affronts to their sense of professional pride', but the defendant for the Finnish National Theatre had not come to discuss 'the dozens of plays offered up that would have caused more of a commotion if we actually chose to stage them. As a critic you can probably hazard a guess as to what they were like'. The reporter was on the Finnish National Theatre's side.[17] The discussion did not end the feud, but its moral stance was opened to wider discussion.

In the end, the Finnish National Theatre's cautious approach was vindicated by a study that took the whole of Finland into account and catalogued the all Finnish plays staged around the country's theatres, analysing the standard and quality of the on-stage drama. Though Finnish drama was witnessing a creatively fruitful period when it came to plays about people's everyday problems, "big Finnish dramas" were decidedly lacking, which was a challenge both for the Finnish National Theatre and Finnish playwrights.[18] The Finnish National Theatre had to stage plays that not only resonated with the viewer outside of localised topics, but also possessed dramatic ability. The fact that a lot of new Finnish drama was first shown on the Small Stage, and later the Willensauna stage, shows how hard it was to find interesting Finnish plays that would fill the

Main Stage auditorium. The Main Stage was the beacon for the Theatre's entire public image, and writers also made more money there. The challenges of staging new Finnish drama and Finnish drama in general were also linked to the Theatre's deficit of experienced stage directors. Traditionally, it was the stage directors who had played a key role in ensuring the success of Finnish national drama on-stage. But, the Theatre only had a small pool of regular stage directors, and for them to have any real impact on the staging of national Finnish drama they would have to be committed to the Theatre and its goals for the long-term. Once the number of permanent directors went down, this became increasingly challenging.

Even after the 1970s, the Finnish National Theatre's repertoire elicited public discussion and criticism, but the issue of staging Finnish drama was only periodically revisited in the press. When a new generation of dramatists took over the National Theatre's smaller stages in the early 1990s, the proportion of Finnish drama tipped over into one-third of all programming for the first time. During the era of this study, no notable Finnish plays were written that became part of the dramatic canon, but by the end of it there was a cohort of emerging Finnish playwrights who would go on to have a significant impact on Finnish drama.

Crossing the border between high and low art

'The traditional boundaries of high and low art are difficult to maintain when it comes to assessing popular and folk culture,' writes Simo Häyrynen; this statement also applied to the Finnish National Theatre and its activities.[19] Researchers of popular drama and theatre observed that many critically acclaimed plays positioned themselves surprisingly near the popular end of the scale and frequently leveraged popular features.[20] The Theatre and its audiences did not always see these boundaries in quite the same way. Traditional dividing lines did not always dovetail with the changing mores of what constituted good or successful theatre.

The requirement that the Finnish National Theatre focus on providing 'quality' programming and what exactly that entailed can be teased out by looking at the boundary between "high" and "low" art, even though the boundary itself is unstable. The former is most readily represented by texts that have an established position in the canon, whereas the latter is more reliant on contemporary (fluid) criteria. The Main Stage productions were visible representations of the Theatre's national character, and it was also on the Main Stage where programming conflicts and a need for hit shows were more acutely felt. On any given night of a production, the Theatre had almost a thousand audience tickets to sell in the main auditorium, which required the Theatre to reach a broad audience and made maintaining consistent artistic "quality" challenging.

Until the 1960s, in order for a play to be accepted as a significant piece of drama, it had usually undergone a literary or academic assessment, even when the piece itself was primarily known through performance, not as a text. Success on the stage and praise from theatre critics were no guarantees of dramatic recognition if the play went against societal norms or contemporary politics. Being staged at the Finnish National Theatre was another way to increase a play's prestige, but even then its connection to the *literary* canon remained paramount. The 1980s was a significant era when it came to theatrical research. Drama and performance studies became increasingly distinct from literary studies and contemporary theatre research emphasised staging by highlighting performance methodologies. The stature of popular art improved and reception studies underlined the status of the audience.

The Finnish National Theatre's policy and position were inextricably linked with how the dramatic canon in Finland developed. The Theatre's mandate to show both domestic and international dramatic classics guaranteed the showing of already established texts, but the National Theatre also had the power to renew the canon by highlighting texts it in turn found important. Frank Kermode highlights how literary and academic attention are central to a text remaining in the canon, but also that only adaptations of the text itself keep it alive from one generation to the next.[21] A solid literary reputation and pertinent academic studies can permanently solidify a playwright's standing, but it is the theatres themselves that determine how their plays live on in their dramatic form. A desire to renew and re-invigorate is not in conflict with establishing a canon as Robert Alter states. According to Alter, attempting to destabilise the canon might even help the canon maintain its hold on power as a source of collective memory. The canon is 'a dynamic transhistorical community and not a timeless inscription of fixed meanings'.[22] In theatres, canonical considerations span both programming choices as well as performance style; at least one of these needed to shake things up in order to maintain canonical authority and align the canon with contemporary demands.

Staging internationally significant dramas was one of the National Theatre's tenets: for the most part, this meant plays from the Western dramatic canon (including classic Russian drama). Throughout the 1970s, the Finnish National Theatre attempted to resolve the tension between tradition and innovation through changing a playwright's established image by staging their lesser-known texts, with varying degrees of success. Later on, the Theatre moved on to staging new interpretations and adaptations of some of the more well-known plays. This was especially the case when it came to staging modern classics.

This same mandate held true for Finnish dramatic classics. The small number of Finnish classics was an ongoing dramatic challenge. The Finnish dramatic canon had been built under the tutelage of the Finnish Theatre and the Finnish National Theatre. Dramatic works by Finland's national poet, Aleksis Kivi, were pivotal to the development of Finnish-language drama and literature in the latter half of the 19th century. Plays by Minna Canth represent the dramatic mood of the late 1800s when Henrik Ibsen was especially influential and new Russian ideas like Tolstoy's philosophy were gaining ground in the Nordics. Playwright Maria Jotuni represents the modernism of the 1910s. All three Finnish playwrights were accepted into the literary canon early on, and it was expected that the Finnish National Theatre would continue to stage their plays on a regular basis. During the 1970s the Finnish National Theatre attempted to enlarge the accepted view of the national dramatic canon by bringing plays to the stage that, although they might have been staged at the time of their publication, had since been neglected and had been primarily circulated in academic and literary historic circles. This project was not met with great enthusiasm. Most of Finnish drama inhabits a grey area where theatres decide on what gets staged and the audience decide on what is popular.

During the early days of Savola's role of Director of the Theatre, the most successful plays from an audience engagement point of view were plays that often inhabited the boundaries of folk drama. This type of folk drama did not need to be Finnish; rather, the aim was to cover a universally interesting topic and deliver 'good drama'. The definition of what constitutes folk drama is open to interpretation and largely dependent on the national context. At the Finnish National Theatre it was simultaneously defined by the people making decisions on the Theatre's programming, the critical press, and the general public. In Finland, a universally accepted form of Finnish folk drama with national characteristics had started to emerge.

Bertolt Brecht's *Notes on the Folk Play*, written in Finland in 1940, is a testament of the challenges of defining national, popular, and folk theatre, and how these definitions are always wrapped up in the culture of the time. Brecht contrasts crude and humble old folk drama with revue drama that is popular in larger cities. Brecht writes about the necessity of retiring 'old folk drama', but also that revue drama, though full of possibilities, has also failed to reach people. Brecht felt that 'we need a theatre that is simple but not primitive, poetic but not romantic, based on reality but not pandering to the political flavour of the month'. He wanted a dramatic style that was both artistic and natural where the art controls nature'.[23] Brecht's 'old folk drama' was probably a reference to a drafted play that Finnish playwright Hella Wuolijoki plucked from her desk that would eventually become the inspiration for *Mr Puntila and his Man Matti* that was written during the year he spent in Finland as a refugee.[24]

The type of 'old folk drama' outlined by Brecht was still staged in theatres around Finland, though seldom at professional theatres and not at the Finnish National Theatre. Wuolijoki's published plays represented a new type of Finnish folk drama that differed from the old folk drama, but Wuolijoki's work was *not* representative of the new folk drama model put forth by Brecht where 'art controls nature'. The position of Finnish folk drama is best described by the fact that plays were benchmarks and waymarkers for social constructs and morality, and by putting a community's repressed feelings and conflicts out there, they acted as a form of social catharsis.[25] These plays were also thought suitable for the Finnish National Theatre.

This folk drama is central to the Finnish dramatic tradition and relevant to the decades pertaining to this study. In the 1930s director Eino Salmelainen had defined Finnish folk theatre in a variety of contexts: he honed in on the audience and the desire to 'speak about things that are intimately a part of their world'.[26] This type of folk theatre predicated a dignified approach to the characters it portrayed, whereas the 'old folk drama' defined by Brecht primarily depicted comical and predictable national types and simple plot structures. According to Paavolainen, the folksy style of theatre championed by Salmelainen as the Theatre Director of Tampere's TTT Theatre had a big impact on the 1960s's definition of folk theatre. Salmelainen favoured depictions of Finnish history alongside plays about contemporary societal problems. Folk theatre was different to avant-garde with its own distinctive drive towards 'consensus, a hope for harmony and a better future'. It also differed from – borrowing from Pierre Bourdieu – the folk theatre as defined by intellectuals: a folk theatre that emphasised formal rebellion, counterculture, and the destabilisation of the values held by intellectuals.[27] Many of the plays staged on the Main Stage at the Finnish National Theatre that depicted Finnish history and Finnish characters from history represented this Finnish folk theatre tradition.

The fourth dramatist right at the heart of the Finnish dramatic canon, Hella Wuolijoki, had to wait a little longer for her position to be solidified. The trajectory of Wuolijoki's productions illustrate the importance of shifting social mores when it comes to a dramatic work being accepted as a national masterpiece. From the latter part of the 1930s onwards, Wuolijoki had been Finland's most popular playwright. However, Wuolijoki's public image, her left-wing dramatic dialogue, and the way that her female characters expressed independent thoughts that were in direct conflict with contemporary nationalist

Figure 6.1 Actors on the National Main Stage, *Kolmekymmentä hopearahaa*, 1982

feelings were all significant barriers to her being accepted to the dramatic canon. Wuolijoki's public activities became mixed up with how her plays were received, ultimately stalling the final acceptance of her work, including at the National Theatre.[28] The gatekeepers of the canon only accepted her as a major national playwright in the 1950s, once her political activities had ceased and she was not far from death.

The valuation of drama as either high art or entertainment could also lead to the rejection of plays previously thought of as classics. The Finnish National Theatre faced its most thorny programming challenges when it chose to stage farces and musicals. In many of those cases, even the international reputation or prestige of the playwright or the Theatre's investment in how the performance was staged did not always stem criticism. The 1970s had insisted on drama with a social or political message and entertainment drama continued to be assessed from this point of view. The message to the Finnish National Theatre was a moral one: the content of the plays was simply not serious enough. Despite the critics' dismissal and rejection of these genres, the plays themselves continued to attract large audiences, proving that professional theatre critics alone could not decide on what was suitable programming for the Finnish National Theatre.

As the 1990s approached, folk drama at the National Theatre's became more intellectual and theatrical as defined by Brecht. At the National Theatre, this shift culminated in the staging of Jouko Turkka's *Valheita* (*Lies*). The national image was still naturalistic, but the style was theatrical. Art controlled nature. From a methodology perspective, they were moving towards a Brechtian 'new folk theatre', but the social gestus was given little importance or left out completely.

Notes

1 Sauter places these in the conceptual and conventional context of a theatre performance. Cf. Sauter 2000, 9–10.
2 Leena Kulovaara, *Teatteri*, 2/1976, 4.
3 Press coverage of the opening of the Finnish National Theatre's seasons, press cuttings 1974–1977, Finnish National Theatre Archives.
4 Paavolainen 1992, 208.
5 Panu Rajala, *Teatteri*, 1980:5, 4–10.
6 Jyrki Vesikansa, *Uusi Suomi*, 20.4.1985.
7 Outi Nyytäjä, *Teatteri*, 5/1984, 7–9.
8 Kyrö 1984, 52.
9 Anneli Kanto, *Kansan Uutiset*, 7.5.1985.
10 Juha-Pekka Hotinen, *Teatteri*, 14–15/1985, 14–15.
11 Harju, Hannu, *Teatteri*, 7/1990, 14–16.
12 E.g. *Taide- ja teatteripoliittinen ohjelma*, 1975, 12.
13 *Theatre Statistics*, Finnish Theatre Information Centre.
14 Finnish National Theatre Archives Archive. Finnish Dramatists' Union board meeting memos, 21.10.1975, 11.11.1975, 2.12.1975. Finnish Playwright Association Archives. The disagreement in more detail: Koski 2019, 61–64.
15 News across different papers, 8–9.11.1975, The Finnish National Theatre Archives
16 Leena Kulovaara, *Teatteri*, 18/1975, 3.
17 Jukka Kajava, *Helsingin sanomat*, 14.12.1975.

18 Hilkka Vuori, *Me naiset*, 8/1976, 58–59.
19 Häyrynen 2015, 52.
20 E.g. Mayer 1977, 265–267 and Goodlad 1971, 178, 189–192.
21 According to E. Dean Kolbas, Kolbas 2001, 33.
22 Alter 2000, 18–20.
23 Brecht 1967, 142–143.
24 During his years as a refugee Brecht lived in Finland for a year and Brecht and his entourage spent the summer of 1940 living in Hella Wuolijoki's villa. Wuolijoki had also written an invitation to Brecht back when his position in Sweden had started to feel precarious. Finland had signed a truce peace treaty with the Soviet Union, and the war started up again once Brecht and company had left the country.
25 Cf. Goodlad 1971, 189–192; Mayer 1977, 265–267.
26 Salmelainen 1957, 108.
27 Paavolainen 1992, 210.
28 Wilmer and Koski 2006, 79–81. For more on the political assessment, see e.g. Koski 1992, 98–107. Wuolijoki's reputation was at its lowest in the mid-1940s when she was accused of treason after she met a Soviet spy and was sentenced to several years in prison.

7 Highs and lows in the context of the domestic repertoire

The Finnish National Theatre traditionally played a significant role when it came to providing a space for domestic national drama to be developed and staged. The 1970s were an exploratory time for the Theatre where it searched for its own angle on national dramatic classics, and the dramatic successes of the next decade were enabled by the advent of a new generation of stage directors and an increasingly flexible approach to performing classics. The Finnish National Theatre has always been a home for Finnish folk theatre, even though the role of folk theatre was often down-played. The new theatrical leadership openly welcomed the folk theatre genre and championed folk formats that resonated with contemporary society and the national mood.

In order to differentiate itself from other Finnish theatres the Finnish National Theatre invested in exacting performance standards and championed unique programming choices. Plays passed the "national" test more readily on the Main Stage compared to the National Theatre's other smaller stages, but at the same time the size of the Main Stage auditorium brought its own challenges when it came to attracting and engaging a large audience. The Main Stage frequently staged drama that looked at national populations, national characters and grand national themes. Dramas about relationships were often staged on the Small Stage.

The challenges of updating traditional classics

A series of classic Finnish dramas started with a dramatisation of Maria Jotuni's novella *Arkielämää* (*Ordinary Life*) as the 1976 autumn season's Main Stage opening production. The premise was promising: Jotuni's plays were canonical dramatic classics, she was a very renowned writer, *Arkielämää* was on the syllabus at a lot of schools, and one of the dramatists, Professor Irmeli Niemi, was known for her work as a Jotuni scholar. The adapted text co-created with dramaturg Terttu Savola was a warm depiction of a village community 'where everyone knew their place and everyone was an individual, respected as a person'.[1]

The descriptions of the production bring to mind another Finnish National Theatre performance from the previous spring: a visiting British production of Dylan Thomas's *Under Milkwood*. Set designer Pekka Heiskanen had situated

DOI: 10.4324/9781003047667-9

the *Arkielämää* village community on a round stage, and the music for the production was produced by one of the top Finnish composers, Ilkka Kuusisto. Performing Jotuni was a singular and welcome challenge for actors thanks to its distinctive language. The layered and sensitive performances and the way in which the possibility of pain peaked through from underneath the lighter touches differentiated Jotuni's work from traditional folk drama.

The production's hesitant atmosphere was beguiling, though it did not please everybody. Critics from different generations had different expectations, which is very evident and noticeable in the production's critical reception. The headlines of some of the reviews illustrate the two extreme ends of the scale. 'Everyday is Sunday in a Savonian Arcadia' writes experienced theatre critic Katri Veltheim, whereas younger critic Kirsikka Siikala goes with the scathing 'Everyday life without the everyday and without the life'.[2] The play was a mediocre hit with audiences.

Two years later Arvid Järnefelt's play *Kanneviskaali Samuel Kröll* (*Samuel Kröll Prosecutor*) was plucked from Finnish history, depicting the legal battles of an attorney hunting down corrupt officials. The production's aim was to draw parallels with contemporary politics. Despite brave directing from stage director Eugen Terttula the connection was flimsy and the production came across as an interesting historical curio. The awakening of the play's protagonist Samuel Kröll to Tolstoy's teachings reflected the playwright's own interest in Tolstoy's philosophy at the end of the 1800s. Kauko Helovirta did an impressive job of enacting this journey but contemporary parallels remained very surface-level. However, contemporary views underlined the very things that both Järnefelt and Tolstoy resisted in their philosophy, instead of forgiveness the play was seen to emphasise wrongdoing and bitterness. Contemporary ideals and the ideals of the play did not correlate.[3]

Kasimir Leino had been an important public figure in the Finnish dramatic circles of the early 1900s. His play *Lehtolapsi* (Lovechild) was resurrected and staged two years later at the National Theatre in the spring of 1980. Like Järnefelt's play this production was also destined to remain a curio. There were high hopes that the production's depiction of the Finnish nation would appeal to the general public which was evident in the Theatre's choice of stage director: Vili Auvinen, a permanent director at the Tampere's Työväen Teatteri (Tampere Workers' Theatre, TTT), was chosen as the visiting director for this production. Sadly, the stylised and controlled dramatic art of the *Lehtolapsi* production was not enough to make up for the play's dated story of a cigarette factory clerk who seduces a mother, whose daughter is in turn seduced by the clerk's successor.

These plays plucked from Finnish theatre history painted a picture of the Finnish nation that seemed distant and literary, especially when compared with productions of Finnish drama at other Finnish theatres in the 1970s. A stark point of comparison were the radical and politically charged productions directed by Jouko Turkka at the neighbouring Helsinki City Theatre. Theatre critic Aarne Laurila was constructive and described the elements of the *Lehtolapsi* production that had worked on stage, but even he questioned whether the production could really be justified other than by a desire to plumb the depths of Finnish national literature for real and timeless human emotions.[4] The plays did not resonate with their audiences and they were quickly forgotten, just like they had been when they were first written. After these experiences, the Finnish dramas staged on the Main Stage tended to either be popular dramatic classics or folk dramas.

The first classic Finnish play that had continuously belonged to the Finnish National Theatre's standard repertoire over the years entered the stage in the autumn of 1978 when Minna Canth's *Papin perhe* (*The Vicar's Family*) was staged on the Small Stage by visiting director and Finnish drama expert, Matti Aro. The play unpacks the family conflicts in a conservative pastor's home against a backdrop of mounting 19th-century Finnish nationalism and religious conservatism. As society changed around it, the text had retained its relevance. The play's themes were evidently still relevant in 1970s Finland, and the production was a hit with audiences, but its radical message was submerged underneath a cultural reading of the play. The problems depicted in the play were still considered fresh, but they stayed on a conceptual level and did not interact with people's contemporary realities and everyday lives. The main advocates for this National Theatre production were likely to be found among people who understood the pastor's conservative worldviews. The production's aim at cultural restoration is also evident in the fact that the production's style was found to be useful for school audiences and students of theatre history.

When it came to classic drama from women playwrights, the 1980s meant a shift towards the contradictory characters sketched by playwright Jotuni, without forgetting the Main Stage requirements and the conventionality expected of performances that were still largely aimed at the general public. Jotuni's plays represent a satirical take on society and the family unit. When looking for international playwrights for comparison, Jotuni is more like August Strindberg than Henrik Ibsen. In Jotuni's plays the action is driven by women whose power is centred on their courageous ability to recognise their own situation and its limiting boundaries. As a repertoire choice, choosing Jotuni's plays was not a particularly subservice choice as over the decades Jotuni had attained the position of an established playwright and her plays were frequently staged in theatres up and down the country – more often than not for artistic rather than social or political reasons.

In the autumn of 1980 the Main Stage production of *Kultainen vasikka* (*The Golden Calf*) tells the story of a mother who throws herself with abandon into the rampant stock exchange speculation happening at the tail end of the First World War. The play had first premiered at the Finnish National Theatre in the autumn of 1918 when post-civil war Finland was also going through a period of want and speculation. The critical reception back then had been contradictory, though the production was praised and it fared pretty well with audiences, some critics were affronted by the play's overall depiction of human character.[5] This time round the production of the play was a success thanks to both the text and the way in which the production had been directed in order to appeal to audiences. Stage director Laine's artistic vision returned the play back to its original historical context, and rejected rather than embraced drawing contemporary parallels, but the text's incisive analysis of society and self-serving people could not be easily erased. Jotuni was a formidable challenge for an actor thanks to the nature of her language and its irony, and all three generations of women actors excelled in their performances. The production was firmly on "national theatre level", though it was unlikely that it would have universally struck a chord with critics who were on the lookout for fresh approaches to drama. As it happens, the spectrum of critical reception for this production is muted because the opening night coincided with a press strike, leaving many critics unable to attend the show.

Jotuni's comedy *Tohvelisankarin rouva* (*The Hen-Pecked Husband's Wife*) staged in the autumn of 1985 was directed by new resident National Theatre stage director Markus Packalén. This was one of Jotuni's most biting satires. The play tells the story of a forest magnate who has been fired from his position while his family are yearning for financial freedom. The "death" of a wealthy brother gives the family false hope of a more carefree future and they celebrate their imminent inheritance in bacchanalian style by dancing around the coffin of the said rich dead uncle. The celebrations are cut short as the supposedly dead body of the uncle wakes up from a drunken stupor in his coffin. The play's first premiere at the Finnish National Theatre in 1924 had caused a sensation that went all the way to the Finnish parliament. Then, the production had also been praised, but in its contemporary context the play's blatant eroticism and its lines about death challenged critics' conceptions of good taste. The public scandal caused by the production interfered with its initial success and sidetracked the play until the 1960s, when it finally returned to the Finnish National Theatre to great success.[6] The 1980s production underlined the play's grotesque elements but in a controlled way as to avoid resistance. The production was staged – just in case? – on the Small Stage.

Tohvelisankarin rouva has an exceptionally multifaceted female protagonist. Actor Tea Ista who established her reputation during the post-war years of new drama played the play's most central role, Juulia, the forest magnate's wife who married her henpecked husband during her 'last bloom of youth'. Ista's sketch of Juulia represented the hard pith of Jotuni's plays: her character saw and accepted the cruel facts of life, including the decay and dystrophy brought on by ageing, making her performance almost tragic. Ista's performance was openly abrasive and compelling. As an actor Ista was separating herself from the elegant style that had long characterised her range as an actor. At the same time, Ista's public image of a composed "national theatre actor" was transformed.

The choice of stage directors for Canth's and Jotuni's plays is a reflection of the way that dramatic classics were approached at the time. First, there was a need to ensure reliable quality, and slowly there was also an appetite for shocking the audience. As we enter the 1980s, the new generation of stage directors means that directors are getting younger and attitudes are becoming freer, though none of the Finnish National Theatre productions of Finnish

Figure 7.1 Tohvelisankarin rouva 1985. Tea Ista and Yrjö Järvinen
Photograph by Johnny Korkman

dramatic classics go down in theatre history as being particularly successful. None of the directors of classic texts were women, despite women dramatists being a prominent feature of Finnish drama.

During the timeframe of this study, it is especially notable and unusual for national poet's Aleksis Kivi's plays to be absent from the National Theatre stage in the 1970s. Kivi's comedy *Heath Cobblers* and dramatised versions of his novel *Seven Brothers* had always been central to the Finnish National Theatre tradition, with the former being last staged in 1965, the latter in 1962. The absence of works by Finland's national poet tells of a reluctance to compete with the most sensationalised stage directors of the time. In Turku City Theatre *Seven Brothers* directed by Kalle Holmberg premiered in 1972 and it had been consistently filling the auditorium since then. It earned a place among the most praised theatrical productions in Finnish theatre history and has repeatedly been shown on national television. At the Helsinki City Theatre *Heath Cobblers* was staged in 1975, sensationally directed by Turkka. In 1984 Kivi's *Heath Cobblers* was finally staged at the Finnish National Theatre as part of Kivi's 150-year celebrations.

Heath Cobblers was written by Kivi in 1864. It was the first Finnish-language comedy ever written and the text has retained its freshness and its standing ever since. The play depicts the failed romantic quest of a man called Esko, who hails from a family of rural cobblers. In the play, Esko attempts to go a-wooing to a neighbouring village, only to find his intended bride is celebrating her wedding to somebody else. After getting into a fight Esko returns home empty-handed after getting drunk for the first time in his life. *Heath Cobblers* was performed at the Finnish Theatre for the first time in 1875, and after its premiere it was included in the Theatre's repertoire almost non-stop until the advent of the next century. Throughout the 1900s the play had been reimagined at the Finnish National Theatre at least once a decade, though the 1970s were skipped.

The production directed by Markus Packalén was the type of folk drama that was deemed suitable for the Finnish National Theatre's Main Stage. The play's raucous atmosphere was underlined by the musical numbers composed by conductor Atso Almila. Aulis Peltonen had choreographed the dance numbers for the production and was responsible for the production's movement. 'Karri's wedding is celebrated against a giant white sheet and the tavern at the halfway mark is ringing with the drunkenness of a thousand bottles', wrote Jukka Kajava in *Helsingin Sanomat*. Kajava felt that when the production 'went back to the original', such as in Esko's famous drunkenness scene, then the production really soared. Problems arose as soon as you stopped to wonder what it all meant.[7] In Laurila's words 'the play thins out: when it is spread wider on the outside it gets narrower on the inside'.[8]

Olavi Veistäjä from *Aamulehti* compared this production with Eino Salmelainen's 1950s attention-grabbing vision at the TTT in Tampere. He felt (justifiably) that the two productions were polar opposites of each other. Both productions attempted to see the classic in a new light, but from opposite angles. Delving into the characters' psychologies and underlining the destructive nature of alcohol in Salmelainen's version extinguished the comic elements of Kivi's drama, whereas Packalén's rustic fun completely sidelined the tragic subtexts of the comedy. The audience was alienated by the former, and critics saw the inadequacy of the latter.[9] This National Theatre production differed even more radically from Turkka's production at the Helsinki City Theatre and the way in which it exposed the brutal double standards of the Finnish national character.[10]

The role of Esko in *The Heath Cobblers* is the Hamlet of Finnish theatre. Seppo Pääkkönen's winning performance of Esko was based on the character's physical strength, his skills as an artisan, and his guileless way of interacting with the world around him. It was hard to reject the obvious appeal of the Finnish National Theatre's production of the play, but it seems to have been equally hard to accept the sidestepping of the deeper undertones of this Finnish classic.

Despite their topical themes these productions of dramatic classics did not excite much public debate or tend to draw parallels to the world around them. The National Theatre was fulfilling its most basic mandate and it tended to excise elements from these productions that might shock audience members. Social and political commentary had to be extracted from productions and performances purposefully embraced the lighter elements of these plays. But the shifting landscape can already be spotted in this production of *Heath Cobblers,* and the emphasis on the stage director's vision and the advent of a new

Figure 7.2 Nummisuutarit 1984, Seppo Pääkkönen as Esko. photograph Leena Klemelä.

generation at the Finnish National Theatre is further elucidated by the production Teuvo Pakkala's play *Kauppaneuvoksen härkä* (The Bull of the Commercial Council) that was part of a group of plays known as the 'small Finnish classics'.

Like many other writers of the early 1900s, writing drama was an interesting side gig for Pakkala. The appeal of dramatic writing was the ability to support a nationally significant Theatre without having to concern oneself with serious literary pretensions. Stage director Arto af Hällström took the *Kauppaneuvoksen härkä* script "as it was" and underlined his choice with a petty bourgeois set design in the naturalist style, refusing to cut any of this national comedy's heavy dialogue. He did however bring his customary "French" reactions to the play: irony and underlined overreactions. Naturalism was transformed into the theatrical.

Arto af Hällström was one of the main theatre influencers from the generation that followed the more radical 1960s generation; he brought the Finnish National Theatre fame as a champion of the younger generation. In his production of the play *Kauppaneuvoksen härkä* the limits of carnivalesque were pushed further than ever before, with the surprising result of making the text more recognisable as topical. The production's success was based on multi-layered *haunting*: the audience were familiar with the stage director and his style, and televised political satires of the time provided a familiar interpretative framework. In the early 1990s, *Kauppaneuvoksen härkä* was once again seen as topical and even the most critical commentators noted that this old play was still a forceful satire capable of finding its mark.

The same irreverent spirit was present in the 1991 production of Kivi's unfinished play *Selman juonet* (Selma is Plotting). The play's tone was set by stage director Markus Packalén and actor Heikki Nousiainen who had successfully delivered on a number of big roles. The play's unfinished ending had been brought into the production and made into a powerful feature. The set designed by Hannu Lindholm was 'a rough city look in an otherworldly bar' and Almila's 'over-the-top by a country mile music' was fun and detached. Critic Marketta Mattila felt the style was Western European and ironic.[11] Actors were able to be innovative with their performances. However, in *Selman juonet* there was one actor above all others. 'If all Finnish actors could act as well as Nousiainen, then theatres would be pretty lucky', wrote Kajava. 'His greedy and miserly performance of a character living on interest is classic comedy: full of vigour that is directed by skill and real thought'.[12]

The Finnish people on stage

In Finnish theatrical circles the boundaries between folk theatre and high art were slippery and audience preferences often differed from those of artistic taste-makers such as researchers and literary critics. A production that unexpectedly also exists on this Finnish dramatic boundary is the collaborative play *Puntilan isäntä ja hänen renkinsä Matti* (*Mr Puntila and his Man Matti*) by Bertolt Brecht and Hella Wuolijoki (Wuolijoki was born in Estonia but later became Finnish). This play indisputably is high art and belongs to the canon of major dramatic works. When the play was staged for the first time at the National Theatre in the autumn of 1975, the production emphasised the play's folksy features and underlined connections to the text's country of origin. This makes it possible to study the play in the context of depictions of the Finnish people. Looking at the Finnish National Theatre production it becomes impossible to determine why the National Theatre had previously rejected the play over its supposedly unflattering portrait of the Finnish people.

The Finnish National Theatre's Director Arvi Kivimaa had rejected the play back in 1950 in the format finished off by Brecht because some of its characterisations were deemed offensive to the members of the audience that the National Theatre respected. Wuolijoki had also shown Kivimaa an earlier version of the play in Finnish translation in the 1940s known as *Iso-Heikkilän isäntä ja hänen renkinsä Kalle* (*Mr Iso-Heikkilä and his Man Kalle*), and the Theatre board's literary department did not see a significant difference between the two texts. Both versions were rejected.[13] The fate of this text illustrates the Finnish National Theatre's ideological priorities and the ways in which they shifted. Wuolijoki was accused of treason and imprisoned in 1943, eventually being freed at the end of the war. At that time her plays disappeared from the Finnish theatre scene for several years. In Finland Wuolijoki was more political than Brecht, although the 1940s version of the text had been rejected in 1940s Finland on artistic, rather than political grounds. Salmelainen who had stage directed Wuolijoki plays in the 1930s writes in his autobiography that he was offered the chance to direct the play at the National Theatre during the directorship of Eino Kalima. He refused on the grounds that he felt that he could not make a success of the production, owing to the clear differences and unevenness in the text caused by its two authors. Wuolijoki would probably have not allowed the text to be freely edited and Brecht was already in America.[14] By the 1970s the play had entered public consciousness, often just under Brecht's name, and it was staged at multiple Finnish theatres.

The 1975 production of *Puntilan isäntä ja hänen renkinsä Matti* directed by actor Lars Svedberg filled the Small Stage auditorium for many years and for a grand total of 120 shows. The critics at the production's opening night inevitably placed the production in the context of its textual history and its relation to the Brecht canon. The critical reception was unanimously positive even though there were some minor qualifications: some people felt that the set and the directing of the actors were uneven. The show 'reached out into two directions at the same time' wrote Sole Uexküll from *Helsingin Sanomat*.[15] The production's style sat somewhere in-between the strict Brechtian attitude of German directors (such as Wolfgang Pinzka's production at Turku's City Theatre in 1965) and the realistic style of a folk drama (such as Salmelainen's *Iso-Heikkilän isäntä ja hänen renkinsä Kalle* from 1969).

In the Finnish National Theatre's production Brechtian concepts and the contextual elements relevant to a Finnish viewer did not entirely mesh together. On the one hand realism and the Tavastian identity of the play dominated the production, something that Sole Uexküll felt 'compromised the knifeblade of the play's ironic dialectic' as 'Brecht's Puntila has been firmly placed back in his home Tavastia'.[16] The new much-praised translation from Elvi Sinervo underlined the play's Tavastian nature by simplifying some of the German language. Artist Björn Landström's naive and fairy-tale-esque stage set brought out the jovial folksy side of the play's setting: the Finnish county of Tavastia. The scenes painted on canvas were stunningly accurate and differed greatly from a Brechtian staging style that was often poster-like and preferred to hint at spaces rather than describe them.

The production's most successful element can be found in the actors' performances. Puntila and Matti played by Kauko Helovirta and Esa Saario were clearly and consistently accepted as Tavastians. Drunken Puntila was a vibrant character full of vitality compared to the other side of his character, the sober and selfish landowner. Matti was analytical and economical with his gestures: a strong counterbalance to his exuberant master. Even the smallest parts of the play were played by experienced actors. Pentti Siimes as diplomat Silakka, Puntila's prospective son-in-law, was elegant rather than sardonic, and the women from the Kurkela village who Puntila had betrothed were played by experienced actors who usually played starring roles. The experienced actors on stage did not quite all fit into the same frame, even though their performances provided exquisite details. The audience did not seem to find this troubling. The play was set in "Tavastia", which despite its geographic context was

Figure 7.3 Mr Puntila and His Man Matti 1975. Kauko Helovirta with Maija Karhi, Marjukka Halttunen, Ansa Ikonen and Eeva-Kaarina Volanen
Photograph by Timo Palm

situated in the past, somewhere outside of the audience's actual frame of reference. The play was also alienated from any actual tensions between master and servant.

The Finnish National Theatre also brought back two Wuolijoki plays to its repertoire: *Justiina* and *Juurakon Hulda*. In the 1930s the Finnish National Theatre had been one of the only theatres in Finland to reject Wuolijoki's work, though it did stage her *Niskavuoren nuori emäntä* (*The Young Lady of Niskavuori*) in the autumn of 1940 (a play set in the 19th century amid burgeoning Finnish nationalism), and a socially elevated version of *Juurakon Hulda* called *The Parliament's Daughter* was staged at the end of the decade. The former was the ideal play for the peace-seeking nation that had just come out of the Winter War, and the latter could have been a gesture of goodwill towards a writer who now yielded political power during Finland's 'years of danger'. (The period of time between Finland losing the war against the Soviet Union and the signing of a final peace treaty). Wuolijoki's particular strengths as a playwright included characterisation and the liveliness of dialogue, and many of her plays had a strong social or political message. During the Kai Savola era the National Theatre staged the two plays from Wuolijoki's 1930s output that had working class protagonists, though it must be stated that these choices did not lead to especially working class-spirited productions.

The play *Justiina* was directed by Laine for the Small Stage in 1977. Laine knew Wuolijoki's work intimately and he was known for his folksy and patriotic takes on the labouring classes. The choice of stage director shows that the production was not an attempt at shocking the National Theatre's core audience segments. Terttu Savola's dramatisation of the text had excised a lot of its political declarations, and Laine's directing ensured that the final "red" colour of the play was drained away from the class-conscious lines spoken by the play's protagonist, as the actor Tiina Rinne who played the play's namesake puts it in her memoirs.[17] When the play was first published in 1938 it had prompted a public conversation about left-wing politics, and in later years it was to prove a popular play for workers' theatres. Now, all that commotion had died down. Understandably Wuolijoki seemed much tamer in the left-wing friendly atmosphere of the 1970s.

In the play the protagonist Justiina has given birth to a lovechild, a boy, and is now working as the housekeeper at Harmelius manor. The child's father Chief Justice Harmaalahti (the name has been changed from its original Swedish form into a Finnish version, as part of the Finnish-language nationalist movement) inherits the mansion and arrives to take control of his land with his frivolous wife. Justiina's social idealism rubs off on the Chief Justice who after a series of rapidly developing events abandons his wife and chooses a "real" life by Justiina's side. According to the National Theatre's pre-show publicity and the stage director, the play was about the love felt by two different kinds of women and the emotional maturing of a weak-willed man caught between them.[18] During rehearsals the exchanges between actor Rinne playing Justiina and stage director Laine became heated; Laine had excised the play's lines to reduce Justiina's characterisation to a portrait of a wronged woman. Rinne wrote in her memoirs about her displeasure at playing a "loser".[19] The awkwardness lasted a long time as the show transferred from the Small Stage to the Main Stage and altogether was staged a hundred times. The production was a success despite the cuts made by its director, or perhaps they formed part of its appeal.

A slightly earlier televised new generation version of the play ended with a shot of a class-conscious Justiina walking down the birch tree lane away from the mansion and out into society. The choice to end the story in that fashion might have been influenced by something Wuolijoki herself said in her memoirs: she had been inspired to write the play after seeing Eugene O'Neill play *Mourning Becomes Elektra* at Helsinki's Svenska Teatern. She could not accept the fact that the play's characters were unable to leave their destructive home.[20]

Especially for the younger critics, Laine's take was clearly behind the times. The text had not been updated to reflect contemporary reality. Wuolijoki's concept of the "Finnish people" had already been idealised and Laine was not able to, or was reluctant to, update the vision to be more in keeping with contemporary mores. (However, naturally, any television drama's "contemporary take" also presents an idealised view of the Finnish people, albeit from a different angle). The success of the National Theatre production seems to have been largely centred on the audience's hunger for romance: Justiina had been a victim, and the unfolding events were reparations that made up for the past. The play was not an artistic triumph, but it did elucidate a successful formula for producing popular theatre. The next Wuolijoki play *Juurakon Hulda* was produced directly for the Main Stage.

Juurakon Hulda was staged in the Autumn of 1986, directed and newly dramatised by experienced dramatist Terttula who was an expert in both epic theatre and Brecht. The old hit play's romantic undertones had been significantly cut and a fundamental shift was made from comedy towards serious drama. Even though the production did not test the boundaries of performance conventions, the Finnish National Theatre did try to actively avoid copying and repetition.

The play tells the story of a country girl who ends up as a maid in the urban establishment of a bachelor judge, Soratie. The maid studies for a Master's degree alongside her work and begins a political career on the moderate left. The play's original double helix plot – the story of a rural girl climbing up the social ladder and a love story – was eradicated in this production. Judge Soratie did not marry Hulda as in the original play, rather he continued on with his various conquests among his own social class. Hulda on the other hand chose her own path as an independent woman and a politician. Romance was relegated to the sidelines and the focus was on Hulda's development instead. Hulda played by Karin Pacius was a serious minded country girl.

There was no need to court success with a romantic ending, although it had always been part of the play's appeal. Back in the 1930s when the character of Hulda first debuted, she had quickly become a role model for women seeking social advancement and betterment. The multitude of letters from women who

Figure 7.4 Juurakon Hulda 1986. Jarno Hiilloskorpi, Karin Pacius and Simo Tamminen
Photograph by Leena Klemelä

Figure 7.5 Valheita 1990. Merja Larivaara, Yrjö Järvinen and Tero Jartti.
Photograph by Lena Klemelä

saw the play in the Wuolijoki archives tell of the play's encouraging example.[21] The story was still relevant, even though the Finnish National Theatre production did not always manage to contextualise the play's setting; and even when the contextual setting was right, the story did not quite manage to expand into a coherent universal message.

This Main Stage production of *Juurakon Hulda* was the last play Associate Theatre Director Terttula directed before his illness and death just over a year later. The production was a unanimous success, critics praised it and it was a hit with audiences. The national image in the play resonated and audiences kept coming back. When Terttula died, his absence was felt: his strong presence left a hole at the Finnish National Theatre and the stage director's role as a champion of the Theatre's artistic vision visibly narrowed for a few years.

Alongside individualist dramas, the Finnish National Theatre eventually also succeeded in its depictions of nationally important ideological movements. The tensions between people and the old elite were a contemporary preoccupation and when these issues were transferred to drama, success was guaranteed. To end the 1982 autumn season a production of Heikki Ylikangas's *Kolmekymmentä hopearahaa* (*Thirty Silver Coins*) was put on the Main Stage, becoming a smash hit of its time. Ylikangas was known as an opinionated and respected professor of history whose subjects of study were often chosen from the social history of the Ostrobothnian region. The play had been inspired by Ylikangas's research into Ostrobothnian pietism published as *Körttiläiset tuomiolla* (1979). For stage director Laine the central element of the play was its religiosity that was also "national" and favoured by popular movements. In a press interview Ylikangas admitted that play also had some genuine religion in it 'if that even exists', but he made questions of 'power, scheming, and jealousy towards a popular leader'[22] central to his production.

Kolmekymmentä hopearahaa depicts the religious debates between evangelical pietist priests in Ostrobothnia where the beliefs of two historical people are pitted against each other. The popular pietist Niiles Kustaa Malmberg is contrasted with Gustav von Essen and his connections with academia and the official Church. Malmberg's popularity with the common people is set against the official and upper-class Church. Even though Malmberg appears to lose the battle in the play for the sake of 'thirty silver coins', his ethical victory is clear. In the production Malmberg's triumph is underlined by him exiting the stage in the final scene to a crowd singing hymns. The picture the play painted of the nation and its religious landscape were easily recognisable, and many had a personal relationship to the events depicted.

This production of Ylikangas's play is a prime example of the contradiction inherent to evaluating drama: when analysing a play, critics of aesthetic and dramatic form use totally different criteria to the general public. The theatre critics wanted more on-stage dramatics; supposedly there was more drama attached to the theatrical event than drama in the play itself. The production did however find its own core audience: people who would have probably found the latest dramatic trends confusing rather than inspiring anyway. A large proportion of the audience was made up of groups who had come to see the show in the spirit of spiritual pietism, many of them from the Ostrobothnian region. The play did not alienate the religious communities it depicted, and many of the religious community members who came to see the play were probably seeing a theatrical play for the first time in their lives.[23] Ylikangas's ideas were viewed through the lens of Laine's religious idealism.

Critics found many issues with the production. Alongside dramaturgical issues they highlighted the problematics of the black-and-white nature of the production's stage directing. Laine reinforced elements that were already amply present in Ylikangas's text. Laine himself was also one of the reasons for the production's success; the national reputation attached to his name helped legitimise the production and his no-nonsense stage directing made following the sequence of events easy. The production looked like its director: it was down-to-earth, solid, and knowledgeable, but also predictable in its effects and stolid in its rhythm. Despite initial reservations the production resonated in a number of ways and many of the critical reviews mentioned the enthusiastic foot stomping of the audience at the play's opening night. Researcher critic Panu Rajala referenced Ylikangas's own view that he had hoped to popularise his research without attempting anything too artistically ambitious. He surpassed himself. 'Night after night a dense mass of populus turn up to listen to the professor's dramatised lecture on pietist power struggles in mid-19th century Osthrobothnia' writes Rajala. 'The connection with the audience has not been severed. People come to the Theatre like they go to their prayer meetings, only the critic is found to be awkwardly yawning (and not entirely without reason)'.[24]

Among the central performances Saario's believable and humane portrayal of Malmberg stands out. Thanks to Saarnio's performance the play amplified itself, pondered Outi Nyytäjä who saw the play well after its opening night and commented on the audience's unusual reaction: audience members started singing a hymn, doing 'something that is real; something real has happened inside the Theatre, something that contradicts its environment'.[25] Pietism was a populist movement and through it the production was also building a boundary between the elite and the people. By throwing itself in with the people the production differed from the contemporary concept of a social didactic where the elite educated the common people on their rights.

Similar to the opera *Viimeiset kiusaukset* (*The Last Temptations*) by composer Joonas Kokkonen that told the story of pietist leader Paavo Ruotsalainen, the production itself became a type of cultural phenomenon. The writer, the play, and the production were extensively covered in print up and down the country and the Theatre was visited by busloads of people who were interested in the fame and the cultural resonance of a national figure. For some people the ability to join in with the final hymn might have been the most moving part of the whole production. 'Heikki Ylikangas found the beats of the national pulse in the play, the questioning and searching of our times as Finns' wrote a pietist priest Paavo Maunula who suggested that the play was something that people came to see 'in large groups' from around the country in the same way that people went to the opera at Savonlinna's Opera Festival, or to see *Viimeiset kiusaukset* in Helsinki.[26] The play is also part of the series of new popular plays at the Finnish National Theatre about Finnish history.

Laine as a stage director represented the Finnish tradition of broad brushstrokes and his retirement age directions resonated with the general public. He continued to work right up until his very last moment. Ilmari Turja's play *Särkelä Itte* that had toured many Finnish stages was Laine's swan song production staged to celebrate his 60 years in theatre, right before the director's death. The show was like a farewell to a world gone by through which most Finnish people had travelled.

That a new type of radical folk theatre was emerging was evident the following year when the Finnish National Theatre staged Turkka's play *Valheita* (*Lies*) which he directed himself. Turkka had been sending shockwaves through Finnish theatrical circles for the past few decades. The speed of television entertainment and its character variations had deeply impacted young theatre companies, but alongside these influences there was also the strong pull of Turkka's mode of physically manifesting emotions known as the 'Turkka mode'. At the time Turkka's career was going through a transitional stage which can be seen in the fact that he was directing his own plays (including this production at the Finnish National Theatre). In its own way this was about Turkka returning to his roots: when he was younger Turkka had worked as an assistant for the National Theatre's Director Kalima, during a time when Kalima was stage directing his final Chekhov productions that ended up solidifying his international reputation. Turkka's own theatre directing training at the Finnish Theatre School had culminated in a final showcase piece: Ernst Toller's *The Machine Wreckers* that had been staged on the Small Stage of the Finnish National Theatre.[27] Despite his reputation as a vanguard, Turkka can be situated in the long line of Finnish theatre directing as a disciple of legendary stage director Salmelainen who settled on intense realism via expressionism and worked in the name of folk theatre.

As its name suggests, in the play *Valheita* the truth was something to be played around with. Actor Tea Ista played herself and a Lady, Yrjö Järvinen was 'an old patriarch', Merja Larivaara a female prisoner, Tero Jartti played the conductor Vesa-Pekka Salonen (compare this with actual conductor Esa-Pekka Salonen), and Markku Nieminen played Kake; and they all also played other characters. The production was (too) long and meandering, but Turkka's 'relentless magic of a theatre-man' acted as a counterbalance and the intensity carried on through to the end. The production built an image of Finland in the spirit of Turkka. Despite the public sensation it caused, Turkka's director visit did not lead to any serious criticism or resistance (as often happened with Turkka). The carnivalesque production still elicited lots of discussions about not only the production itself, but about the spectacle of a playwright-director.

The *Teatteri*-magazine covered the show over two extensive articles. It had invited Professor J.-P. Roos, who had adapted Pierre Bourdieu's models to come and evaluate the production's cultural standing and to help explain audience attitudes. The headline 'The new middle class is not provoked by an old enmity' already hints at the results: the new middle class wanted to mark cultural territory without heavily investing in cultural capital or a deep cultural background. Turkka's attempt at breaking out of the chains of high art was problematic and socially unfinished according to Roos. Turkka was not accepted as an interpreter of feeling by either the elite or the people. According to Roos, *Valheita* was an example of 'overcultivated theatre'.[28]

Juha-Pekka Hotinen's critical review dove into Turkka's role in Finnish theatre overall. This production was an attractive adaptation with a sprinkling of naughtiness according to Hotinen, but it was also numbing. Turkka's relationship with the cultural elite was contradictory and marred by jealousy. The play's Vesa-Pekka Salonen (or Esa-Pekka Salonen) had no intimate relationship with the "people", but it was unlikely that Turkka really thought that he himself or his theatre had a real relationship with them either, other than traverse column inches in gossip magazines. Hotinen felt that the Finnish people loved the myth of the genius, and it was fortunate that they had found one. He confessed that he himself was chained by the Turkka myth and that Turkka was only partly to blame for the position he now found himself in. Turkka had been called Finland's Münchhausen but he 'hadn't had to pull himself up by the scruff of his neck for a long time now. It's all been done for him'.[29] Hotinen was referencing an interview by Kirsikka Moring in which Turkka had pronounced that he will show 'what we were, what Finland of the masters looked like'. Theatre saved itself from death only by going back to 'magic, ecstasy, and spells'.[30]

Turkka was also placed within the context of the international world of theatre when visiting Professor Erika Fischer-Lichte analysed the *Valheita* production. She grouped Turkka with Giorgio Strehler, Peter Brook, and Ariane Mnouchkine and their desire to renew folk theatre. Fischer-Lichte picked up on Turkka's habit of making the stage into a locus of change where actors change genres, scenes, and roles. The performance was porous and did not give the viewer a clear frame of reference. The continuous references to history and the theatre worked in tandem with the viewer, and thanks to the multiplicity of viewing experiences, this happened in multiple different ways. Fischer-Lichte justified her point of view: 'Theatre should not be about solving problems and giving answers to political, social, or economic questions. Its aim is to build a connection'.[31]

Turkka moved Finnish folk theatre towards a more carnivalesque direction, and eventually the Finnish National Theatre was also part of the shift, though it cannot claim to have been the catalyst for change. The new direction was theatrical and therefore "danger-free" in the sense that it did not incite people to rebellion (not immediately at least). Social and political theatre had become elite in a new way; it was no longer about giving people instructions, but about subtle messages that were only being intelligible to people with a specific cultural background. The Finnish National Theatre picked up on the new group theatre spirit. The new generation had taken over Finnish theatre, the Finnish National Theatre included, and Turkka brought his own contribution to the generational shift. Throughout his career he had mainly stuck to Finnish texts, embedding international influences in his methods. The national turned out to be international.

The Finland of poets

The art of theatrical recitals has a long tradition in Finland. Helsinki University founded its own speech technology and recital department back in 1928 and the Finnish Reciter's League was founded ten years later. After the war, reciting has also been taught at central arts schools and colleges. Full-time recital artists have always been responsible for organising their own shows, but Finland had plenty of recital hobbyists and a variety of recital and speech choirs. Some of the most renowned recital performers started their careers in the theatres, and for many actors recitals have been a hobby that sits alongside collective theatrical work.[32] Performers have been responsible for spreading Finnish poetry and many of the shows have happened in conjunction with national holidays.

At the Finnish National Theatre, there were frequent poetry evenings on the Small Stage and on the Willensauna stage. On the border between recital art and theatre a new form of dramatised performance was created that underlined the actors own oral delivery. This was a form of drama that especially allowed the National Theatre's experienced women actors to expand their range. One of the Finnish National Theatre's most lauded actors, Eeva-Kaarina Volanen, was renowned for her skilled recitals, and she also produced a monologue play titled *Eeva Maria Kustaava* that was recorded as a television special. Rinne performed in *Naismetsä* which was called a prose ballad or a monologue short story: the text was written by one the most important poets and dramatists of the time, Paavo Haavikko. *Mesikämmen and Mustarouva* performed by Risto Mäkelä and Ritva Ahonen was the married couple's interpretation of a sensationalised love affair between two writers from the turn of the century. The story was reconstructed from letters, diaries, and textual extracts from the writers' works. Mäkelä was a Finnish National Theatre actor, and Ahonen one of the country's most famous recital artists.

Nationally important dates and years were commemorated with visiting productions and joint evenings of poetry. In the spring of 1990 Yrjö Jylhä's *Kiirastuli (Purgatory)* poetry collection was used as the basis for a show to commemorate 50 years since the end of the Finnish Winter War. In the production the group of male actors and recital artists from the Finnish National Theatre and the Helsinki City Theatre sat on the darkened stage of the Small Stage in their army woollen shirts and recited Jylhä's post-war texts in a steady flow of poetry, accompanied by Tapio Tiitu's organ music that set the scene. In this impressive show that slid seamlessly into pathos, Jylhä's pacifism inspired by the horrors he experienced during the Winter War was tangible. The Finnish National Theatre also participated in the national poet Kivi's and the national epic's *Kalevala's* anniversary celebrations with poetic ensembles that were created in collaboration with the Theatre's actors and recital artists. The production of *Poems from Kanteletar* was engaging and enlivening and the show was punctuated by artists and performers reciting alone and together, even singing as they sat on a variety of chairs in the vicinity of the ramp.

Actor Volanen frequently performed with two recital artists Ahonen and Aino-Maija Tikkanen, performing new and old Finnish poetry. In the autumn of 1988 they put together a night of poetry from Helvi Hämäläinen's poetry collection *Sukupolveni unta* (*Dream of My Generation*) that had won awards that same autumn as a serious book with plenty to say. The poems were about the Winter War, concentration camps and wars, but as well as being about private and collective grief and suffering, the poems were also about connecting with nature and its different forms, even covering the threat of environmental destruction. *Sukupolveni unta* reflected the social movements of its times and despite its focus on the Winter War, it was very much connected with the political turbulence of the late 1980s. For the writer it was about freeing herself from a period of silencing, cleansing herself, and reminding people of the fate of Estonia. As well as going over the events of the war, Estonia was brought to the surface in a strong way, connecting Estonia to the events going on in the rest of Europe.

These recital evenings highlighted the Finnish National Theatre's importance as a guardian of national culture, but the collaborative approach of working with other artists and even performers from competing theatres disrupted the image of an insular institution. Inside the building of the Finnish National Theatre even the occasional pathos was given a convivial connection that made it seem justified.

Notes

1 Katri Veltheim, *Uusi Suomi*, 9.9.1976.
2 Katri Veltheim, *Uusi Suomi*, 9.9.1976; Kirsikka Siikala, *Helsingin Sanomat*, 10.9.1976.
3 Pirkko Koski, *Demari*, 21.12.1978; Irmeli Niemi, *Helsingin Sanomat*, 24.11.1978.
4 Aarne Laurila, *Demari*, 22.3.1978.
5 Koskimies, 1972, 70–71.
6 Koskimies 1972, 162–164.
7 Jukka Kajava, *Helsingin Sanomat*, 8.12.1984.
8 Aarne Laurila, *Suomen Sosialidemokraatti*, 8.12.1984.
9 Cf. Koski 2005a, 146–148.
10 Cf. Paavolainen 1987, 101–103.
11 Marketta Mattila, *Uusi Suomi*, 20.4.1991.
12 Jukka Kajava, *Helsingin Sanomat*, 20.4.1991.
13 Arvi Kivimaa's letter to Hella Wuolijoki 16.5.1950. National Archived, Hella Wuolijoki's Archive 602:133, 29. See also Koski 2010b, 73.
14 Salmelainen 1968, 25.
15 Sole Uexküll, *Helsingin Sanomat*, 5.9.1975.
16 Ibid. The play is set in the Finnish region of Tavastia, an area with a recognisable regional character that would have resonated with the play's Finnish audiences.
17 Rinne 2003, 255–260.

18 Tuula Saarto, *Ilkka*, 28.10.1977.
19 Rinne 2003, 256–59.
20 Wuolijoki's original description about the importance of O'Neill's play as an influence was printed in the programme for the play's premiere, but the extract was also printed in the Finnish National Theatre production's programme.
21 Hella Wuolijoki Archives, National Archives. Also Koski 2000, 131–133. When it comes to audience engagement, I can share the following memory: as we moved into the interval during a Saturday afternoon matinee I heard a middle-aged woman behind me say that she really felt like expressing her support aloud and encouraging Hulda to study. And this was the 1980s.
22 Pentti Kirstinä, "Kansallisteatterin syksy. Hopearahaa kertoo valtataisteluista ja uskosta." Press cutting, Finnish National Theatre Archives.
23 E.g. Koski 1997, 670.
24 Panu Rajala, *Parnasso*, 3/1983, 171–173.
25 Outi Nyytäjä, *Teatteri*, 5/1984, 8.
26 Paavo Maunula, *Vaasa*, 27.11.1982.
27 C.f. Paavolainen 1987, 17; Koski 2013, 602–606.
28 Hannu Harju, *Teatteri*, 8/1990, 10–12.
29 Juha-Pekka Hotinen, *Teatteri*, 8/1990, 6–9.
30 Kirsikka Moring, *Helsingin Sanomat*, 9.9.1990.
31 Erika Fischer-Lichte, *Helsingin Sanomat*, 27.10.1990.
32 Kajas 2013, 301–303.

8 Finnish history without a nationalist slant

From the 1960s onwards, in theatres across Finland, as well as more widely across Finnish society, there was an increased desire to examine recent national history. This was coupled with a dramatic desire to explore the great societal crises of the past century. At the Finnish National Theatre, dramas about Finnish national history explored historical figures as well as national events. Positioned between East and West, Finland had continuously been caught up in war zones and been forced to fight for its position. Unsurprisingly many of the dramas staged explored 20th-century wars.

Plays that dramatise history 'are aesthetic adaptations or revisions' of past events that we intuitively know to be real, or that a general consensus helps us to accept as real, theorises Freddie Rokem. In a historical play, 'the historical events are, rather, performed again' as history *haunts* the dramatic event. Experiences from the past have been responsible for collective identity building and drama 'participates in the ongoing representations and debates about these pasts, sometimes contesting the hegemonic understanding of the historical heritage on the basis of which these identities have been constructed, sometimes reinforcing them'.[1] Rokem's study honed in on plays that depicted events that affected the whole of Europe, but the same conclusions can be made on a national level when looking at one nation's experience with plays about its own history.

When it came to historical plays, the Finnish National Theatre also tended to favour new plays and premieres. What was desirable was drama that in some way challenged accepted and entrenched narratives of a grand national destiny. Every generation rewrites history, and drama is no exception; critical reception itself is also never homogenous. Examining national Finnish history and its role in a domestic setting did not exclude the crossing of geographical borders when it came to the historical people, events, and ideas depicted. Finland emerged as a country where the history of the East and West collided.

Historical characters from across the decades

When it comes to national characters, recognition trumps reality, argues Joep Leerssen.[2] When examining the concept of the popular, John Fiske writes that recognisability cannot be dictated from the top down; rather, it is a collection

DOI: 10.4324/9781003047667-10

of impressions: 'our truth' that is also susceptible to becoming a norm.[3] Leerssen has also found that a defining feature of national characters is their Janus-like personalities where underneath universally admired characteristics nationally repressed characteristics can be glimpsed.[4] When you examine the portrayal of historical Finnish figures through these lenses, a few themes emerge: notoriety, the potential standardisation of a public image, the meaning behind contradictory traits, and the success of the staged version or a contradictory critical reception. During the years pertaining to this study, the National Theatre did not put on any shows about historically significant women.

Historical turning points create a fertile ground for drama, but they do not necessarily guarantee success. This is borne out by the staging of Eila Pennanen's *Ministeri murhataan* (A Minister is Murdered) at the end of the Finnish National Theatre's 1977 spring season. This new Finnish play made for the Main Stage was about the 1922 assassination of Finland's Minister of the Interior Heikki Ritavuori. After Finland's 1917 independence from Russia and the ensuing civil war, a group of right-wing activists attempted to extend Finland's Eastern border into Soviet territory through military action. An advocate for due legal process, Ritavuori condemned the military activity, and generally, his work and principles made him an obvious target for right-wing radicals. A young right-wing activist Ernst Tandefelt shot him at his front door in front of many witnesses who happened to be on the scene. A political assassination is an unusual event in Finnish history and Ritavuori's death is common knowledge, though it has received little continued attention in Finland.

When the play came out, Eila Pennanen was one of the most renowned prose writers in Finland. Pennanen's reputation secured a general level of interest towards the play, but the production did not become part of the tradition of depicting great men or re-interpreting history. The central victim of the events, Minister Ritavuori, was not even the play's protagonist. Pennanen spoke in a contemporary interview about the desire to explore how a normal person becomes a political assassin.[5]

Contrary to historical fact, the play's murderer was an 'anonymous': a fictitious character surrounded by real historical figures. The production's social commentary remained scant and its events were not tied to a specific point in time, which resulted in the production building empathy towards the protagonist. The reason for the murder was given as a temporary aberration of the mind (which is what actually ended up happening to Tandefelt after many years of imprisonment). When there is an actual public event behind the performance, the murder cannot be simply reduced to a one-off drama between individuals, and the production was unable to bring these two elements together. The critical reviews reveal that the play did not fulfil the requirements of a historical drama, but that its historical setting also meant that it could not be seen as a psychological drama either.

Ministeri murhataan is a good example of the inherent risks of staging historical drama. As a historical event, Ritavuori's assassination from the early 1920s did not successfully dovetail with national history-making. From the 1970s onwards, there had been a lot of literary and dramatic explorations of post-civil war Finland, bringing alternative narratives to the fore, often highlighting new sides to the opposing political camps at the time. Pennanen's play also included encounters between different social classes, but the catalyst for the play's events, the government minister's assassination, did not embody the two ideological camps present in Finland's great national myth. Activists were part of a marginal story, and tensions were born mainly inside the ruling class. In order to have succeeded as a play about an individual historical personage, the individual would have had to be famous and occupy a substantial position in the national historical narrative.

Even the most famous national figures did not guarantee dramatic success, when the event was more well-known than its central figure, or especially when an established national narrative was sidestepped. In the spring of 1984 Antti Tuuri's play *Mannerheim Puolassa* (Mannerheim in Poland) focused on the Finnish national hero Field marshal Carl Gustav Mannerheim, but the play depicted a part of his career that was alien to most Finnish people and the play's Mannerheim figure remained distant. The audience's appreciation of Mannerheim and his history did not include the phase staged in this play.

Mannerheim is one of the most mythic figures of Finnish history, and his national image is full of intriguing contradictions, infinitely fascinating from a dramatic point of view. He was a member of the Finnish-Swedish nobility and before the Russian revolution he had made it to the rank of General in the Russian army. He was the supreme leader of the 'Whites' during the Finnish Civil War, feted in the Spring of 1918 as a hero among the people who had won the war (rather a different story among the losing 'Reds'.) The Winter War that had started in September 1939 with Soviet aggression had united the Finnish nation and had softened the left's attitude towards Commander-in-Chief Mannerheim. His national reputation peaked in the 1950s as shown by his elaborate funeral and the way in which places that had been significant to his life were turned into museums. A mounted statue of Mannerheim was placed in a central location in Helsinki. At the end of the 1960s, there were renewed discussions about Mannerheim's role as the Commander-in-Chief for the Whites during the Finnish Civil War; this facet of Mannerheim was emphasised by Communists and impacted pacifist youth movements and left-wing cultural circles' attitudes towards Mannerheim. From the 1980s onwards the interest in Mannerheim continued, but with less of the two extremes.[6]

These fluctuations in Mannerheim's reputation have inspired artists, and he has appeared as the title character and as a cast member in numerous dramas. These plays tended to make the most of the contradictory nature of the Mannerheim myth. The cautious national attitude can be seen in the Finnish National Theatre's decision in the 1960s to only stage journalist-playwright Ilmari Turja's Mannerheim-critical play *Päämajassa* (In The Headquarters) after it had already had a successful run in Tampere at its Työväen Teatteri (Tampere Workers' Theatre, TTT) after its premiere.[7] During Kai Savola's era at the Finnish National Theatre, there were no on-stage character portraits from Mannerheim's glory days, but as a figure Mannerheim garnered attention and apologists whenever his idealised portrait was questioned, even when he merely appeared as a minor cast member. The pull of Mannerheim can be seen in the fact that *Mannerheim Puolassa* was the fourth Mannerheim-production for its director Eugen Terttula.

In Tuuri's play, Mannerheim is a Russian officer among the cosmopolitan Polish upper-class right before the outbreak of the First World War. Tuuri said that his play was about peace; the fact that a nation should develop its sciences and its arts, its own culture, rather than rely on its armed forces. According to the ample pre-show material, Poland's position was a mirror for 1980s' Finland.[8] Judging from the play's critical reception, the portrait of a known historical "great man" who had gained his reputation based on his wartime feats was a poor choice as a carrier for a pacifist message, nor did it manage to reflect European or Finnish politics of the mid-1980s.

Central to Tuuri's play is the love triangle between Mannerheim, Polish baron Lubomirsk, and his wife, that takes place in the heady atmosphere of people waiting for war. Letters between Mannerheim and Marie Lubomirsk have survived to this day, and some people, especially in the artistic circles, have drawn far-reaching conclusions from their exchange. Historian Henrik Meinander has analysed them in the context of epistolary conventions of the time and feels that other explanations are at least possible.[9] However, this presumed historical romance brought a mythical sheen to the play; after the breakdown of the marriage he had formed in St Petersburg, Manneherheim's relations with women were a mystery, as were practically all details of his close personal relationships.

The critical reception of the opening night proved that in the Finnish dramatic imagination, Mannerheim was firmly established as a much more one-dimensional figure than the real man. Plays with themes that ventured outside the established Mannerheim-myth were poorly received. References to the time in which the play was set and its real historical people, the audience's knowledge of what came next, the play's romance, or even its sharp aphorism-style dialogue were not enough to elicit the required levels of dramatic tension. The play was missing a link in the great Finnish story, yet Mannerheim was too big of a figure to get around, and the playwright's desire to explore themes of pacifism and art were overshadowed by the looming figure of Mannerheim.

Aleksis Kivi born in 1834 was another historical figure whose public image had taken on mythical dimensions. Even the characters in his tragedy *Kullervo,* comedy *Heath Cobblers* and novel *Seven Brothers* had become national figures themselves, and Kivi was stamped with the label of literary genius who suffered from poverty and mental health problems. In the mid-1980s the Finnish National Theatre started to question some of these entrenched beliefs. The 150th anniversary of Kivi's birth was celebrated during the 1984–1985 Small Stage season with two premieres of plays about Kivi. The critics felt that the plays were topical and that the shows were a success, but the general audience was less enthused about these new kinds of depictions of the Finnish national poet.

In his play *Yössä Gehennan* (*In The Nights of Gehenna*), Ilpo Tuomarila imagined a fictitious meeting between Kivi and Finnish-Swedish J. J. Wecksell in the Lapinlahti mental asylum. As far as the historical records go, this meeting never happened, but all the characters in the play down to the hospital's senior physician were real historical figures. Wecksell was the first author to write a Finnish tragedy in Swedish, and he spent the last years of his life in Lapinlahti. Kivi was also sent to Lapinlahti before his death. Tuomarila was an experienced writer who had visited the topic of Kivi a number of times already. Tuomarila saw both Kivi's and Wecksell's decisions as a form of escape, and drew parallels with other artists who chose death. Historical accuracy was not essential to the play.[10]

Director Katariina Lahti was in charge of the show's integrity and its rich field of associations. 'The directing enters the mind bit-by-bit without resistance and with blunt energy; using often terrible, searing tableaux', wrote Timo Tiusanen.[11] Pekka Autiovuori as Kivi was not a true "likeness" whereas the figure of Wecksell played by Lars Svedberg would have been one the audience would have struggled to recognise anyway. The differing social backgrounds of the characters as a country boy and an urban person of quality as well as their differing literary linguistic foundations were part of the fundamental make-up of these two national characters.[12]

The production was described in colourful terms, such as brave, fierce, coarse, discordant, rich, and insightful. It seemed that Tuomarila had brought his best work to the fore and contributed to the contemporary practice of portraying artists with a play that delved deep into the spiritual landscape of the people involved. Maija Savutie commented on the ongoing discussion surrounding Finnish drama in general: 'What if someone writes, or directs, in an unconventional way, [...] do crowds flock to the theatre, excited to broaden their horizons? Isn't it more likely that outraged writings will appear in newspaper comment sections?'[13] Savutie was correct about audience success and she also partly correctly predicted negative audience reactions to the production. Despite praise from the theatre critics, the show had a lukewarm reception from the general public.

Arvo Salo's play *Yks perkele, yks enkeli* (One Devil, One Angel) re-examined the relationship between Kivi and Professor August Ahlqvist. Within the arena of accepted Finnish cultural history, Ahlqvist is largely remembered for his harsh review of Kivi's extraordinary Finnish novel, *Seven Brothers*, when it first came out and the potential role that his judgement played in Kivi's premature death.

Salo's play, directed by Terttula, was a dramatic exploration that managed to successfully shake up the Kivi myth. The dialogue in the play was witty, playful and full of aphorisms – lines were delivered at a record pace. Jukka Kajava felt that 'for once here's something that is both cruel and impressive'.[14] Tiusanen felt that Salo had brought the relationship between Ahlqvist and Kivi (played by Martti Järvinen and Seppo Pääkkönen) 'into the present-day, freeing it from history and bringing it to the audience'. The actors were able to portray the crushing nature of the two mens' destinies in a nuanced way.[15]

Figure 8.1 Yks perkele yks enkeli 1985. Seppo Pääkkönen and Martti Järvinen Photograph by Leena Klemelä

Salo had written *Lapualaisooppera* (*The Lapua Opera*) in 1966: a play whose opening night had become known as a turning point for 1960s theatre. Salo was known to be a social democrat and a cultural and political thinker. As well as the show itself, Salo's own political reputation raised inevitable comparisons with contemporary politics; Salo's reputation is also another potential reason why the play did not become a hit. The core audience demographic of the Finnish National Theatre were unlikely to be either champions of Salo, or champions of the carnivalisation of national figures. The show was to be found lacking, but perhaps its biggest problem was that it was situated in the "wrong place", namely at the Finnish National Theatre. Outi Nyytäjä reflected the opinions held by professional theatre critics by finding in Salo's work a sign of a new artistic direction where perspective, analysis, and orientation are intrinsically linked to a play's language. Reading the play was a refreshing experience.[16]

These depictions of Finnish national figures on-stage at the Finnish National Theatre did not conform to normative views of national monuments, but rather challenged the national narrative about that person, or placed themselves in conversation with already established views. The disjuncture between critical and public opinion shows that even though theatricality and the breaking of dramatic conventions were appreciated by the critics, recognisable elements and norms were also needed to attract wide-spread audience success.

War history and contemporary politics on stage

Finnish society in the 1970s was ready to look back at its national history from a diverse range of angles and free itself from nationalist revisionism. Theatres had a central role when it came to interpreting and depicting wartime events, including teasing out contradictions and adding flesh to the bones of the social context of war. Re-interpreting did not always lead to a change in individual opinions, but the processing of wartime events and analysing their social context raised new questions.

The Second World War left deep scars across Finland. Väinö Linna's realist war novel *The Unknown Soldier* was published in the early 1950s, portraying Finnish soldiers as independent agents and disrupting the national narrative of patriotic heroism. Edvin Laine developed the novel into a film that largely eschewed any of the war's more controversial elements, and slowly this cinematic version became part of the national story too, displacing the novel itself in many ways. Finland had yet to process the long shadow of the 1918 Finnish Civil War when everybody, including the losing side of the Civil War and even the Finnish communists, were suddenly ready to join forces in the 1939 Winter War against the Soviet Union. Alongside warfare, other times of crisis in Finland's history surfaced in drama, either as central themes, or as the social context to historical plays.

Daniel Katz's play *Miten kalat suutelevat* (How Fish Kiss) in the Autumn of 1974 was a revised version of the production shown in Tampere at the TTT four years' previous. The original play was a domestic drama about a Finnish-Jewish family during the Second World War who had escaped to the country to avoid the bombings in the city and were preparing to leave the country in case the situation got worse. Even though Finland fought against the Soviet Union on the side of the Germans, Finnish Jews participated in the war alongside other Finnish people. The general consensus is that German requests to Finland to hand over its Jews had fallen on deaf ears. This National Theatre adaptation of the play added quasi-absurdist elements to the plot with a political parody exploring Himmler's visit to Finland and the ensuing conversations about Jewish question, somewhat changing the tone of the play. The play tied Finland's history to Germany in a much more concrete way than Finnish public opinion and conversations had previously done, making the play's sense of danger even more palpable.

Katz had risen to fame at the end of the 1970s with his debut novel *When Grandfather Skied to Finland*. His absurdist and scatological style had successfully differentiated him from the Finnish mainstream. His depictions of the Finnish-Jewish community were seen as part of a new wave of successful American-Jewish authors. The original Tampere production of *Miten kalat suutelevat* had been a success and had gone on to tour at five city theatres around the country, but the additions made by the National Theatre did not lead to a renewed national interest in the play at other Finnish theatres.

Daniel Katz and the play's director Lisbeth Landefort were both Jewish, exonerating them from accusations of cultural appropriation. (Landefort had settled in Finland after escaping Austria as a teenager in 1938). Some of the critics felt that the absurdist parody added to the production by the Finnish National Theatre was inappropriate in the context of the grim Jewish question, though nobody denied the fact that the production was very powerful, and it's likely that the parody would have been welcomed in other contexts. Sole Uexküll from *Helsingin Sanomat* justified the exaggeration from a cultural viewpoint. Uexküll felt that it might be referencing a characteristic of the Jewish tradition, 'a humour that is fed by self-preservation, tough resilience, and the desire for survival'.[17] The general critical confusion exemplifies the difficulties of cultural appropriation and the challenges of interpreting parody.

The show was a success thanks to its humour, not its historical frame of reference. The play was put on almost a hundred times to an almost packed-out auditorium. 'It's been awhile since I've seen an audience having as much fun as I did on the National's Small Stage', wrote a journalist in *Me naiset*-magazine.[18] Parody distanced people from the play's possible theme of the position of Jews in a wartime Finland that was fighting on the side of the Germans. The production did not become part of an analysis of Finnish wartime history or post-war discussions about the fate of the Jews. Finland's role in the Jewish genocide had not yet received much attention, and it was not until a few decades later that a public conversation about the eight Jews that Finland handed over to the Baltics, or the fact that a Jewish refugee ship was turned away from Finland's port, was initiated.[19]

In the Autumn of 1979, the National Theatre put on a new dramatisation of Ilmari Turja's play *Jääkäri Ståhl* (Jaeger Ståhl). Set in early Spring in 1918, it tells the story of the Jaegers' return to Finland after receiving military training from the German army. Men from across the social spectrum had secretly left the Russian Grand Duchy (as Finland was back then) to receive military training to facilitate Finland's break from Russia. By the time they returned, Civil War had erupted in Finland and the Jaegers found themselves fighting against revolutionary Russian infantrymen as well as the Red Finnish People's Army. The Commander-in-Chief for the Whites was the Finnish General of Russia's Imperial Army, Carl Gustav Mannerheim. The dramatic tension in the play comes from the intense rivalry between Finns of differing backgrounds: the Russian Tsarist officers and the German Jaeger officers, as well as from the fact that Jaeger Ståhl and many of his fellow Jaegers quickly discover they are in a civil war against their own relatives. Turja was both a writer and a journalist who had plenty of experience of dealing with nationally sensitive social problems in the public eye. Despite the play's title, a lot of the attention in the play was reserved for Mannerheim.

The divide between Mannerheim and the Jaeger officers was still an unacknowledged facet of Finnish history in the 1970s. The play's representation of historical events was faithful, though the later historical theory that the Finnish Civil War for Mannerheim was part of a larger project to re-install old Russian rule, was not yet known. The Mannerheim myth that had gone from strength to strength after the Second World War had eradicated the possibility of having that conversation when the play was staged.[20] The play's events troubled not only the people who wanted to uphold the Mannerheim-myth, but also left-wing commentators who felt that the themes surrounding the re-assessment of the Finnish Civil War that loomed large in public discourse at the time were sidelined.

The play's premiere at Vaasa's City Theatre two years previous had elicited political commentary, which inevitably coloured attitudes towards the play now that it was being shown at the Finnish National Theatre. The Vaasa production had garnered negative press for twisting the narrative about the Jaeger movement and their supposed high-minded desire to free Finland from the Russians by leaving out what happened after 1918.[21] The aftershocks of the Finnish Civil War had only been properly examined in the few decades preceding the production, which initiated an escalating awareness of the atrocities committed by the winning side. Turja's play did not glorify the victors, but in Vaasa the enthusiasm for the play in right-wing circles impacted the way in which radicalised left-wing theatre enthusiasts approached the play.

Terttula directed the play at the Finnish National Theatre in the spirit of epic theatre by leveraging the historical context in many ways, and the production's programme redacted by Terttu Savola was a thorough and informative package on the play's background. 'Out of hard-to-process ingredients (…) a prestigious national play' was built by the National Theatre, praised ex-diplomat turned journalist Heikki Brotherus. 'That is what the mission of the National Theatre is: fostering national dramatic arts and exploring our own national identity'.[22] Critical opinions oscillated from the negative to commendations: opinions were often influenced by the critic's age and the newspaper's ideological stance. On the one hand (mainly in the right-leaning press), the feeling was that this cavalcade-style historical documentary had been mined for maximum dramatic value, bringing new material to light and 'hinting at the future mission'[23] of the National Theatre. The show was seen as a prime example of how theatre can be used to flesh out the narrative of Finland's independence. On the other hand, contemporary political debates and the debates that had sprung up in the theatrical circles post-Vaasa coloured some of the reviews. Some of the reviews appealed directly to the audience: 'It's worth coming to see Turja's Ståhl from near or far as it's deeply compassionate and moving'.[24] And this is exactly what happened: despite a lack of critical consensus the audience filled the auditorium on a regular basis.

Marshal Mannerheim was one of the characters in the play, and putting Mannerheim on stage always elicited opinions (and still does): the last scenes in the play highlighted some of the inherent contradictions of the Mannerheim-figure. Having risen to the position of the most lauded actor at the Finnish National Theatre, Heikki Nousiainen, played a Mannerheim 'that was developed in an intelligent manner, sensitively and believably building up a character portrait'[25] sprinkled with 'moments of brash impudence'.[26] The defenders of Mannerheim's dignity were also outspoken, like journalist Eila Jokela who felt that 'his caricature of a portrayal of the White General betrayed the writer's lifelong antipathy towards Mannerheim'. She would have preferred the play to

Finnish history without a nationalist slant 105

have a more suitable interpreter such as Laine, the director who was known for his popular and uplifting portrayals of Finnishness.[27] However, the Finnish National Theatre's mission to encourage national self-reflection was fulfilled.

The enduring interest in Finland's wartime history meant that productions that were even more documentary-style than Turja's play were also set up for on-stage success. The Winter War that started in the autumn of 1939 provided a stronger and more coherent national narrative than the Civil War. The spring 1989 play *Tie talvisotaan* (*The Road to the Winter War*) by Professor of History Heikki Ylikangas told the story of the discussions the Finnish government had behind closed doors during the autumn of 1939, secret discussions about the Soviet Union and the threat of war. From a structural point of view the play is reminiscent of the British National Theatre production of David Hare's *Stuff Happens* depicting British and US cabinet discussions about the possibility of an attack on Iraq (although Ylikangas actually preceded Hare).

The Soviet Union actually attacked Finland on the last day of November in 1939, and, after a hundred days of fighting, a (temporary) peace treaty was signed that forced Finland to sign over some of its territory to the Soviets; the Finnish population promptly left these areas to settle elsewhere within the borders of Finland, but Finland itself was not occupied. There was widespread international attention throughout the duration of the Finnish Winter War. One example is the April 1940 Broadway show set during the Finnish Winter

Figure 8.2 Tie talvisotaan, 1989
Photograph by Leena Klemelä

War titled *There Shall Be No Night* that went on to win the Pulitzer Prize for Drama the following year. In a dramatic reversal of theatre politics, the show had to be cancelled in December 1941 when the Soviet Union joined the War against Germany.[28]

Ylikangas's play created a space for a dialogue between the viewer's own historical knowledge and the history being depicted on-stage, and part of the show's success was this productive tension between fiction and fact. The critical conversation by researchers and academics that surrounded the production only served to increase its popularity with audiences. Ylikangas's version of events broke with the historical national myth of an unpreventable war that was endured thanks to the happy uniting of the Finnish nation.

The choice of director, Sakari Puurunen, emphasised the production's documentary-style: Puurunen had fought and been injured in the war against the Soviet Union. The play brought to light (and the stage) some more controversial interpretations of events, and offered an insightful glimpse into discussions that had previously remained "secret". Thanks to the political thaw at the end of the 1980s, the subject matter was particularly pertinent in the Baltics at the time, highlighting a key difference between Finland and the Baltic countries who, unlike Finland, handed over military bases to the U.S.S.R. in 1939. In the show's programme, Seppo Zetterberg, an expert in Estonian history, described what happened to the Baltics in 1939. Zetterberg ended with 'The next stage in the U.S.S.R.'s dominance over Estonia, Latvia, and Lithuania came into effect in 1940 when it annexed them and made them part of the Soviet Union'.[29]

Ylikangas's established public image as a radical writer and historical revisionist, as well as his previous dramatic success with his play *Kolmekymmentä hopearahaa*, affected the centre of gravity of various critical conversations about the play. Just as audiences often view a play in light of their previous theatrical experiences, seeing similarities with the actors' or the director's previous work, now Ylikangas and his strong personality impacted his play's critical reception.[30] Dramatically, this was a rare occasion where a play's social reality is impacted by ideology and value-laden emotions. The play's overall documentary-style mixed with the national context became even more poignant when the play was being staged at the Finnish National Theatre.

Ylikangas's central hypothesis that he had already outlined in his book on the matter, *Käännekohdat Suomen historiassa* (1986), was that 'the Winter War started by accident, without either side really wanting it to happen'. Finland did not agree to the proposed exchange of territory demanded by the Soviets that would have resulted in a reduction of Finland landmass, but as Moscow did not send a clear ultimatum as a sign of an imminent attack, the Finnish government did not really believe in the prospect of war. Moscow wanted to be able to defend itself from the Baltic Sea and had failed to communicate the importance of these territorial negotiations. The Finnish government made a critical error. At the same time, the Finnish government acted in a way that was in line with Finnish national character, to avoid the War altogether would have demanded that the Finnish people themselves were different.[31] In the play Ylikangas also hints that some people in Finland knew about the contents of a secret adjunct dossier to the Molotov-Ribbentrop pact signed on 24 August 1939 that outlined Germany's and the Soviet Union's border deal. Different points of views on these issues were aired in writings about the play, and even the Finnish National Theatre set up an alternative sequence of events in the play's programme.

Theatre critics homed in on the production's atmosphere and the way in which actors played famous figures. Critical opinions varied: this was not meant to be a documentary about the onset of the Winter War, but rather a series of imagined conversations rooted in reality; when focusing on fleshing out the story's characters the play hung together well, but the maps and crests tended to give it a rather stuffy atmosphere; the most intriguing element was how the actors played famous politicians. The show was most successful when it focused on colouring in familiar and known historical events. The historical message was also problematic as the audience were in possession of later knowledge about the time in question, making it hard to view the drama from purely the lens of its contemporary context.

Many critics felt that the show's central problem was the fact that the actors largely stayed within the accepted physical representation of the character they were playing. Physical similarities or lack of thereof was something that could distract the viewer from the dramatic unfolding of events. The extreme manifestation of this was evident in the portrayal of Commander-in-Chief Mannerheim who had become a significant national figure. In his autobiography, Mannerheim's actor Tapani Perttu confesses to having thrown himself into the myth. For Perttu, Mannerheim was his favourite role and his attitude to the role accurately depicts the intensity of the values wrapped up in a performance like this. 'When I got the role I tried to channel the sensitive, spirited, and great person that Mannerheim really was behind the exterior pomp', Perttu reminisces. He felt that the production was very similar to the Finnish spirit itself: usually gruff, sometimes friendly.[32]

A lot was written about the play, and not just critical reviews either, and the Theatre's auditorium kept filling up. The show stayed in the Theatre's repertoire for three years. The wider conversation about the play did not revolve around formal questions, but centred on questions of national memory, values, historical fact/interpretation, and the recognisability of the characters depicted in the play. Plays about Finnish history, and especially its wartime history, had previously had success on the Finnish stage. Usually writers of these plays had come from literary or theatrical circles and looked at the subject from an artistic angle. Now the historical "facts" played an increasingly central role.

In the public discourse both researchers and other commentators made themselves heard. According to the main editorial in *Liitto* magazine, judgements that had the benefit of hindsight were mixed in, in an apparently deliberate move.[33] Critic Jyrki Vuori stated that as there was no access to Moscow's archives, the chain of events were just as much opinions as historical fact.[34] Journalist Benedict Zilliacus conceded that agreeing to the Soviet demands in the Autumn of 1939 might have stopped war from erupting in November–December, but also questioned how long that peace would have actually lasted. Zilliacus also criticised Ylikangas's reluctance to factor in superpower politics into the unfolding of events.[35] Ylikangas generally responded to criticism, and this production was no exception. He professed to be a believer in one single truth, even if it might be impossible to actually pinpoint the truth. Anybody working on a historical novel or play had to respect historical fact.[36]

Members of Helsinki's War Veteran Association came and watched the play, and on the whole, the play was accepted by them. The experiences of the people who had actually lived through the war were recounted in the veteran magazine: 'None of us veterans were there to witness what happened in government councils, the President's Residence, or in cabinets. And neither did Ylikangas, so from this perspective the play is fiction, imaginary'. The actors impressed the audience and in the paper they were interviewed on the backgrounds of their performances.[37]

Finnish National Theatre productions that examined Finnish history proved that in order for people to recognise themselves in a dramatised version of their national history the plays had to focus on the big picture, provide lots of context for public discussions, and be organised around subjects rather than themes. For example the play *Kohti maailman sydäntä* (Towards the Heart of the World) by Juhani Peltonen that was staged on the Willensauna stage in 1977 told the story of Finnish officers captured as prisoners of war in early 19th century Russia, but as the play was written by someone who was known for his work on "new drama" and because the events took place so long ago, the production got no critical attention as a representative of the genre of historical drama. 'The play depicts trekking and arriving at your destination; the characters in the play provide both a mirror and a map for attitudes both then and now. Thematically, the play unequivocally stands on the side of people and peace' wrote Kajava in his review of the play.[38] The production was praised and it was a success, filling Willensauna's small auditorium year after year. But it was not the play's national element that resonated with its audiences.

Based on the plays depicting 20th-century Finnish history, the Finnish National Theatre attempted to contribute to conversations about national identity, as well as the challenging of nationalist points of view. The National Theatre managed to attract both positive critical attention, as well as praise from the general public, though when it came to staging national crises, this was not always simultaneously achieved. Staging political history became a significant contributing factor when it came to guaranteeing audience success. An academic and research-led approach also leant extra credence and weight to the genre of national drama.

Notes

1 Rokem 2000, 5–6.
2 Leerssen 2000, 276.

3 Fiske 1989, 6.
4 Leerssen 2000, 276.
5 "Eila Pennanen Kansalliseen. Poliittinen murha suomalaisittain." *Helsingin Sanomat*, 7.5.1977.
6 Meinander 2017, 297, 303–307.
7 Eino Salmelainen's letter to Ilmari Turja. The Finnish Literature Society's Archives.
8 Linda Iranto, Uusi Suomi, 10.3.1984.
9 Meinander 2017, 87–88.
10 Rauni Paalanen, *Oma markka*, 7/1984, 9–10.
11 Timo Tiusanen, *Uusi Suomi*, 30.11.1984.
12 Pekka Autiovuori, interview, 29.4.2014.
13 Maija Savutie, *Kansan Uutiset*, 1.12.1984.
14 Jukka Kajava, *Helsingin Sanomat*, 28.4.1985.
15 Timo Tiusanen, *Uusi Suomi*, 28.4.1985.
16 Outi Nyytäjä, *Arsis*, 2/1985, 11.
17 Sole Uexküll, *Helsingin sanomat*, 27.9.1974.
18 "Naurun paikat." *Me naiset*, 18.10.1974.
19 Finland welcomed 500 Austrian refugees in 1938. Of them, 350 were moved on and 150 spent the wartime in rural Finland. Out of the eight Jews handed over to the Germans by the Finnish state police, only one survived. Later on, the public discourse also extended to the Jewish Soviet prisoners of war that Finland handed over to Germany.
20 Of Mannerheim and the Jaeger Movement: Meinander 2017, 95–97.
21 In Vaasa, Kari Väänänen, who played the title role, said that it was his most miserable, horrible, and worst performance. E.g. *Vaasa*, 25.1.1979. The Finnish National Theatre's actors had predicted that this might turn out to be a 'problem play'. Notes from a Finnish National Theatre Actors' Association meeting, 17.12.1979.
22 Heikki Brotherus, *Helsingin Sanomat*, 27.11.1979.
23 Katri Veltheim, *Uusi Suomi*, 30.11.1979.
24 Ilari Piipponen, *Turun Sanomat*, 30.11.1979.
25 Katri Veltheim, *Uusi Suomi*, 30.11.1979.
26 Jukka Kajava, *Helsingin Sanomat*, 30.11.1979.
27 Eila Jokela, *Uusi Suomi*, 8.12.1979.
28 Bigsby 1985, 1; www.wikipedia.org/wiki/There_Shall_Be_No_Night. 24.5.2020. Theatre Guild's (nowadays the Neil Simon Theater) opening night for the production was at the Alvin Theater, 29.4.1940. The stage director was also the actor playing the lead male role, Alfred Lunt, with other central roles played by Lynn Fontaine, Charles Ausley, and Montgomery Clift. The play depicts how even a pacifist sees the necessity of the Winter War. A television version in 1957 situated the play in 1956's Hungary and the country's revolution. In June 1941 Finland attacked the Soviet Union with support from Germany. (Finland signed a separate peace treaty with the Soviet Union in 1944 and committed to driving the German troops stationed in Lapland out of the country. Finland now lost the territories that it had won back and also had to pay heavy war reparations to the Soviet Union. However, Finland was never occupied.)
29 The play's programme included lots of historical background to the performance. The Finnish National Theatre Archives.
30 See Carlson 2001 and Quinn 2010.
31 Ylikangas 1987, 192, 195.
32 Grahn 2014, 154–56.
33 "Talvisotaa 'ajan henkeen'." *Liitto*, 16.4.1989.
34 Jyrki Vuori, *Turun Sanomat*, 9.4.1989.
35 Benedict Zilliacus, *Hufvustadsbladet*, 9.4.1989.

36 Ylikangas 1988, 97–98.
37 "Tie talvisotaan." *Pääkaupunkiseudun sotaveteraani*, 3/1989.
38 Jukka Kajava, *Helsingin Sanomat*, 29.9.1977.

9 Significant literary works as national interpretations

In their book *Kolonialismin jäljet: keskustat, periferiat ja Suomi* (*Traces of Colonialism: The Centre, the Periphery, and Finland*), Mikko Lehtonen and Olli Löytty locate Finland's modernisation strategy in the copying of societal models from Western centres of power and in Finland's adoption of a Western geographical identity. In Finland importing culture has always been much more significant than exporting it, and Finnish national culture has been largely cosmopolitan in its nature.[1] This is evident in the extensive translation of classic drama into Finnish at the end of the 19th century. During the Cold War in the 1970s and 1980s Eastern European classics continued to be popular in Finland, forming a bridge with pre-Revolutionary Russia.

A theatrical production is always tied to an event and a specific cultural setting, and to maintain its position in the dramatic canon, a play must be recognised, interpreted, and re-interpreted.[2] As a traditional national institution, the Finnish National Theatre had the power to influence what is artistically appreciated in Finland, but when it came to its dramatic choices, these choices also tell a story about its values and its position in the national cultural landscape. During the era of our study, the Finnish National Theatre continued to fulfil its traditional role to a satisfactory extent, and during the 1970s it particularly succeeded in ensuring a continued interest in classic drama that would have received little attention otherwise.

From the 1970s until the early 1990s, the Finnish National Theatre kept up its strong Shakespeare and Molière tradition, with both playwrights being well-represented in productions, especially Shakespeare, but there were relatively few premieres of other classic drama. From the Classics, only Sophocles's *Philoctetes* had its Finnish premiere on the small Willensauna stage. The productions of classic drama were only partly successful, but a few of them managed to reflect contemporary realities, garner attention, and become audience successes.

Shakespeare as a contemporary mirror

Putting on plays by Shakespeare has always been the central spoke of the National Theatre's project of staging dramatic classics. In the 19th century a

DOI: 10.4324/9781003047667-11

series of translated Shakespeare plays had first appeared in Finland and the Finnish Theatre that preceded the Finnish National Theatre had included about 30 Shakespeare productions or revivals in its programme. By 1912, Paavo Cajander had translated 36 Shakespeare plays into Finnish.[3] The Finnish National Theatre was the country's premier Shakespeare advocate, and following its lead, Shakespeare's most famous plays were put on at all Finnish theatres, including as popular amateur theatricals. In total, Finnish palimpsests and translations of Shakespeare's plays numbered 56 by 2020.[4]

From the end of the Second World War until 1974 the Finnish National Theatre staged 16 premieres of Shakespeare plays, but only two of these productions were plays that were not regularly staged. *Julius Caesar* was almost solely produced by the Finnish National Theatre, and *As You Like It* was only staged on a few occasions elsewhere before or after its sole Finnish National Theatre production. It was apparent that up until the 1970s the Theatre's long-term goal seemed to be the continuation of the accepted repertoire of Shakesperian classics, rather than the expansion of the existing Finnish dramatic canon. Despite this evidence, the Finnish National Theatre had not formally or informally determined its own definitive way of staging Shakespeare.

Once the Theatre Director changed in the 1970s, there was an effort to shake up the Theatre's long standing repertoire of Shakespeare plays by selecting texts that were previously unknown or rarely staged in Finland. By modernising the accepted Shakespearean canon, the Theatre simultaneously fulfilled its traditional role as a champion of culture, as well as attaining its other mission of staging new dramatic texts. In practice, this was only partly successful: though the theatrical circles got a more nuanced view of Shakespearean drama, the new productions did not lead to the permanent adoption of these "new" Shakespeare plays into the Finnish dramatic canon. But by the end of the decade, the Finnish National Theatre had broadened its scope to include some of Shakespeare's more well-known texts.

Looking at this Savola-era from the viewpoint of the Theatre's Shakespearean traditions, if we include the five foreign Shakespeare productions that visited the Theatre, the proportion of Shakespeare productions remained roughly level with previous years. Any shift from previous Shakespeare conventions hinged on the choice of plays, not the number of productions. Amongst the nine National Theatre productions, only three were plays that were frequently shown in Finland: *King Lear*, *Macbeth*, and *Midsummer Night's Dream*. There were three Finnish-laguage premieres: *All's Well That Ends Well*, *Timon of Athens*, and *The Comedy of Errors*; though the *Comedy* was only staged in 1992 after the Theatre's Director had already changed. *Measure For Measure* had only previously been staged in Finland twice (including once at the Finnish National Theatre in 1944), and there had only been ten Finnish productions of *The Winter's Tale* in the preceding hundred years (once at the National Theatre in 1940). With the exception of *The Comedy of Errors*, the previously unknown Shakespeare plays did not fare particularly well, though the press had good things to say about the new productions and were even enthusiastic about a few of them. *King John*, adapted by Friedrich Dürrenmatt, was also staged in Finland for the first time. Visiting Shakespeare productions from abroad included *Hamlet, King Lear, Macbeth, Coriolanus* and *The Winter's Tale*.

The Finnish National Theatre's nine Shakespeare productions had eight different directors, four of them international. The plurality of directors meant that it was not possible to form a universally coherent way of staging Shakespeare at the Finnish National Theatre. Out of the visiting directors from abroad, only Declan Donnellan's *Macbeth* represented the British Shakespeare tradition. László Marton was Hungarian, Radu Penciulescu Romanian, and Robert Sturua came from the Soviet Union – all three were Eastern European. Out of the three, Georgian Robert Sturua who directed *The Comedy of Errors* at the Theatre was the most renowned Shakespearean dramatist.

The first notable Shakespeare production of the Savola-era was Friedrich Dürrenmatt's adaption of *King John* in Autumn 1975, directed by Eugen Terttula. Terttula was known as a Brecht-expert and a director of Finnish epic drama, but there were only a few classic plays in Terttula's stage directing career. However, the adaptation was close to Terttula's overall style of directing, and, thematically, *King John* fitted in well with the rest of the National Theatre's repertoire at a time when war and anti-war sentiments were being examined from multiple different angles.

The play tells the story of the 12th-century battle for the crown of England, fought between King John (known as John Lackland) and the natural son of John's brother, Richard Lionheart, the 'Bastard' in the play. The battle for power is bloody and like most plays about kingship, the play ends in bloodshed. Timo Tiusanen who has studied Dürrenmatt felt that the adaptor's mark is most discernible in the play's ending, its textual anachronisms, in the grotesque ways that harmony is broken in the play, and the way in which stylistic boundaries are crossed. The characters had become symbols for societal forces in the spirit of epic theatre and its principles. For Dürrenmatt the play was about Vietnam and Czechoslovakia. The adaptation had premiered in 1968 and was influenced by the late 1960s German wave of documentary and political drama. The play's political ties were highlighted in the programme for the German-language premiere of the play by mentioning historic peace treaties like the 1919 Treaty of Versailles, Yalta in 1945, and Bratislava in 1968.[5]

All this led to the production being labelled as being unusually violent. The characterisation was sharp and individual scenes were built with broad brushstrokes, the director's vision was complimented by Esko Elstelä's witty translation and the ample costumes and set-design from Romanian Dan Nemteanu transmitted a "Shakespearean" feel. In an interview, set-designer Nemteanu explained how the production's visual world had been created to capture Dürrenmatt's distinctive way of using anachronisms to support his pitiless depictions of people. The whole ensemble worked well together, complemented by Heikki Nousiainen's great performance as King John, who had just joined the Theatre and had been immediately given starring roles.

The production was also a success with the audience. Even though the more overt political messages Dürrenmatt had tried to convey were lost on the National Theatre audiences, the playwright was still known in Finland thanks to his own plays. His name and reputation for being a social commentator *ghosted* the production's success and created the sense that even when staging a classic play, the Theatre was tapping into the latest dramatic moment.

Alongside *King John*, the best way to renew the received image of Shakespeare in Finland was through new productions of his most famous plays. *Midsummer Night's Dream* directed by Kurt Nuotio in 1980 was staged on the new Willensauna stage as a joint production between the National Theatre and the Theatre Academy. These were opposing institutions, the Theatre Academy was labelled as left-wing, even communist, in right-leaning circles; and the Finnish National Theatre was accused by the left of being conservative and stuck in its ways. The show was a meeting of different acting generations as well as a spatial experiment. The students were joined on stage by two of their teachers who also belonged to the National Theatre's acting ensemble, Eeva-Kaarina Volanen and Hannu Lauri, who were joined by another Finnish National Theatre actor, Juha Mäkelä. The show was directed by one of the teachers at the Academy, Kurt Nuotio. The production used music composed by composer Esa Helasvuo who had taught at the Academy, and glass artist Oiva Toikka designed the cushioned and deep arena stage that also extended out to a system of ropes on the roof and clandestine routes snaking underneath the padded arena.

In the critical reviews, mentions of Shakespeare were incidental, as the production itself and the background of its performers took centre-stage: the physical joy of the young actors, the surrender of the teachers who were swept up in the performance, and the refreshing nature of the collaboration. Thanks to the Finnish translations of books by writers such as Peter Brook and Jan Kott that had revolutionised the way Shakespeare was staged, Finland was already equipped to see Shakespeare in this new light: the production managed to hold its own. 'Great dramatic entertainment, the best in town [...] It makes you sigh with pleasure'. Jukka Kajava from *Helsingin Sanomat* titled his review with '*Midsummer Night Dream* transformed into a charming ruckus'.[6] Special attention was paid to the Finnish National Theatre's Grand Lady Volanen and her erotic romp as the Queen of the Amazons and fairies that was laced with humour.

Three years later Jotaarkka Pennanen directed a production of *King Lear* for the Finnish National Theatre's Main Stage. Not long before, Pennanen had become famed for the *Romeo and Juliet* he directed for the Turku City Theatre, and Shakespeare as a whole was not an unfamiliar topic for him to tackle. At the Finnish National Theatre Pennanen was known for his 1980 feat of directing Albert Camus's *Caligula* in a startling Willensauna production that became the theatrical event of the year. Expectations for his latest production were two-fold: a continuation of his previous directing work on Shakespeare and a contemporary re-interpretation of the text using dramatic methods.

The productions of *Caligula* and *King Lear* can indeed be seen as sister productions thanks to the way in which Pennanen's style as a director and Pekka Heiskanen's visual world as a set designer are threaded through the both of them. *King Lear's* stage included a mirror image of the auditorium, and Pennanen's directing choices tied the production to its contemporary context: dead cast members would first sit in this on-stage auditorium, then end up back on stage in civil dress. The production started with a stylised masque, and Lear even entered the stage on a live horse for a pivotal scene. Shots were fired from Finland-submachine guns and in the final scenes the walls of the on-stage auditorium came crashing down.[7] There were many points of contact between *Caligula* and *King Lear*. Even though Pennanen had previously directed many Shakespeare plays, these connections displayed Pennanen's overall style as a director.

The show was described as impressive, jagged, uneven, topical, influential, and living, breathing theatre. It started as a grotesque folk tale and ended with shock tactics from the present day. The Theatre of the Absurd slipped into contemporary society and genre boundaries were crossed. The contemporary connection was universally understood, but many felt that machine-gun fire and Finnish military dress were too close to the bone. Kajava from *Helsingin Sanomat* felt that the production was full of child-like underscoring and 'the instructions from Jan Kott on how to create a grotesque Lear were always present'. As a whole the production offered 'a welcome instability that eschewed ceremonial pomp, bringing a humane glimmer to an inaccessible tragedy'.[8] Timo Tiusanen felt that the director's vision was missing one level: complete asceticism. All critics praised the way in which the performers had been directed to act.

The Lear played by Risto Mäkelä was a creative and accurate representation of a tyrannical king who only through suffering reveals himself to be a lovable character. The role of the Fool was played by a visiting actor, Veijo Pasanen, an old Tampere colleague of Risto Mäkelä, mirroring Lear's and the Fool's age and long shared life.

In his memoirs, Jotaarkka Pennanen references Ingmar Bergman's Swedish *King Lear* and the thematic choices and violence present in Japanese Akira Kurosawa's King Lear film. He felt that these interpretations reflected the play's concept of time and that they had accurately captured the problematic nature of the play's denouement.[9] Bergman's production from Stockholm's Dramaten Theatre came to Finland a few years after the Finnish National Theatre's premiere, and many reviews compared the two productions. Both productions were strong examples of director-led drama, both had a strong artistic voice threaded through them. Bergman's stage was stripped back and the costumes were in the voluble Renaissance style. The play's action was depicted from a distance and with biting cruelty. This contrasted with Pennanen where even in their cruelty, characters remained humane, and emotions had not been completely cut away. Critic Maija Savutie from *Kansan Uutiset* could see the difference in theatrical cultures: the Swedish tradition of court theatre contrasted

Figure 9.1 King Lear 1983. Veijo Pasanen and Risto Mäkelä. Photograph by Johnny Korkman

with the Finnish folk theatre tradition. The Finnish actor acted more as an individual and inhabited their role instinctively and emotively, rather than through conscious thought.[10] At the end of Pennanen's production the audience was pulled into the play through the staging, whereas Bergman's paired-back stage distanced the audience into voyeurs and witnesses.

A similar boundary-breaking production was Donnellan's 1986 *Macbeth* on the Small Stage. Usually, a visiting director from abroad directing an internationally recognised masterpiece would have been more suited to the Main Stage. In this case, there was a clear justification for choosing the Small Stage, as Donnellan as the leader of the Cheek by Jowl theatre company, was known to be a director disciple of experimental theatre. Also, the production itself required no complicated set design or staging. The production was the perfect fit for a theatrical audience who knew their drama and who appreciated experimentation.

Before *Macbeth's* opening night in autumn 1986, the papers covered Donnellan's and set designer Nick Ormerod's backgrounds and Cheek by Jowl activities. The pair of visitors described how they were aiming for a no-frills performance that stimulated both the audience's and the actors' imaginations and honed in on Shakespeare's text without any other devices. Rehearsals started with two weeks of improvisation and casting was only done afterwards.

Significant literary works as national interpretations 117

The visitors felt that Finnish actors differed from British actors only in the sense that they were less neurotic, as the actor residencies in Finland did not create the tensions inherent in the intensely competitive British acting industry. Actor Martti Katajisto stated that the visiting directorship turned out to be a great opportunity for further professional development. The cast worked well and were able to keep up with the director's constantly shifting requirements.[11]

The set was a large arena around which actors, dressed in grey, waited for their scenes. There were very few props and the performance space was created through sounds made by the actors, and objects themselves were imagined through movement. One of the other ways that the production differed from the expected, was that the playtext chosen was the most complex and archaic possible: Paavo Cajander's Finnish translation from the 19th century, though the text was edited and adapted by Rauno Ekholm. Even with all the experimentation the text was central to the production and the director did not want it abridged. As Donnellan did not know any Finnish, he was not able to judge how the language of Cajander's adaptation of the play was hitting the Finnish audience, but even as a non-Finnish speaker he was able to insist on the correct rhythm for dramatic dialogue.[12]

The production divided opinions. The bare stage and grey costumes had been designed to give space to individual expression and clarify the performances

Figure 9.2 Macbeth 1986. Markku Maalismaa and the ensemble
Photograph by Johnny Korkman

themselves, but the on-stage contacts did not always play out in the desired way. Most critics felt that the mechanical elements had drained the play of its tensions and changed its tone to something more academic, though it was noted that both Risto Aaltonen's Macbeth and Elli Castrén's Lady Macbeth were impressive. The most enthusiastic supporters felt that the greyness sent out sparks, whereas elsewhere it was dismissed as posturing. All critics felt that the production and its style were brave, something that was universally admired.

Finnish touring theatre had gone through a renaissance during the previous decade and the Finnish translation of Brook's *Empty Space* had been passed from hand to hand in theatrical circles, making the principles of Poor Theatre well-known and its methods widely accepted. This included guiding the play's cast and crew through experimentation and improvisation to culmination in a final production. Finnish group theatres had transformed necessity into opportunity when funds for technological experimentation ran dry. A single performer within a space took centre-stage.[13] Yet this was all still novel and news-worthy in the context of the Finnish National Theatre; *Macbeth* was still quite a distance from Finnish "Poor Theatre", but it was evidence that a production that heavily relied on the actors' performances could be achieved without adapting or shortening Shakespeare's text to make it more in-line with contemporary language. The production offered an interpretation that focused on aesthetics when Finnish theatre had long been emphasising social relevance and hard-hitting dramatic tableaux. The actors were also given a taste of the British Shakespeare tradition, as the production advanced scene-by-scene the unique nature of these classic texts and their pitfalls were brought up for discussion.[14]

The Finnish National Theatre's Shakespeare productions were an example of how canonical texts retained their relevance when there was an emphasis on diversity and opportunity in how they were staged. A director with an innovative perspective and reputation was also an important factor, and the status of the playwright alone was not enough to guarantee success.

The cultural heritage of Continental Europe

Traditionally the Finnish National Theatre had regularly staged dramatic works of art from the German-speaking parts of Europe, and this continued to be the case, although the number of new productions was modest. French classics were more frequently staged, and these productions also tended to attract more attention. Dramatic classics from other Continental European countries were few and far between, in contrast to newer European drama that was widely staged.

The two previous Theatre Directors of the Finnish National Theatre had been experts in French drama, and many of the Theatre's actors had been famed for their "French" roles as characters from Molière. Now there also possessed a talented translator, Elstelä. *The School for Wives* in 1976 and *The Hypochondriac* in 1987 exemplified the change that the Finnish National Theatre and other Finnish theatres had undergone during the ten interceding years. They were also evidence of the timeless nature of a dramatic classic.

Figure 9.3 The School for Wives. 1976. Set design by Miklós Köllö

The School for Wives was directed by Hungarian László Marton, with support from set designer Miklós Fehér and choreographer Miklós Köllö. The production was diffused with a Hungarian flavour through János Gonda's music used in the pantomime scenes. Marton was riding on the coattails of a previous successful production at his home theatre of Vígszínház that had also been his first production of a classic drama.

The School for Wives was a modern reimagining of the play, which usually meant taking the play's protagonist seriously. In this production, rather than a silly old man falling for a young woman, we see a mature man falling in love with a younger woman in a serious but possessive way, and the ways in which he fails to assert his power. The production's staging brought its own nuance to the performance, as instead of historic interiors the stage was dominated by an actual cage and a fence to protect young Agnes from the outside world and its bad influences. Servants rushed on stage to serve their masters through a hatch underneath the round stage. The spatial metaphor brought to mind contemporary Eastern European drama and it was possibly interpreted as a political message.

Leif Wager's Arnolphe was in many ways a new type of Molière-figure that broke the usual character mould by building on the character's internal conflicts. Repressed desire and sensuality battled against conservative morality and a patriarchal view of women. This conflict was reinforced by on-stage pantomimes depicting his thought processes and the final devastating denouement that culminates with him hanging himself. Following this production's line of interpretation, one came to understand that after defeat there is nothing. The extremity of Arnolphe's internal conflict was comical, and the character's tragedy did not come from external factors, but from the character himself. The personification of healthy and youthful love, Horace, functioned as an opposing force to Arnolphe, and through misunderstandings he was a vehicle for comedy too. The same sincerity was present in the character of Agnes. The play's main comic elements came from the 'juicy hand-to-mouth morality of the servants'.[15]

The production's black humour might have interfered with the audience's ability to identify with the characters in the play, but it was also an opportunity for the production to function as a mirror of contemporary society. Katri Veltheim, *Uusi Suomi* critic, mentioned in her review that Arnolphe's tyranny sometimes went so far that the viewer was left pondering what the production was really trying to say.[16] Was the critic referencing the fact that perhaps the director wanted the production to be seen as a metaphor for the current political situation in Hungary? Did she see national borders in the on-stage cage? The production was praised as fresh and modern, and it must have in large parts recreated the director's previously successful Budapest production. Traditionally in Hungary political metaphors were commented on, but a direct political reading of the play was not evident in any of the Finnish critical material.

The other Molière comedy, *The Hypochondriac* in 1987, was Finnish stage director Arto af Hällström's National Theatre debut. Not long after this production he was made a resident stage director at the Theatre, and this production was also chosen as the last play he directed before his retirement in Spring 2015. When comparing af Hällström's production to Marton's 1976 production, it's obvious that Finnish theatrical attitudes had softened in the intervening period. A lot of the reviews referenced af Hällström, who was known as a reformer of dramatic performance and a director at Ryhmäteatteri, in their headlines but the actual content of the articles reveal that the production belonged to the actors. This was especially the case with actor Pentti Siimes who had originally been classically trained, but had distinguished himself in modernist productions. The production was a celebration of both him and the acting prowess of Paula Siimes who was in one of her first big roles. We had moved from a director's theatre towards an actor's theatre. Arto af Hällström had the ability to inspire actors and also leave space for their individual performance. It was no surprise then that actors roundly came out in favour of af Hällström's permanent residency at the Finnish National Theatre.

Paula Siimes played the maid Toinette who represented common sense, and her acting was irreverent, fast, and uninhibited. Pentti Siimes played Argan who used hypochondria to control his surroundings, and his Argan was an insightful performance down to the very smallest details. The situational comedy in this production was strong but it 'bubbles up from deep inside, from the endless well of comedy. After laughter, tears easily follow as you are led to encounter such rich and poignant depictions of humanity', wrote Harry Sundqvist from *Aamulehti*.[17]

Contemporary theatre critics still struggled with the production's lack of a clear political or social message, and the most enthusiastic reviews could not resist a little barb aimed at the Finnish National Theatre: 'What a wonderful *Hypochondriac*, a comedy classic and an irreverent lark in the same breath!'

wrote Riitta Wikström, going on to say 'Dare I say a Molière-esque enema to enliven the old cripple of a National Theatre!' She felt that Arto af Hällström had brought some Ryhmäteatteri spirit to the proceedings.[18] The frothiness of the production was based on real depictions of human character – a deep undertone that some critics who were used to more direct messages were perhaps unable to pick out.

The difference in acting generations and their performance styles was most clearly discernible in productions of classic verse tragedy. Throughout the years, longstanding National Theatre actors had had plenty of experience with the type of verse drama that received little attention in other Finnish theatres, owing to a lack of classical programming. The contrast was particularly stark in the production of Pierre Corneille's *Cid*, directed by Polish director Adam Hanuszkiewicz. Marian Chwedczuk's set design was simple but glowed with colours and textures. Xymana Zaniewska's costumes delighted with their shapes and the surprising ways in which they differed from their historic period. Even the music composed by Jerry Satanowski was Polish. Despite an impressive production, the focus of the story remained at a distance, and the production presented a variety of challenges for the actors, some of them unsolvable. This production favoured those who had experience of performing in verse, and Elstelä's free translation of this French classic written in verse was as new to the young actors as the director's ways of working. Their delivery came out as slightly flat: the text and the tempo were mastered, but there was no extra energy left for freeing up expression or delivery.

Out of all the old German-language classics staged at the Finnish National Theatre, only Friedrich von Schiller's *Don Carlos* in 1981 had become a permanent fixture in Finnish theatres. The production's director, Patrik Drake, had graduated from the Theatre Academy only a few years previously, and his experience of classic texts and the requirements of the Main Stage were evidently still limited. The experienced actors of the National Theatre were demanding. Hannes Häyrinen, who played Filip and had a long acting and directing career behind him, was especially strong-willed. Tensions swirled around the production.

The production was visually impressive, and Markus Sandberg's music attempted to move towards a new type of expression by using instruments like four saxophones that were from the "wrong era". Some critics felt that production did not quite feel finished on its opening night. The play had been shortened with textual requirements in mind. There had either been too many cuts, or the cuts had been made in a way that affected the play's balance.

Häyrinen chose Filip's role in *Don Carlos* because he felt it suited an older actor, but the play had plenty of other fine roles to choose from. In the role of King Filip, Häyrinen became the focal point of the production, both thanks to directorial decisions and the actor's own charisma. However, Häyrinen's strength as an actor destabilised the entire cast and especially complicated Ahti Jokinen's performance in the starring role. Conversely, Häyrinen's on-stage relationship with Risto Mäkelä who played the Grand Inquisitor in the play was especially impressive. According to Kajava, it wasn't until the denouement and Mäkelä's entrance that any really impressive drama took place: 'He is like the beast in a mask play, inexplicable and scary, just like the play itself when it is not being unduly simplified'.[19]

Old Russian classics

By the end of the 19th century Russian artists had a strong reputation in Finland, as they did in the rest of Scandinavia. Aleksandr Ostrovsky's plays were staged at the Finnish Theatre and the Finnish National Theatre before the Russian Revolution. Nikolai Gogol was renowned, principally thanks to his plays like *The Government Inspector,* but his novel *Diary of a Madman* was also dramatised before the Russian Revolution. After the Russian Revolution and once Finland became independent, the cultural ties to the Soviet Union were almost severed and Russian plays dropped out of theatrical repertoires. After the Second World War, the classics came back and many of them were adapted for the stage and directed by world famous Russian directors. This included dramatisations of Dostoevsky's novels that were better known as prose texts than stage adaptations in Finland.

The Finnish National Theatre's 1978 autumn season started with an impressive visiting director when an old classic got Georgi Tovstonogov's fresh and contemporary re-interpretation. Critic Pentti Riitolahti felt that Ostrovsky's play *Enough Stupidity in Every Wise Man* managed to touch the viewer's reality: 'Go to the National Theatre – and go into yourselves! Both journeys of discovery might potentially be very healthy and call you through to healing'.[20] The play's antagonist, Glumov, has become frustrated with his poverty and he starts socially climbing by determinedly using all available methods, from flattery to bribery. He is successful in his endeavours and is surrounded by increasingly keen fellow 'climbers' who are also helping themselves by helping him. Glumov's determination finally gets the better of him when Glumov's detailed notes end up in the wrong hands and reveal unsavoury revelations about everyone involved.

In this production the moral message of the play was heavily underlined. The rotating stage created by set designer E. S. Kotzergin flitted between sets of rough dives and elegant salons at a comical pace. L. Schwarz's music both reflected and facilitated the narrative's development. The director's vision was particularly apparent in the acting and the ways in which actors approached their roles. 'When the Finnish National Theatre's acting ensemble that was once declared dead does performance work like this, the work of the director becomes secondary to analysis, despite his solid grasp of the production', writes critic Hilkka Eklund from *Demari.* Eklund often had very sharp critical opinions. She felt that 'the Finnish National Stage is for once filled with on-the-nose characterisations that have been done with care'.[21]

The historic play had been transported to the past using visual means, but the performance and its characters remained connected with contemporary realities.

Tiina Rinne who had just become a resident actor at the Theatre displayed her ability 'to switch her voice from a deep, titillating pur to the frenzy of revenge, to measured casually seductive movement' as Katri Veltheim from *Uusi Suomi* wrote.[22] Jarno Hiilloskorpi played Glumov at a dizzying speed. The actor's natural charisma that tended to soften his delivery had been stripped away, adding a hard edge and determination to his comedy. Olavi Veistäjä from *Aamulehti* described the actors' delivery as excellent stylised Russian theatre where the act of performance is highlighted and shamelessly underlined. The show's best part was wealthy and hard-as-nails Mamaev played by Pentti Siimes: a comic, imaginative, and polished character that was reminiscent of the great Finnish comic actors who had already moved into the annals of theatre history.

Pentti Siimes himself has described how he created his asthmatic, sweaty, and wheezy character. The director had to accept the characterisation. 'Georgi Tovstonogov had two habits that we picked up on pretty quickly. One was a disembodied *vot* sound that would sporadically emanate from the auditorium, and the other was long sighs. When I first offered up the character I had created, *vot-vot* could be heard from the auditorium'. The character was "bought" and my interpretation was approved by the director.[23]

The next director was not Russian, but nevertheless shared Tovstonogov's generational experience and considerable celebrity. Film director Vojtěch Jasný, who had left Czechoslovakia for the West, directed Georgi Tovstonogov's dramatisation of Dostoyevsky's *The Idiot* in January 1981. In the 1980s Dostoyevsky's reputation in theatrical circles reached new heights thanks to director Kalle Holmberg's productions that were based on a variety of his texts. Many of Dostoyevsky's works had been translated into Finnish, but only a few people were familiar with the novels' content in great detail. Tovstonogov's dramatisation picked out individual elements from Dostoyevsky's novel that described St Petersburg's social elite and Prince Myshkin, but some of the events might have been obscure to those who did not know the novel very well. The critical assessment of the production was divided and depended on whether the critic focused on the director or the performance. All critics agreed that the production's beginning was impressive.

The critical reviews are a great example of how seasoned critics like Katri Veltheim from *Uusi Suomi* and the newer critical generation differed in their conception of what made good theatre, or at least in the ways they thought and spoke about it. Veltheim felt that the show only came together on stage thanks to the intense exertions of the actors. Out of the younger critics, Kirsikka Siikala felt the production lacked passion, Juha-Pekka Hotinen felt that cutting the text had made some of the roles too thin, and Eklund only had praise for one performance, that of Risto Aaltonen as the anti-hero Ragožin. Nevertheless, the play was a success with its audiences, and although originally opening on the Small Stage, was transferred to the Main Stage. A difference in opinion between critics and the general public can be placed in the context of the wider changes happening in Finnish theatre at the time; amateur theatre enthusiasts did not change their opinions as quickly as the critics or the professionals did, for them the director's style represented a fundamentally familiar type of performance.

The subsequent visiting directors represented a new generation of innovative Eastern European stage directors. Lev Dodin's vision was evident in his 1987 production A. N. Ostrovsky's *Bankruptcy*. 'The Finnish National Theatre ensemble are all breathing in the same rhythm and you can almost pick up each individual actor's creative breath', Kai Tuovinen wrote.[24] Ostrovky's play about a Moscow bankruptcy scam turned into an exceptionally interesting production. This was especially evident in the final scene where the collapse of the uninspiring scenery simulated the story. The old was rotten, but when the cards were redrawn the future did not look too bright either.

Amongst the critical chorus, Eklund only had unreserved praise for the director. She felt that the group of actors were 'mediocre' and that Dodin was in the wrong theatre. Helsinki's City Theatre would have had far more suitable and capable talent. Eklund felt that the actors should have communicated with the director, giving him an overview of Finnish society at the time, as he was not familiar enough with the ideological landscape of capitalist societies and thus was not able to convincingly anchor the production in social or political commentary.[25] Eklund's review was intransigent and inordinate.

The next Russian production was directed by Yuri Lyubimov with his own adaptation of Dostoyevsky's *The Raw Youth* in the autumn of 1991. By this point, Lyubimov had risen to global fame and the National Theatre production was the world premiere of this text. The early 1990s were full of political and social upheaval, and the 73-year-old director could similarly boast a colourful life. For this production, Lyubimov created a coherent work of art for the stage, where Edison Denisov's music played a big role in the drama, and Andrey von Schlippe's staging and costumes both reinforced and provided a framework for the on-stage action. In this production, movement was constant, rhythm carefully considered, and drama entwined together through music. Tragedy and farce intertwined seamlessly, as did pondering psychologisations and emotive melodrama. In the play a young boy named Arkadi (played by Markku Maalismaa) finds himself caught between two different attitudes to life as he dreams about riches and independence. Out of the critics, Wikström saw an analogy between the play and Russia in-crisis; Lyubimov himself had a turbulent relationship with his home country that had been tried by various crises.

Only one stage director from the Finnish National Theatre was responsible for the staging of a Russian classical work, Gogol's *The Diary of a Madman*. The text was well-known in Finland, including in its dramatic form, and the year it was shown at the Finnish National Theatre other dramatisations up and down the country had also been staged. Eugen Terttula's dramatisation was performed by Tarmo Manni, a charismatic actor who had the tendency of placing his fellow actors in challenging situations. The production reflected its star actor, and the show was one that tended to suck the audience in. The production went on tour outside of Finland, though it did not tour the U.S.S.R., where a more traditional approach would have been expected. In this dramatisation Gogol's depiction of how a small-time civil servant ends up in a mental asylum was told as a medicalised narrative and the background as to why he fell ill had to be pieced together as the story unfolded.

Stage director Terttula's authority ensured that the production remained disciplined. 'When Tarmo Manni's impressive creative force is channelled into a performance that is made up of small gestures that can be externally analysed, and when the majority of his power is transferred into an explosive inner energy, the end product is a soul-shattering experience' Eklund writes.[26] Manni threw himself into his role with gusto and his grotesque humour mixed in with a disturbing performance that pulled on people's heartstrings and kept the viewer transfixed. The die was cast, and what might have looked like overacting for another actor, suited Manni and his absolutism. The show's final monologue had strong echoes of a sensationalised character who had also ended up in an asylum that Manni played in the 1960s in Peter Weiss's play *Marat/Sade*, but there were also echoes of Manni's own personal life as somebody who liked publicity and had built himself a reputation as an eccentric.

Finnish actors were successful at inhabiting Slavic characters. One of the Finnish National Theatre's emerging strengths was its ability to collaborate with Eastern European directors who understood the world of the plays on a deep level. Ostrovsky was a great example of how timeless classics are, and the interest in Dostoyevsky was based on the continued relevance of the questions raised by his writing and thinking.

Notes

1 Lehtonen and Löytty 2007, 110–112.
2 Alter 2000, 18.
3 Keinänen, 2010, 21.
4 Ilona database.
5 Tiusanen 1977, 336–37.
6 Jukka Kajava, *Helsingin Sanomat*, 15.12.1980.
7 Keinänen 2010, 159.
8 Jukka Kajava, *Helsingin Sanomat*, 23.9.1983.
9 Pennanen 2010, 214.
10 Maija Savutie, *Teatteri*, 8/1985, 8–9.
11 Maija Paavilainen, *Kotimaa*, 8.5.1987.
12 See Markku Maalismaa's email to Pirkko Koski, 3.1.2017.
13 Kyrö 1984, 41.
14 Jukka Rantanen's email to Pirkko Koski, 1.6.2016.
15 Sole Uexküll, *Helsingin Sanomat*, 30.1.1976.
16 Katri Veltheim, *Uusi Suomi*, 30.1.1976.
17 Harry Sundqvist, *Aamulehti*, 27.11.1987.
18 Riitta Wikström, *Ilta-Sanomat*, 26.11.1987.
19 Jukka Kajava, *Helsingin Sanomat*, 23.1.1981.
20 Pentti Ritolahti, *Kotimaa*, 20.10.1978.

21 Hilkka Eklund, *Demari*, 23.9.1978.
22 Katri Veltheim, *Uusi Suomi*, 15.9.1978.
23 Meri 2002, 165–66.
24 Kaj Tuovinen, *Tiedonantaja*, 8.5.1987.
25 Hilkka Eklund, *Suomen Sosialidemokraatti*, 5.5.1987.
26 Hilkka Eklund, *Suomen Sosialidemokraatti*, 2.10.1980.

10 Modern dramatic classics

Modern drama at the Finnish National Theatre during the post-war Directorship of Arvi Kivimaa generally meant Western dramatic connections and Nordic co-operation. Kivimaa had started his career as a writer in the modernist circles of the 1920s, and by the 1940s he was already known as an advocate of New American Drama, though the Finnish National Theatre also staged new European drama. And rather than stage the grand historical and ideological dramas by notable turn-of-the-century European dramatists, it was generally their more naturalist and symbolic works that were chosen for production. At the same time, after an initial severing of dramatic ties by the Russian Revolution, there had also been a renewed interest in early 20th century Russian drama at the Finnish National Theatre. Generally, the Finnish National Theatre had reacted cautiously to the rising popularity of Bertolt Brecht in 1960s Finland.

Theatre Director Kai Savola had started his own theatrical career in the late 1950s during a transitional era marked by second wave modernism and dramatic experimentation on the Finnish National Theatres's Small Stage. Savola did not reject the modernist leanings of his predecessor when he became the Theatre Director at the National Theatre, but as with the rest of the programming, he started by re-angling it towards finding slightly rarer dramatic works. With the completion of the Willensauna stage and the Omapohja studio space, familiar texts were experienced in a new context and in a more intimate relationship with their audience. The Theatre's programming focused on analysing the human condition in often unspecified environments and historical contexts.

A generation of Masters

In his *Drama from Ibsen to Brecht*, Raymond Williams examines Henrik Ibsen, August Strindberg, and Anton Chekhov under a chapter called 'A Generation of Masters'. Ibsen's and Strindberg's plays had always belonged to the core repertoire of the Finnish National Theatre, and many of their works had been produced at the Theatre not long after their world premieres.[1] Eino Kalima, a director from the Finnish National Theatre, had been personally responsible for creating a strong Chekhov tradition in Finland.

DOI: 10.4324/9781003047667-12

After the Second World War, small-scale dramas by Henrik Ibsen and August Strindberg with their depictions of problematic characters resonated with post-war Finnish society. The roles in these plays provided an opportunity for theatrical stars to be born, both on and off-stage, and specifically at the Finnish National Theatre. However, first came August Strindberg's *Erik XIV* on the Main Stage in 1977, and then Henrik Ibsen's *The Lady from the Sea* in 1980. As smaller stages multiplied small-scale dramatic works with problematic characters were increasingly staged; plays such as Ibsen's naturalist *Ghosts* and Strindberg's plays *Miss Julie*, *The Father* and *The Dance of Death* which had been staged in Finland soon after they first came out, but had not become popular at the Finnish National Theatre until the 1950s.[2]

Unlike Strindberg's other history plays, *Erik XIV* had rarely been staged in Finland, but thanks to its depiction of complex personalities it had become part of the interest in 1940s Modernism.[3] The success of the Finnish National Theatre's new production was due in large part to the intense relationship between Pentti Siimes who played the King and Risto Aaltonen who played the King's secretary, Göran Persson. Dressed in an old grey cloak, Aaltonen made Persson into a thoughtful and quietly deliberative character, whereas Siimes's King was simultaneously a jester and a wise man, both dangerous and fascinating. Director Eugen Terttula had taken the text and coolly and deliberately honed in on individuals. The production's message seemed to be: will these power games and man's desire to rule ever end?

The production was in-line with the Finnish National Theatre programming strategy that stipulated that a significant ideological drama should be annually staged on the Main Stage. Like many other productions, Strindberg's play could be interpreted as a political statement in a contemporary climate coloured by both the Vietnam War and the Cold War. Even though the play was set during a time when Finland was part of the Kingdom of Sweden, the complexity of its characters did not lend itself to a nationalist or heroic historical interpretation.

Jack Witikka's swan song production in the autumn of 1980, Henrik Ibsen's *The Lady From The Sea*, was even rarer on the Finnish stage than Strindberg's play. The play depicts family tensions and the hold the past has over people and where the realist plane intersects with the mythical plane, mixing in everyday reality and metaphor. In her Witikka research, Maria-Liisa Nevala found that for Witikka this play had been 'a play about liberation and freedom'. It had also been an intensely personal production, as the role of Ellida was played by his wife, Tea Ista, who had joined the National Theatre's staff as soon as she graduated from the Finnish Theatre School in 1956.[4] The play was not unfamiliar to Witikka who had built his reputation on being an expert in modern drama, but staging the production on the Main Stage was a departure from his usual scale. Witikka's biggest dramatic hits had been on smaller stages. His farewell production can be seen as the end of an era and the end of the road for a dramatic tradition that had favoured modernist mysticism and the absurd.

Critical opinions on the production differed greatly, with a clear divide across generations. Critic Heikki Eteläpää, who had been building his own conception of drama since the 1950s, thought that the play's central spiritual development was gracefully depicted and that Tea Ista performed her role with expressiveness and a charged intensity. Younger critics thought the production was 'deadening', presumably a reference to Peter Brook's seminal *Empty Space*.

Other Nordic modern classics were staged on the Theatre's smaller stages. Unlike other Ibsen plays that had been staged not long after their premieres, *Ghosts* had been a poor candidate for the national cultural project back in its day thanks to its references to sexual disease. By 1983 on the Small Stage it no longer delivered any particular shock value, and it also failed to particularly interest audiences. Another play that did not fare well was an old post-war favourite, Strindberg's *Miss Julie* that was staged in the spring of 1984. Conversely Strindberg's *Father* directed by Ritva Siikala staged in the autumn of 1985 was a dramatic production that was praised for its strong performers and the subtle hints of tragedy that were injected into the production by Eeva Ijäs's harmoniously beautiful set.

Any critical verdict on Strindberg's naturalist plays was inextricably linked to the question of how women were portrayed in them. In the case of the *Father* the position of men came up alongside the position of women, something that critic Kaj Tuovinen picked up on in his review. He felt that the female perspective of the director had wronged the play's male dynamics. In the cruel power struggle between the married couple of the play the child and fatherhood are both weaponised; the mother (Laura) is able to capitalise on these themes with more success. These were some of the strongest years of actor Risto Aaltonen's career, and his role as the Captain undermined the authority of the female perspective. 'In the Captain he goes through the thought processes of a soldier, an ambitious scientist, father, and a man: all of these coming together in a multi-layered way' Hilkka Eklund writes.[5] The misogyny associated with Strindberg had become mythologised, often obscuring the texts themselves and the strong female roles offered by his plays. As women neared middle-age available acting roles for them tended to dwindle, and this was one of the reasons why Maija Karhi saw Strindberg's Laura as a new and interesting challenge: 'it had something wild and eternal, at the same time some kind of awful humanity, a fight for justice and a defence of your own territory'. She also admired soon-to-be-retired actor Pia Hattara who played the play's wet nurse both devastatingly and exquisitely, especially in the final scene where she wrapped the Captain in a straitjacket.[6]

The Finnish National Theatre has a long history of staging plays from Anton Chekhov: the third dramatist from Williams's 'generation of masters'. By 2020 an impressive total of 261 Chekhov productions had been staged in Finland.[7] Kalima, a stage director and long-standing Director of the Finnish National Theatre itself, had already staged Chekhov's *Uncle Vanya* and *The Cherry Orchard* in the 1910s. After a gap of three decades he returned to Chekhov at the end of the 1940s, and during his last years as Theatre Director and after his

130 Finland's National Theatre 1974–1991

retirement he directed all of Chekhov's central plays, some of them multiple times. He was even renowned as a Chekhov director outside of the borders of Finland. During the 1900s the Finnish National Theatre staged Chekhov's four central plays a total of 16 times, of which ten were directed by Kalima, the last one being in 1966. After him, *The Three Sisters* was staged by visiting Russian director Georgi Tovstonogov in 1971.

From the 1970s onwards the Finnish National Theatre's role as a place to see Chekhov was impacted by an increasingly deeper understanding of the writer in Finland, and Ralf Långbacka's influential literary and on-stage adaptations and productions. After Kalima the Finnish National Theatre did not have a resident Chekhov expert, and the directors who tackled Chekhov tended to be visiting ones. At least the Finnish National Theatre had "authenticity" on its side: a working relationship with talented new Soviet directors.

The Cherry Orchard directed by Russian Anatoli Efros in 1983 was an impressive production. The production was visual and highlighted the physical gestures of the actors. The set design by Valeri Leventin included a backdrop of a redundant cherry orchard in bloom in front of which a faux burial mound kept moving on a rotating stage. Efros himself said that he wanted to really hone in on the ideas in the play, bringing a fresh psychological perspective to the table. To borrow Pushkin, the play was about 'partying whilst the plague rages on'.[8] Contact between actors on stage was minimised which contributed to the play's overall message. The director abandoned the play's apparent surface naturalism and brought out the tragic tones of the play by upping the ante on conflicts. Theatre in Finland generally at this point was moving towards finding more intimate on-stage portraits of people. The production was in tune with this cultural moment. Tea Ista played Ranjevskaja at full-volume and was able to capture the horror-laden tragedy of her role that the production demanded.

Efros was a demanding director and he had an innovative creative approach to his work. Actor Soila Komi has told the story of how after the first read-through Efros played all the roles out to the group of actors, telling each of them what their character was like and what their role in the play was. Efros had been fired up with new ideas off the back of his previous productions of the play. In Japan, one of the actors from his production had been borrowed from the circus across the road from the theatre, and the same level of physicality was now expected from Komi in the role of Charlotta. The actor was expected to drive a bike, and Efros wanted a live dog on stage. Efros also insisted that Charlotta have a knitted scarf that had to be taken back to the costume department four times because more layers were needed and the scarf needed to be bigger and bigger still.[9] The embodied loneliness that had been carefully built into the character of Charlotta resonated with the audience.

Efros's directing style with its emphasis on spatial metaphor is reminiscent of the theatre companies who visited Helsinki in the 1980s from the other side of the Iron Curtain and their Chekhov productions pulsating with hidden political messages. In an Estonian *The Three Sisters,* directed by Adolf Shapiro, the three

Figure 10.1 Cherry Orchard 1983. Paula Siimes, Terhi Panula, and Soila Komi
Photograph by Leena Klemelä

sisters representing the old order were crammed into a smaller and smaller space in their own house, finally ending up in their garden hemmed in by a high board fence in the final scene. In *Uncle Vanya* directed by Lithuanian Eimuntas Nekrosius the professor moved his young wife about by pulling her by the neck using the hand rest of his walking stick. In the final scene of *The Three*

Sisters directed by Hungarian Tamás Ascher the military orchestra did not leave town, but drowned out Olga's soliloquy about a better future with their increasingly loud playing.

The next day after its Finnish National Theatre premiere *The Cherry Orchard* was staged at the Helsinki Lilla Teatern directed by Kaisa Korhonen who had been one of the most vocal figures of the 1960s generation. In comparison to Lilla Teatern's production, Efros's production underlined the tragedy of the final scene. At the Finnish National Theatre the student Trofimov was keen, but a joint future with Anja 'evaporates into a joint miserable apathy'.[10] In the Lilla Teatern production the youngsters go trustingly off towards a better future, with Lopahin even secretly giving them some money for their trip. In his study Seppo-Ilmari Siitonen analysed the social and political messages in both productions 'two different ways of grabbing society by the shoulders', and two ways of looking at the inevitability of change. In Korhonen's production people were encouraged to change, whereas in Efros's hope is possible only when a person bravely confronts their inadequacy.[11]

The next Chekhov production was *The Seagull* directed by Kurt Nuotio in 1985 which the critics saw as a departure from, or an attempt to depart from, the Kalima-tradition that the rest of Finland had already long ago left behind. The production was built around Chekhov's mention of a comedy, and many of the actors were profiled as comic actors. Unfortunately, it seemed like the play's audiences did not really have a lot of fun, and the actors did not really light up the stage.

Uncle Vanya was staged at the National Theatre in 1989 when it was directed by Ritva Siikala. It was the second time Siikala worked on this play: she had directed it for the Ryhmäteatteri theatre company ten years previously. Since her first *Uncle Vanya* she had become renowned as a character-led director. Since that first production she herself had matured, which might be why the production was particularly aimed at a middle aged audience at least according to its programme. The show especially appealed to Riitta Wikström who felt it was both eviscerating and sensitive and a deep surgical cross-section of midlife crises. The production was carried by the play's central characters, Vanja played by Heikki Nousiainen, Astrov by Risto Aaltonen, and Sonja by Terhi Panula. The play's centre of gravity revolved around the apathy of the two men and the lack of opportunities. Sonja was played as open and resilient, a counterforce that balanced the production out.

Anglo-American relationship drama

The Finnish interest in Anglo-American new drama that had gathered momentum after World War II had its origins in the 1930s. Now in the 1970s and the 1980, Anglo-American plays entered the Finnish National Theatre's repertoire in accordance with an accepted formula: first the 'big' dramas that had been rarely staged in Finland before were shown on the traditional stages, and then from the 1980s onwards, known and popular plays were staged as more intimate productions on the Theatre's smaller stages. The small stages re-welcomed known plays by Tennessee Williams, Edward Albee, and Arthur Miller. The Theatre of the Absurd took on a new form.

The Main Stage opening show of the 1975 autumn season was Eugene O'Neill's *More Stately Mansions*: a traditional production directed by Esko Elstelä. The production was over-long and the critical reception was as muted as its audience success. The play's message about monied power having its comeuppance did not resonate with its audience. Another play directed by Esko Elstelä a few years later, G. B. Shaw's *Heartbreak House,* was a hit thanks to clever comedy acting and the allure of seeing 1920s British upper classes on stage. However, younger theatre critics found fault with the production, either rejecting it or belittling it.

Shaw's irony and long lines had often presented challenges for Finnish theatre practitioners, and *Man And Superman* staged in the autumn of 1982 was especially problematic with its expansive musings. However, this production was a hit, and it was shown on the Main Stage for three years. Thanks to the cuts made by director Eugen Terttula and dramaturge Terttu Savola the show went on for three hours instead of the original five. The play's message about morality, politics, and the power of money was delivered in an entertaining way that felt relevant according to contemporary theatre critics. Thanks to its philosophising, the story of uber-mensch-like John Bernard Tanner played by

Figure 10.2 Man and Superman 1982. Ismo Kallio and Risto Järvinen

Ismo Kallio and the woman who had chosen to be his wife, Anni, played by Marjukka Halttunen, resonated with the viewer. The play's philosophical focus was the hell scene that was often cut from other productions;[12] but this one kept it in, and surprisingly it became the very scene that allowed the actors to enrich their characters. The rhetorical duel between the devil played by Yrjö Järvinen and Kallio's reborn Tanner was impressive, fervent, sparky theatre. The production's success was especially tied up with Kallio's rendition of Tanner.

An exception to the rule that emphasised novelty was Eugene O'Neill's *Long Day's Journey into Night* staged two years later. It had been a hit play on Finnish stages since its premiere in 1965. 'Too much of one, and too little of everything else' wrote critic Jukka Kajava, referring to the centrality of Mary Cavan Tyrone played by Kyllikki Forssell in this production directed by Edvin Laine. 'Theatre that revolves around one talented star has passed us by: a single butterfly fluttering against a gray backdrop is no longer enough to fill an evening'.[13] Laine was not gifted at depicting modern and problematic characters. The production meandered along with the story without really analysing its meaning. Out of all the critics, Timo Tiusanen analysed the production the most closely as befitting his status as an O'Neill researcher. He felt that Forssell's performance grew into its majestic and shocking full height especially in the third act, but Tiusanen would have wanted a few more humdrum features.

American social drama resonated with audiences in an entirely new way when realism was explored in an intimate performance space. This was especially evident in Ritva Siikala's direction of Arthur Miller's *The Death of a Salesman* on the Willensauna stage in 1984. The play had been a success all over Finland since its premiere and at the time it was part of theatres' standard repertoires. Staging the play in the small space of Willensauna was new, but the production was also brave thanks to its traditional realism: audience members were so close they could see even the tiniest of gestures. Still, as Tiusanen wrote, the wide stage also witnessed its fair share of sound and fury. The production had the potency of a classical tragedy.

The play's two starring roles were played by two of the most significant post-war performers of the Finnish National Theatre. Willy Loman played by Pentti Siimes brought out the character's futile dreams, delusions, and heroism. Willy was a lonely character, but Siimes's connection to the other performers on stage was strong. Eeva-Kaarina Volanen playing Linda Loman had turned sixty: Volanen had now fully transitioned from playing bright young roles of girlhood and elegant roles of middle-age to the powerful portrayal of a mature woman. 'Again that ideal combination: vulnerability and power used in unerring proportions. Nothing beats that when it comes to depicting the human character', wrote Olavi Veistäjä.[14] The performance was simple, straightforward, and direct.

As the acting troupe at the Finnish National Theatre became younger in the early 1990s, classic modern drama offered challenging roles for younger actors who had found the style of great tragedies alienating. Performing on the smaller stages helped actors focus on characterisation. Eugene O'Neill's

Modern dramatic classics 135

Figure 10.3 The Death of a Salesman 1984. Eeva-Kaarina Volanen and Pentti Siimes

Mourning Becomes Electra directed by Kari Paukkunen in the spring of 1990 was taken as evidence of a renewed Finnish National Theatre. In the play, young people were played by young people, which was also true of Arthur Miller's play *The Crucible*. Miller had dissected his experiences of the McCarthy era by transposing them on a 17th-century witch hunt. The Finnish production of *The Crucible* in the spring of 1990 was seen as a more generalised declaration of freedom and righteous justice. The production was co-created with the Theatre Academy and it inevitably underlined the age of the actors involved. Alongside the young actors some of the main roles were played by experienced Finnish National Theatre actors. More than one critic referenced the fact that the play's director, Anita Myllymäki, came from Ostrobothnia, a region of Finland that had a strong religious history which might have given her extra insight into understanding evangelical religion. *The Crucible* was the first stage of the long-awaited and debated collaboration with the Theatre Academy.[15]

Realism had returned to the stage with a new sense of purpose, but not even the absurd came across as mysterious anymore by the 1980s. Edward Albee's *Who's Afraid of Virginia Woolf* has been part of the standard repertoire of smaller Finnish stages since the 1960s, and Jack Witikka's 1962 National Theatre production was one of the most prestigious ones. In 1987 a Small Stage production directed by Paukkunen was an impressive show of force of what two strong actors can do together: Pentti Siimes's performance was made up of small gestures and an internal intensity, Martha played by Tiina Rinne was strong, open, monstrous, and finally lonely and fearful as well. The production came across with clarity and finesse.

Martin Esslin brought Albee's play into the orbit of the absurd in the way that he broke the theatrical illusion and used ritualist elements in his work, unlike Harold Pinter who merited a whole chapter as an absurdist. The two Pinter plays staged at the Finnish National Theatre were not part of Pinter's early plays that were better known in Finland.[16] Soon after its premiere *Betrayal* was staged on the Willensauna stage in 1979, and *No-Man's Land* was staged on the Small Stage in 1991 two decades after it had been first written.

In directing *Betrayal* Jack Witikka was in his strongest suit as a stage director with this play, and critics recognised that. He also had two of his most trusted actors who were both skilled in modern dramatic performance to work with. Alongside talented Pentti Siimes and Tea Ista, Risto Aaltonen offered the ideal counterbalance to them both with his rugged manliness. The production became a mirror of its time, a play about values and the fraudulence of life. The show became a hit. In the play *No-Man's Land* directed by Arto af Hällström, Aaltonen and Pentti Siimes played two writers, the former subsisting in carefully constructed drunkenness, the latter hiding something sinister underneath his busybody comedy. Neither of these productions caused any consternation over their form or contents. The absurd had become generally understood.

Social commentary from behind the Iron Curtain

The Finnish National Theatre was also intrigued by the innovative atmosphere of the early years of the Soviet Union. Nikolai Erdman's Soviet satire *The Suicide* that he had written in the 1920s had been banned in the Soviet Union for political reasons. The play was staged at the Finnish National Theatre ten years apart, in 1979 and in 1989. Chekhov's contemporary Maxim Gorki was a life-long revolutionary which was evident in his creative output both before and after the Russian Revolution. In 1991 amid all the turmoil that was going on in Europe the Finnish National Theatre put on Gorki's play *Barbarians* that he had written in 1906.

The uncensored version of Erdman's play was not seen in the Soviet Union until 1989 as a visiting production from the Finnish National Theatre. Earlier attempts to stage the play had always fallen foul of censure. Erdman had built his writerly reputation with his first comedy *Mandat* in 1925 that had become a dramatic hit when directed by Meyerhold. The play has also been staged in Berlin. Conversely, *The Suicide* did not get permission to be performed at the Vahtangov Theatre, the production directed by Meyerhold only made it to the rehearsal stage, and Stanislavski also rehearsed the play without ever getting permission to show it. In 1969 the text travelled in a Czech dramaturge's bag to Gothenburg in Sweden where it was staged in the same year. The play's reputation got out into the world quickly and an adapted version of it was also staged in Moscow.[17]

Vili Auvinen had directed the play to great success during Kai Savola's directorship at the Tampere's Työväen Teatteri (Tampere Workers' Theatre, TTT) back in 1970, when the text was just beginning to be circulated around the world. Based on the reputation of that production, a lot of critics were disappointed with his 1979 production at the Finnish National Theatre as a visiting director. They felt that the production smacked of compromises. The show was still somewhat of a success, largely thanks to Nousiainen excelling in the role of unemployed Semjon Semjonovitš Podsekalnikov. The role had 'a dose of the eternal, a lonely clown's fantasy, a style that clearly set him apart from the other caricature-like characters', wrote Riitta Wikström.[18] Critics felt that the whole production would fall into place after its premiere, and based on its audience reception, that is what seemed to have happened.

We can assume that the regulars in the Finnish National Theatre audience took this play on as a Soviet satire; part of the production's success was its political attitude, not just its emotive resonance. The theatre critics of the time took up the play's relationship with Soviet drama either directly or indirectly. According to Mikko Heikka, the future Bishop and critic from the *Kirkkolehti* (Church) magazine, the production spoke 'to all of us' and Maija Savutie felt that Nouisiainen's performance brought the play up to the present day. Pirkko Koski pondered the audience's ability to self-reflect and felt that some audience members saw the production as a mere confirmation of their political biases, but regardless, the production's serious message was transmitted with clarity.

The production's tendency towards compromise is evident when you compare it with the 1989 production directed by Hungarian Tamás Ascher who used an earlier Finnish translation that had been edited in accordance with the Hungarian translation of the text. The playtexts behind these two productions had both linguistic and factual differences. The political aspects of the play are much more evident in the latter text and even the word choices used for stage directions imply Soviet realities as characters' names reveal their standing in the political system, and the monologue-style lines in the final scene mimic revolutionary talk. Ascher focused on the Soviet Union as a dramatic environment at the expense of Auvinen's signature vivacious style.[19]

Ascher had directed the play *The Suicide* in Hungary the year preceding the Helsinki production, a production had been named production of the year in Hungary. Amid all the political changes and as the general atmosphere became more free, the play had finally found its political moment. Ascher had long been in possession of a Hungarian underground samizdat-version of the text that he had kept safe throughout the time that a banned Soviet play would have been impossible to stage in Hungary.[20] However, the Finnish National Theatre production did not become a runaway hit like Ascher's previous visit as a director and the production was dismissed as a spectacle. Only Martti Järvinen's performance playing the character of Podsekalnikov stood out as exceptional. The character successfully communicated the 'macabre funniness of being close to death'. Hannu Harju's assessment that the actors' performances tended to fall somewhere in-between absurdist farce and psychorealism and thus were slightly lacking in potency is an accurate description of the overall critical consensus.[21]

Ascher's Hungarian production's presence was felt, perhaps making some of the actors in rehearsals feel like their work was a form of copying. What might have had an even bigger impact on the Finnish production remaining slightly politically obscure was the director's attitude. Ascher felt that as a foreigner he was unable to find ways to ensure that the play was politically topical in Finnish society.[22] Erdman's play had been born out of a political imperative and abandoning here a search for an alternative political message undermined the play. Finnish people looked at the glasnost and the tearing down of the Berlin wall from further away than the Hungarians who had been right in the thick of it. However, Finland was the Soviet Union's neighbour; the problems of its socialist neighbour were deliberately kept at a distance in Finland and ring fenced as the Soviets' problem. In any case, times were changing and the Finnish National Theatre was able to soon put on its version as a visiting production at Moscow's Taganka Theatre.

The two productions of Erdman's plays reinforce the fact that the Finnish National Theatre shunned Soviet art that toed the party line and consistently favoured social satires for its programming. Good drama and plays that were deemed to be classics were usually adapted in order to reflect society around them, though this did not happen with this specific Erdman production. The production was seen in the context of a visiting rising theatrical star. When a play's message was not transferred to the outside world in which it was performed, it lost its political power.

A director's Finnish nationality was no guarantee that the social commentary in a classic text would be successfully adapted to its social context. Maksim Gorki's *Barbarians* staged at the Finnish National Theatre in the spring of 1991 describes the reactions of the Russian intelligentsia and bourgeoisie when their city is selected as the venue for a new railway station. The change brings about accidents and tempts people into committing financial crimes and eloping. Kajava saw contemporary parallels in the play's theme by stating that 'a society shaped by its traditions and habits reacts to strangers with prejudice, just like modern Finland does to Somalians'. Yet he also felt that the way Sakari Puurunen directed the play lacked a clear connection with the culture and the time surrounding the performance, focusing on character studies instead.[23] Puurunen was an experienced theatre practitioner who had directed large-scale productions before, and the fact that the play was staged on the Main Stage shows how the Theatre were hoping for an audience hit. Sadly, this did not materialise.

Modern drama from the Continent

In the September 1976 Finnish National Theatre production of García Lorca's *Blood Wedding* retired grand diva Ella Eronen's role as the play's mother stood out. Her part in the play dominated the production's critical reception and it was one of the main reasons that the play was popular with audiences. The shows were almost all sold out, but they had to be cancelled after a while after Eronen fell sick. She returned to the stage two years later in new roles.

This Spanish drama of passion was not the most typical choice for director Eugen Terttula and the production was a compromise between on-stage poetry and social commentary. The production's strength came from the actors' performances. Eronen's performance was driven by artistic discipline even though her performance was deeply emotive. In the figure of the controlling mother there was a seamless bleed between an Andalusian countrywoman and a great tragic heroine. Marjukka Halttunen built up her bride character with the opposite technique, using strict asceticism. This was a play Lorca had clearly written for women and he gave them a particularly visible position in the dramatic action.

Lorca's reputation in Finland hinged on a few of his core plays, and the playing of passionate female characters tended to attract experienced female actors. This same line was carried through Federico Garcia Lorca's and Sinclair Bailes's *My Brother Federico* that kicked off a series of actor performances in the autumn of 1977. During her trip to Spain Forssell had become fascinated with Lorca and Francisco Goya and on her return she created a show out of Lorca's poetry that was illustrated by Goya's paintings and that also included music.[24] The production got its name from the small Sinclair Bailes play *My Brother Federico* that complemented Lorca's poetry.

It is unclear whether this production's reported 'new perspective' on Lorca was to do with the fact that the performance incorporated his poetry rather than his more well-known drama, or whether it was more about gaining a new perspective on the poet himself. Poet Tuukka Kangasluoma praised the choice of poems in his review, but the play at the end of the poems came across as a morality play. According to Kangasluoma, the overacting in the play and in some of the poems was entirely justified. Lorca was a darling of the left-wing, and the left-wing paper *Kansan Uutiset* critic Savutie admitted that the production confused her. She felt that the small play at the end implied that Lorca died because he was "different", not because of his ideology. Lorca was known for his powerful Andalusian plays, but for many, he was primarily a victim of fascism: a poet killed by Franco's men. For the people who had assimilated this political perspective on his life, the show was bound to raise question marks. (Savutie intimated that Lorca did not die because of his homosexuality).

Modern dramas from the German-speaking world were particularly in vogue in the 1970s. Two dramatists' productions fared especially well. First was playwright Ödön von Horváth who had been influenced by Young Viennese dramatists; he was not very well known in Finland. Then there was Arthur Schnitzler who was part of the Young Viennese movement and whose productions had had their Finnish heydays (with a few exceptions) in the early 1900s.

Von Horváth's play *Figaro Gets a Divorce* at the Finnish National Theatre in 1979 was the play's Nordic premiere and it remained the only Finnish production of the play. The 1930s play inherited its name from Beaumarchais's play *Figaro's Wedding*: in this version its characters return on stage 'sometime after the wedding'. In the play familiar characters move from tableau to tableau in a state of exile.

The production's director Lisbeth Landefort enjoyed working with the famous glass artist and experimental set designer Oiva Toikka. A wall made out of book pages and postcards was a 'paper revolution' and the 'border forest' was created by suspending bags filled with water in the air. The set design was made up of carefully constructed backgrounds, specific scenes, open space, a zip-line, and different types of geometrical shapes.[25] 'Both Oiva and I are refugees. Everyone who has crossed that border knows how strange it is', Landefort explains, referencing her own journey to Finland as an Austrian refugee, and Toikka's background as a Karelian evacuee.[26] Like many other Finnish citizens Toikka had left Finnish Karelia and settled elsewhere in Finland when Karelia was handed over to the Soviet Union as part of the post-war peace treaty.

Landefort had previously directed operas and she worked closely with Gustav Djupsjöbacka who composed the music for the production. The performance was enlivened by Fred Negendanck's choreography and Esko Aho's lighting design. Horváth put his strongest anti-war and pacifist statements into the lines spoken by the four child actors. Heikka sensed biting social satire and a revealing portrait of humanity behind the play's simple plot. What started out as individual human destinies widened out to an examination of the very essence of life: 'Every ideology and every institution – including the Church – has to be judged by how well it respects and values the life of a small human being'.[27]

Von Horváth's other play *Tales From The Vienna Wood* was a social satire, and Hungarian director Tamás Ascher did not attempt to soften its pitiless portraits of people for his autumn 1987 production. Ascher spoke about the importance of rhythm and of how translation made finding the right rhythm and tempo challenging, though there were some benefits to the constraints that language brought. He found the Finnish actors slower and more patient than their Hungarian counterparts (and they were not as prone to fighting among themselves), even though 'the temperaments of Pia Hattara and Kauko Helovirta would not be out of place in Italy'.[28] It is likely that these observations held true to some extent, British director Declan Donnellan had made similar observations about Finnish actors before. Ascher's way of directing the production situated the play within the bounds of realism when considering the plausibility of the scenarios and the actors' performances, but the play's concept of realism nevertheless was quite broad. In practice, there was a tendency to slip from realism towards irrealism from time to time. The show had to resonate, as Ascher put it: 'I want to meet my audience in a dynamic and active exchange. I do not enjoy polite dramas that people get up from feeling full like when they get down from the dinner table'.[29]

From the outside this production was very reminiscent of Ascher's previous production in Hungary from ten years ago. This was especially evident in the alienating Brechtian set design. The director set the overall framework for the production that was then executed collaboratively. According to Ascher 'everything fundamental has to emanate from the actor's person'.[30] In Kirsikka Moring's interview Ascher praised the Finnish National Theatre's production crew for developing a great team spirit so quickly, but he also described working with seasoned actors at his two home theatres: 'Back home I don't have to explain much, the actors already know what I mean'."[31] Ascher knew the text like the back of his hand from the previous production, but the long interval between the productions had brought some distance to his directorial choices.

The production was generally recognised as one of the top dramatic events of the year. For many actors being directed by Ascher was a new fruitful experience. For an actor like Tea Ista who had drifted into staid female roles during her career, being directed by Ascher seemed to have been the permanent turning point for her adopting a bolder performance style. Ista found a new dimension to her acting in the role of a cigarette seller who has accepted the brutal facts of her life that Ista played with revealing accuracy, compassion, and humour.

Arthur Schnitzler's *The Vast Domain* was directed by the 68-year old famous director Otomar Krejča on a visit to the Finnish National Theatre. In an interview in the spring of 1990 Krejča shared his withering opinion of great European theatres. In these grand theatres actors tended to laze about, but paradoxically they were also where the best actors were to be found. The Finnish National Theatre earned his praise: 'Here that lethargy is not yet as deep as it is in many other similar institutions'. Krejča was surprised by the differences between Sweden and Finland: 'People are not as blasé over here as they are in Sweden, here the actors have a lot more fantasy to play with'. At the Finnish National Theatre Krejča felt he was able to work effectively right from the beginning and search for the best way to stage the production together with the rest of the crew.[32] Actor Tapani Perttu described the rehearsals and the director's ability to see behind the lines. He felt that the intense work pace produced a lot of material and that perhaps a Finnish actor would not be able to keep up with that pace in the long-run. Perttu played the play's cynical protagonist, the industrialist Hofreiter.[33]

The play depicts the Viennese upper classes in an ironic style unique to Schnitzler, exploring the core questions of life through tangled Viennese relationships. The set design by Guy-Claude François filled the stage with deep red and icy blue fake flowers, creating a strong backdrop for the play's compelling characters. For Harju the production still represented museum theatre with an old fashioned structure and artificial language. The Finnish National Theatre had done better with other visiting directors and their interpretations of dramatic classics, as well as with other plays about historical subjects. Regardless, the talent of a master director was still impressive. Moring referenced the Finnish connection with the director's background: his Prague theatre had been the mecca for Finnish performing arts students at the end of the 1960s, and its influence had spread to Finland. The director's stage language was light and the rhythm airy. Moring praised the play and the production for the lack of moralising and sensationalism.

The return to absurdist roots

There was a distinct shift in the style of National Theatre productions over two decades, a shift that mirrored the Finnish dramatic scene as a whole. The dramatists and artists became significantly younger and the mood lightened. Not everything had to always be mined for a serious lesson, but a serious message did not lose its potency when it was presented in a lighter way. Attention became focused on performance and its physicality.

The extreme edge of the transformation was represented by Roger Vitrac's French play from the 1920s, *Victor, or Power to the Children,* directed by af Hällström in the spring of 1990 that disarmed even the most po-faced audience member. Nine-year-old Victor is a vulgar, mean, genius, terminally ill model child who terrorises the lives of his parents and neighbour. Their lives are not from the normal end of the scale either: marriages are all over the place and the elegant visiting lady, Mrs Montmart, has the awkward habit of constantly farting. 'The production proves that tacky does not age in 60 years', wrote Teppo Sillantaus. 'The play's beginning in the polite and normal looking Finnish National Theatre' was just the jumping off point for 'abhorrent things served up on a beautiful platter' that were followed by 'perversions, extramarital affairs, farting, military defamation, the breaking of expensive things'.[34]

The way the play was directed highlighted its grotesque and absurd comedy. This classic of European surrealism was a lot funnier and sharper in its surrealism than many of the other classics staged at the Finnish National Theatre. The acting in the production was done with a relaxed and pleasure-seeking attitude. Jukka Puotila as Victor was mesmerising as someone who blasted through official and unofficial relationships and ties and 'pounded token patriotism'. The production was at its best when the child troublemaker duo of Victor and his little sister Ester were on stage.[35]

The play had been staged in Tampere at the TTT back in the 1960s, and it had long been of interest for its director af Hällström. He had read it back in the 1970s, and now the Finnish National Theatre finally had the right sort of actors suited for its roles.[36] The review from critic Sillantaus was titled 'the importance of being coarse' — a reference to af Hällström's style that people knew from his work at Ryhmäteatteri and his production of Oscar Wilde's ironic play *The Importance of Being Earnest*.

The production borne out of the spirit of Vitrac's surrealism is connected to the work of esteemed and influential French dramatic artist Antonin Artaud who was becoming more known in Finland from the 1980s onwards. It can also be linked to the overall splintering of the modern tradition of dramatic performance. Different dramatic movements continued to co-exist, but they lost their overall dominance.

Notes

1. *John Gabriel Borkman* by Ibsen had its world premiere in Helsinki, where it was put on at The Finnish Theatre and Svenska Teatern (Swedish Theatre) on the same night.
2. Strindberg in Finland: Koski 2005b, 6–11.
3. Koski 2005b, 76.
4. Nevala 2018, 276–277.
5. Hilkka Eklund, *Suomen Sosialidemokraatti*, 13.11.1985.
6. Valkonen 2008, 302, 304.
7. *The Cherry Orchard* was the first Chekhov play produced by a professional Finnish theatre. The Finnish Maaseututeatteri Theatre staged it in 1910. It was the second production that became more famous, Kalima's 1916 production. This play was also not staged again until 1951.
8. Liisa Byckling, *Teatteri*, 9/1983, 18–20.
9. Akonpelto and Komi 2011, 30–34.
10. Maija Savutie, *Kansan Uutiset*, 15.11.1983.
11. Siitonen 2007, 74.
12. The small Kansan Näyttämö theatre in Helsinki produced the whole play (including the hell scene) in 1908.
13. Jukka Kajava, *Helsingin Sanomat*, 6.9.1984.
14. Parras, *Aamulehti*, 2.12.1984.
15. Finnish National Theatre's joint advisory artistic board's meeting notes 6/1990. Finnish National Theatre Archives.
16. Esslin 1985, 260–261, 313–314.
17. The Suicide [Programme] The Finnish National Theatre 1991, 12.
18. Riitta Wikström, *Uusi Suomi*, 6.9.1979.
19. The main books of the production. The Finnish National Theatre Archives.

20 Heikki Eteläpää, *Uusi Suomi*, 15.11.1989.
21 Hannu Harju, *Uusi Suomi*, 19.11.1989.
22 Ibid.
23 Jukka Kajava, *Helsingin Sanomat*, 15.3.1991.
24 Forssell and Kinnunen 2007, 249–251.
25 More details about the set design: Savolainen 1999, 258–262.
26 Leena Kulovaara, *Teatteri*, 4/1979, 7, 9.
27 Mikko Heikka, *Kirkko ja kaupunki*, 7.3.1979.
28 Heikki Eteläpää, *Uusi Suomi*, 22.12.1987.
29 Kirsikka Moring, *Helsingin Sanomat*, 11.10.1987.
30 Olga Huotari, *Suomi – Unkari*, 4/1987.
31 Kirsikka Moring, *Helsingin Sanomat*, 11.10.1987.
32 Heikki Eteläpää, *Uusi Suomi*, 27.5.1990.
33 Grahn 2014, 157.
34 *Helsingin Sanomat*, 13.3.1990.
35 Aarne Laurila, *Demari*, 15.3.1990.
36 Kaarina Naski, *Ilta-Sanomat*, 17.3.1990.

11 New Eastern European drama

The Finnish National Theatre staged many productions of new Eastern European drama between 1974 and 1991. In the late 1970s, despite the plays' shared critical indictment of their socialist environments, political critique in the productions tended to be muted and cautious. Theatre Director Kai Savola had previously worked as the Theatre Director of the Tampere's Työväen Teatteri (Tampere Workers' Theatre, TTT), as well as the Director of the Työväen Näyttämöiden Liitto (Union of Workers' Stages). It is clear that Savola's previous roles influenced the way in which Eastern European drama was staged and programmed at the Finnish National Theatre.

When examining new dramas staged at the National Theatre at the time it becomes striking that so few *Soviet* plays aligned with its programming goals. When breaking down new Eastern European plays by their country of origin it becomes clear that Eastern European drama at the Finnish National Theatre did *not* mean Soviet drama. Similarly, dramatic connections with East Germany hinged on one single play about Chekhov. Rather than being seen as Eastern European, Estonian drama was examined through the lens of Estonia being Finland's sister nation, with Estonia occupying its own unique position in the Soviet Union axis. Compared with the National Theatre's repertoire as a whole, the proportion of Eastern European premieres was not particularly substantial, but many of the productions that were staged attracted comment and started lively public discussions. What tended to thematically unite all new Eastern European drama at the time was the examination of an individual caught up in a problematic social situation.

By staging new Eastern European drama of its time, the National Theatre depicted the two decades of social shift taking place in Finland, Eastern Europe, and across a Europe still divided by the Cold War. By offering its audiences international dramas replete with their own complex ideologies, the National Theatre emerged as an alternative to the Finnish theatres that staged drama that overstated and pontificated its political messages. The National Theatre's Eastern European programming reflected the rapid opening up of Eastern Europe after the mid-1980s: from the open (though still largely metaphorical) cultural expression coming out of Hungarian theatres, to the public crisis in the Czech Republic, and finally to the national mourning in Estonia that foreshadowed the collapse of the entire Soviet Union.

DOI: 10.4324/9781003047667-13

Rarities from the Soviet Union

The scarcity of Soviet drama at the National Theatre was in direct contrast with other Finnish theatres, where there tended to be a wider range of Soviet productions. In 1977–1978 a 'Year of Soviet Drama' was organised in Finland. In many ways, the event showed how much the National Theatre differed from general attitudes in Finland at the time. In Finnish theatres very few people knew any Russian, but young theatre directors and practitioners participated in the event with marked enthusiasm. The year garnered lots of positive responses, but it was also quickly forgotten.[1] The event's report directly stated that the interest towards Soviet drama at the National Theatre had been lukewarm. Other Finnish theatres put on plenty of Russian and Soviet drama.[2]

Aleksandr Vampilov, the writer behind the new Soviet play *Duck Hunting* that was included in the Theatre's autumn season of 1974, was not a popular choice of writer as far as Soviet officials were concerned. After the publication of the season's new programme, the Soviet embassy tried to pressure the Theatre into choosing another play. Vampilov was known in the Soviet Union, but he had drowned at the age of 35 during a fishing trip only two years previous to the Finnish National Theatre's production. The writer's international fame was solidified after his death, and his play had been staged in places like London and Washington D.C, though there had been some trouble getting the playwright's plays staged in Moscow and Leningrad.[3] In the play's programme, Vampilov was described as an eccentric playwright whose plays had been translated into multiple languages. Anton Chekhov was named as one of his influences and his plays were described as 'semi-absurd' and as part of the Russian Gogol tradition.

As a text, *Duck Hunting* can be compared to Nikolai Erdman's *The Suicide* as the two plays centre around a protagonist waiting for their suicide. In Vampilov's *Duck Hunting* there is heavy drinking, marital infidelity, a fruitless wait for your own apartment, and generally unexpected behaviour. Yet the characters in the play are intriguing and firmly tied to each other through bonds of friendship.[4] The Soviet embassy's negative attitude towards the play was probably not brought on by dramatic or theatrical considerations, but rather the fact that the play's protagonist was a materialist egoist without a proper moral compass: hardly an appropriate representation of a Soviet person.

As a production, *Duck Hunting* divided the Finnish critics. The text was considered interesting, and the problem seems to have primarily been with the way that Jack Witikka directed the production, whereas the actors were universally praised. The overall critical consensus seemed to be more negative rather than positive, and its audience success was also modest.

The next Soviet play staged at the Theatre in the spring of 1985, Aleksandr Galin's *Retro*, was also a theatrical rarity in Finland. Its cultural setting was deemed too distant to really resonate in the Finnish context. But despite this, thanks to charismatic acting performances, and perhaps even partly due to the distancing, the audiences kept coming back to the Theatre to see the play. The production directed by Terttu Savola was quickly moved from the small Willensauna stage to the Small Stage with 50 percent more audience capacity.

The play tells the story of a widowed retiree who turns up in Moscow to disrupt his daughter's life. In order to rid them of a tricky house guest, his son-in-law keeps looking for potential wives for him. In the production the young people of the play are portrayed as grotesque, whereas the older generation, the widower and the three spouse candidates, come across as clean-cut, wise, and empathetic. The overall effect was rather black-and-white. Timo Tiusanen compared the production to *On Golden Pond* by Ernest Thompson that had been recently staged at the National Theatre: 'Neither Galin (nor Thompson) are in the business of renewing drama. They simply harvest it, working at one of its many facets. With them it's about people-led theatre. It's good that this dramatic avenue remains open to us still'. Tiusanen felt that the production opened up a dramatic perspective that could be traced all the way back to the Gogol tradition. This critical assessment was probably influenced by Kauko Helovirta's performance of the play's widower: his performance deepened from pithy mime acting into a thoughtful character study and a general discussion exploration of life and death.[5]

The season's new East German play was a dramatic hit largely thanks to its Russian connections. Anne Habeck-Adameck's *Chekhov on the Yalta* told the story of the correspondence between Anton Chekhov and Olga Knipper during Chekhov's later years. Two talented character actors, Eeva-Kaarina Volanen and Esa Saario, sat at their own tables at opposite ends of Willensauna's wide stage, writing each other letters. Volanen also performed some parts from Chekhov's plays themselves. The production directed by Eugen Terttula was a success thanks to the way in which the humane and loving main characters were interpreted by a talented pair of actors.

From metaphor to documentary-style

In Eastern Mitteleuropa where the Soviet Union's sphere of influence was pronounced, drama became an important cultural and social battleground. In a temporal art form like drama, meaning and interpretation are always created by (and dependent on) an interaction between audience and performance. Therefore, despite the fact that theatres often had a limited recourse to put on plays directly exploring contemporary politics and society, local audiences were still able to read social and political cues and messages hidden in the productions themselves. The development of metaphorical drama and physical storytelling led to a new kind of dramatic expression that bolstered drama's reputation as both an art form and a viable tool for social change. Poland, Czechoslovakia, and Hungary became focal points of interest for Finnish theatre practitioners and the Finnish National Theatre. Romanian drama also became increasingly significant in Finland at the time by the way of theatre practitioners working in Sweden.

In 1976 a Hungarian play by Lajos Maróti, *The Night After The Last One,* tells the story of Giordano Bruno, an astronomer accused of heresy whose execution by burning at the stake, his auto-da-fé, is delayed by one day, forcing him to spend an extra night in prison. The historic Bruno died in 1600. The play's title character Bruno encounters thinkers from across history, from both before and after his own time period. The play's dialogue is filled with intertextual references, such as extracts from the works of Plato and Copernicus. Meeting Socrates deeply influences Bruno and his desire to defend what is good and true while being trapped in the jaws of Inquisition. Bruno's discussion with the Pope on his last night on Earth highlights the tensions inherent to maintaining an existing system whilst factoring in new knowledge. Lastly, the conversation with Einstein places Bruno's fate in a more universal context, beyond his individual fate. This becomes a structural pivot point of the entire play. Tensions between authority and freedom are brought to the table by Bruno's discussions with Bellarmin, a childhood friend turned informant and Inquisitor.

The playwright had given the play the subtitle 'A definitely unhistorical play in two parts'. Through Socrates and Einstein, Bruno's fate becomes a locus of ideological questioning that looks at freedom, authority, defending the truth, and doing the right thing, and undoubtedly the relationship between the playwright and his own audience as well. Rather than the accuracy or authenticity of the events depicted, the central question becomes: what really matters – a question that Freddie Rokem associates with all historical drama.[6]

The playwright, born in 1930, clearly had a good command of the play's subject matter: any historical discrepancies were deliberate changes. Maróti had previously belonged to the Benedictine Order, worked as a researcher in Radiation Physics, and been in charge of a publishing house specialising in seminal physics texts. Maróti drew a parallel between the play and Hungary's recent history, a time when 'Hungarian Marxism was becoming strongly dogmatic'.[7] The play *The Night After The Last One* had been staged in Hungary in 1972 to great success. The production, directed by Esko Elstelä, was the play's premiere in Finland and it became a success, but the play did not go on to tour other theatres. The three actors playing the central characters played a big part in the play's success: Bruno, Bellarmini, and the Pope were respectively brought to life by Antti Litja, Pekka Autiovuori, and Hannes Häyrinen. Even the play's smaller roles were built to be interesting and engaging.

In the reviews, the play was associated with a series of contemporary Hungarian plays that had been making their mark at the Finnish National Theatre, placing it in conversation with István Örkeny's and Károly Szakonyi's absurdist dramas. At the same time, associations between Bruno and Galileo Galilei and Maróti's play and Bertolt Brecht's masterpiece about Galileo might have strengthened the play's status as a social commentary. The play clearly borrowed Brechtian elements such as curtain texts and the frequent use of comedy and colloquialisms to break out from high moments of drama, but the Brechtian connection was not especially noted by critics and, if mentioned, was briefly passed over. The reference to the historical

Figure 11.1 Viimeistä seuraava yö 1976. Hannes Häyrinen and Antti Litja (The Pope and Bruno) Photograph by Timo Palm

anachronism of Friedrich Dürrenmatt's plays about freedom was perhaps more compelling in this context. These dramatic intertextualities enabled the production to come across as a contemporary, ideological drama, rather than merely a historic play.

However, the Finnish press still avoided approaching the play from an overtly politicised angle. The play's message was interpreted in the context of a wider tension between science and religion, free inquiry versus religious dogma. These themes were seen as distant to the Finnish context where a sense of fruitful scepticism had always prevailed and religion did not actively repress information. When it came to theatrical criticism, an individualist perspective dominated, with commentators largely eschewing interpretations that drew a parallel with the political realities of Hungary. Consequently, an overtly political interpretation of the play was categorically rejected.

The Finnish National Theatre itself underlined, albeit subtly, the play's geographical significance. The play's programme included a Finnish translation of a text that had been published in the Hungarian press as 'Border checkpoint': 'Over the centuries and millennia there have been many ways for society to free itself of those who dare to think that there are things worth knowing outside of the accepted norms and systems: new things that are orderly and may even signal progress'. The text paints a picture of a railway station where the train tracks finally reach their end.[8] When it came to this production at least, it seems as if the Finnish National Theatre was being more openly critical about Eastern European politics than the Finnish press or public debate in general, whether unconsciously or not.

In Finland Hungary enjoyed a particular status because of Hungarian's linguistic kinship with the Finnish language. It might be that this special relationship made Finnish commentators reluctant to highlight the country's problems, even if they were already partly acknowledged. The Finnish National Theatre's reputation as a place to discover fresh new plays was perhaps one of the other reasons why the production was viewed through a dramatic, not a political, lens. This was further compounded by the received wisdom that the Finnish National Theatre preferred "apolitical" theatre. On the other hand, it could be that audiences in the 1970s were simply unable to pick up on the subtle political references of the play.

A month later, Romanian playwright Marin Sorescu's new play *The Source* was the inaugural play for the Theatre's new Willensauna stage. This production was also the play's Nordic premiere. The play depicts the struggle of a woman who holds her child above water when they are caught up in a flood, saving the child's life as the flood claims others around them. During Kai Savola's directorship at the TTT in Tampere, another of Sorescu's plays, *Iona,* had its Nordic premiere in the TTT's Basement Theatre. The choice to stage Sorescu was not only a sign of Savola's expansive dramatic knowledge, the choice was also probably influenced by Savola's previous experience of working with this same playwright and adapting his work to a new studio performance space. Both the TTT and the Finnish National Theatre had the ideal actors for the monologue-style delivery this drama required: Veijo Pasanen in Tampere and Volanen in Helsinki. Volanen's performance was particularly impressive. The play's message was enhanced by the auditory world created by Aulis Sallinen. He was one of the most significant composers of his time who acquired international fame with his operatic work. Some parallels have been drawn between the music at the Finnish National Theatre and the musical world of Sallinen's opera, *The Red Line,* that he was concurrently working on. The opera had its own premiere two years later.[9]

The connotations attached to the performance space and performers themselves shifted the critical reception towards a dramatic and theatrical, not a political, interpretation. The apolitical attitude to reviewing the play held fast with only a few exceptions. Heikki Eteläpää's review referenced the agreement on the sovereignty of national borders and the free movement of people and information that had been recently signed at the 1975 Helsinki CSCE summit. Eteläpää also brought up the fact that the play was banned in Bucharest not long after its premiere. He felt that this 'over-the-top knee jerk reaction from Bucharest is largely down to circumstances, I don't think we can really say that [the main character] Irina stands for the dangerous liberal ideology coming out of the CSCE summit'.[10] The political reasons behind the ban were not common knowledge in Helsinki, but despite its political neutrality in the Finnish context, the play was politically significant in its national (Romanian) context. Sorescu, known for his irony and celebrated as a poet, was a popular writer. He came to be known as the most significant (perhaps the only) Romanian writer of his era who did not go away to exile in Paris, but chose to stay and work in Romania.[11]

In the new year of 1978 the Small Stage celebrated another premiere, this time it was Václav Havel's duo of Vanek plays named *Vastaanotto* (Reception). Choosing Havel was a clear indication that the Finnish National Theatre was happy to offer a public platform to the radical thinkers of Eastern Europe. In the first play, *Audience,* an intellectual Bedrich Vanek, who feels like an outsider and who looks like Havel, is having a conversation in a brewery with its inebriated director. In the second, *Unveiling,* he is talking to two of his friends who have been gripped by a hysteria over the standard of living. In a few short years Vanek's character became a cultural icon; later, he turns up in a third play by Havel, *Protest,* and he also makes his way into another Czechoslovakian writer, Pavel Kohout's, play.[12] The politicisation of the Vanek plays hinged more on Havel's position as a writer in Czechoslovakia than the subject matter of the plays itself.

The play was directed by Lisbeth Landefort who felt that though the two-part play was clearly a very 'socially conscious play, more than anything it's a human play', and that its most important line was 'what do you intellectuals do for me' which is what the well-adjusted brewer demands of Vanek.[13] Actor Autiovuori remembered that the play's rehearsals did not include any discussions of solidarity with Czechoslovakia's imprisoned partisans.[14] Actor Maija Karhi felt that the Vanek plays were more about modern man's sense of alienation and the feeling of being an outsider rather than Czechoslovakia.[15] Vanek, played by Autiovuori, had an important role in pointing out the absurd elements of other people's dialogue and their hilarious irony. Antti Litja's intense depiction of the master brewer summed up the play's energy. The couple obsessed with buying things, played by Maija Karhi and Jarno Hiilloskorvi, brought the play's theme into dialogue with the wider context of a materialist modern society.

Figure 11.2 Vastaanotto 1978. Antti Litja and Pekka Autiovuori
Photograph by Timo Palm

Havel had an established reputation in Finland thanks to the staging of his earlier plays and this new production was firmly placed in that ongoing dramatic context. The interest in Havel's plays was at its peak in the mid-1960s, the years which were characterised by the success of other new drama coming out of Eastern Europe and the overall thawing of the political atmosphere in Czechoslovakia (which ultimately was to be short lived as the tanks rolled in in 1968). In Tampere the TTT had staged the Nordic premiere of Havel's first play, *The Garden Party,* in 1966 which was swiftly followed by a few other Finnish theatres staging his work. In the other Nordic countries, Havel had not yet established a foothold as a writer, contrary to how he was perceived in Finland.

After the annexation of Czechoslovakia and the widespread arrests of people who dared oppose the new regime, Havel's position in his home country became increasingly complicated and his plays were banned. However, he continued to write new plays that found their way out of the country through various clandestine routes. His two playlets, *Audience* and *Unveiling*, were published in the mid-1970s as underground samizdat editions, followed by the slightly later play *Protest*, all three finding themselves staged abroad within a few years. The first two playlets had their world premiere in Vienna in October 1976 and were staged at the Finnish National Theatre in 1978, making the Finnish National Theatre the second theatre in the world to stage them. The Finnish production kicked off a successful run of the Vanek plays in the Nordics.[16]

In the 1970s Havel was known as a disciple of a new wave of drama that Martin Esslin termed 'semi-absurdist' in his discussion of Havel's plays in the chapter 'Parallels and Proselytes' in his 1968 edition of *The Theatre of the Absurd*. Recognising that new Eastern European playwrights touched on the political and social questions of the day, Esslin examines their works from a predominantly theatrical and formal angle.[17] In Finland, these plays also tended to be analysed from a dramatic, not political, viewpoint. The Finnish National Theatre also avoided an overtly political interpretation of the Vanek plays, downplaying politics in the play's publicity, but the Theatre clearly knew it was dealing with a diplomatically sensitive topic as evidenced by the fact that Taisto Tolvanen, a Czech interpreter from the Finnish Foreign Office (later an ambassador) who translated the play with Kai Savola felt obliged to use the pseudonym of 'Taisto Veikkola'.

When announced, the choice of play did not attract a lot of press attention and only a few reviews mentioned Havel's imprisonment or his years of silence and absence from writing.[18] But all was not calm behind the scenes. A state representative for Czechoslovakian culture travelled to Finland to explain why the play could not possibly be shown. The Finnish National Theatre also received several agitated phone calls from the Czechoslovakian Embassy over the issue. Savola defended his programming choice by maintaining that the play represented some of the finest European modern drama out there.[19] The Czechoslovakian ambassador, Antonín Kroutžil, visited the Finnish Secretary of State for the Foreign Office to protest the fact that 'the Finnish National Theatre was going to show an anti-communist play by the Czech dissident Havel at the same time as Finland was due to celebrate the Finnish-Czech week of cultural celebrations', as the Secretary of State recorded in his diary on 16 January 1978. He had promised to look into the matter, but had come to the conclusion that 'interfering with the staging of the play could psychologically worsen Finnish-Czech relations'.[20] It is a paradox of history that the fate of Havel and other Eastern Europe freethinkers was sealed by the 1975 Helsinki CSCE summit's civil rights agreement, which had also been ratified by Czechoslovakia. *Charta 77,* compiled in Prague in 1977 and published in the West, demanded civil rights reforms in Czechoslovakia, referencing both the Czechoslovakian constitution and the agreement from the CSCE summit. Many people who had signed the charter, Havel included, were duly forced out of the country into exile or imprisoned. During the shows at the Finnish National Theatre the events that had transpired around the signing of the charter were only just beginning to be recognised.

The reviews of the National Theatre production referenced the playwright's own biography and Czechslovakian history, but at the same time the production was only localised through the lens of a much more generalised ideology. Havel was seen as a reforming discipline of Ionesco and Pinter. The fact that critics from different generations tended to disagree about the production could easily be interpreted as a generational political divide, but it is much more likely that differences of opinion came from different ways of defining what constituted good theatre. For younger critics, theatre, and the Finnish National Theatre especially, was a serious business: a performance could have rough or jagged edges, but drama had to convey a clear message to its audience.

Equating the production to an examination of how a dissident functions in society was a theme that was exclusively developed by experienced *Uusi Suomi* critic, Katri Veltheim. Behind the character of Vanek Veltheim glimpsed Havel himself and the 'imprisonment, home arrests, and exile orders' he had experienced; we see a writer 'stripped of his position as messenger and intellectual, reduced to an abhorrent troublemaker backed up against the wall, becoming someone potentially dangerous'.[21] Even in a more political review such as Veltheim's, the exceptional nature of the individual prevailed. It is notable that there were no extreme left-wing reviews of the production.

Finland did not accompany Havel's shows with political evenings of support for freethinkers, unlike neighbouring Sweden a few years later. The Finnish National Theatre wanted to support victims of political oppression, but it did not want to do it in an overtly political way. Regardless, the audience would have approached the shows with their own political views and with the contemporary political context in mind. As a neighbour to the Soviet Republic, Finland was well aware of Soviet ambitions and how they affected Czechoslovakia, and it was unlikely that the audience members of the Finnish National Theatre in the 1970s belonged to the branch of radicals who found criticism of Eastern European governments problematic.

Havel and his plays were a part of Cold War international politics. The response to his plays varied from country to country, and even just a few years difference could lead to markedly different reactions of political distrust. In any case, Havel's profile as a dissident from the other side of the Iron Curtain created a persona of somebody tied to a specific time and place, which might have curtailed interest in Havel's work later on, as Michelle Woods argued happened in Britain.[22] It became difficult to divorce the playwright's work from his biography and national identity. Havel became imprisoned by his own historical identity.

Estonian history

Finland and Estonia are neighbouring countries separated by the Baltic Sea with close linguistic ties and a shared chequered history in the time period leading up to World War II. When independent Estonia was annexed to the Soviet Union in the 1940s, relations between the two countries became increasingly challenging, despite periodic moments of political thaw from the Soviets. In the 1980s, cultural relations started to improve and they accelerated significantly mid-decade. One of the first signs of this new era was the Estonia night put on by Finnish National Theatre actors in 1984 where seven actors directed by Volanen and accompanied by music from conductor Atso Almila recited poems from Estonian writers.[23]

New Eastern European drama 155

During the later years of the Cold War in 1988 the Finnish National Theatre staged Estonian playwright's, Rein Saluri's, play *Lähtö* (*Going*). The play is about an Estonian family forced on the autumnal Siberian transport of 1946, centring on the two hours that the family were given to pack up their home and leave it behind for good. Saluri himself had experienced his family's transportation and the play was based on his experiences. The Finnish National Theatre wanted to ensure cultural authenticity by inviting Estonian Mati Unt to direct the play. The production's music was composed by Unt's frequent creative partner, Estonian composer Erkki-Sven Tüür. The rest of the production crew were Finnish, as were the play's audience for the most part, save for individual audience members and a few short-lived shows put on in Estonia.

Unt's artistic vision for the play oscillated between realism and the grotesque in order to contain the play's entire range of emotional intensity. Regardless of its artistic and political aspirations, the play had a tangible emotional intensity that impacted the way that the actors' performances were analysed. But the most impressive feature of the play was its subject matter as its characters were largely predictable. The line between good and evil was clear-cut and the most tangible representation of evil was personified by a man from the village (played by Autiovuori) who actively participated in the deportations. The biggest dramatic tension in this play was created by the fact that audience members and readers could draw a bridge between what they knew to be true and the historic events depicted on stage.

During the year of the *Lähtö* premiere, 1988, events in Estonia started moving at an unforeseen pace: criticism of the communist party in Estonia slowly became overt, the nationalist Estonian People's Front party was formed, and the official Estonian party line underwent a significant transformation. The Estonian deportations had already been called a 'mistake' during the Khrushchev era, but in 1988 they were officially denounced as acts of terror. Saluri's play was one small milestone on the road to perestroika and increased openness. In Finland, the Finnish press increasingly drummed up sympathy for Estonia's plight and also partly reflected on the changes seen in its neighbouring country.[24] The staging of *Lähtö* marked the first post-war contemporary Estonian play to be put on at the National Theatre, despite the fact that relations with Estonia had been activated at the National Theatre since the start of the 1980s (at the same time as many other Finnish theatres had started collaborating with Estonians).

The Finnish relationship with the Estonian family condemned to deportation was largely historical. The National Theatre's artistic team for this production had thoroughly researched Estonian history, and as well as the Estonian director, they were assisted by other notable Estonian cultural figures to help them understand Estonian realities.[25] The individual experiences of actors and audience members, and their understanding of history, greatly coloured individual responses to the play and its ability to function as a vehicle for private and collective memory. Even though deportations were not part of the collective memory of the Finnish audience, by identifying with the play's documentary-style cast, audience members could form a strong experiential link to the past that was stronger than written history. However, this "lived experience" was only created through a contemporaneous experience of a performance, and despite its emotional intensity, the past was not present as an actual memory in Finland. Estonian Lea Tormis put it well when she said that the Finnish audience members watching the play from their comfortable context would not be able to fully appreciate the feelings that a play like this triggered in Estonians. For Estonians, the deportations were a nationally traumatic event that they had been forced to deeply bury for many decades.[26]

By increasing knowledge of Estonia, building empathy for Estonians, and providing glimpses of Estonian culture, the staging of an Estonian play like *Lähtö* at the National Theatre was part of the impending political upheaval that would see a major movement towards a permanent opening of cross-border relations and an overall shift of borders across Europe. The production was a success, but it was the only interpretation of the play seen in Finland, despite the increasingly intense public debates about the Estonian situation. According to the programme at the National Theatre, Saluri himself said that societal events did not leave space for aesthetics: content was what mattered in 1988.[27] Examining theatrical productions that tap into Europe's collective memories, researcher Milija Gluhovic has remarked that in a theatrical context, systematic political persecution by the Soviet Union was not a dramatic message that tended to cross national borders.[28] The production of *Lähtö* is a pertinent example of how challenging it can be to translate national trauma and take it across the border in performance.

The successful transmission of subterranean meaning can sometimes be practically impossible, as the autumnal 1991 staging of the Estonian play *Tohtori Karellin vaikea yö (A Hard Night for Doctor Karell)* exemplified. After many failed attempts, the Finnish National Theatre had finally managed to secure Estonian's most renowned writer, Jaan Kross, to write a playtext for the Theatre. The play was directed by Estonian Mikk Mikiver and the play's music was provided by another Estonian, Lepo Sumera, the latter the Estonian Minister for Culture. Like many of Kross's works, the play is set in the past, the first two acts set during one night in 1855, the third act in a morning in 1879. The play's 'night' is 'hard' because the Russian tsar demands the doctor Karell give him some poison to end his life. The characters in the play were selected from history, including tsars and many St Petersburg officials with Estonian heritage.

When visiting Finland in January 1991, Kross explained that the play is about the doctor's sense of responsibility and Estonian independence.[29] The latter theme is so deeply buried in the play that it failed to transmit to its Finnish audiences. The extensive Estonian expertise helped the production deliver a faithful performance from a content perspective, but as the audience was a Finnish one, critics felt that a Finnish director would have perhaps had a clearer grasp on the audience's ability to make those connections.

Actor Juhani Laitala looked back at the spring of 1991 when rehearsals for the play started amid all the turmoil going on in Estonia; Mikiver had to absent himself from rehearsals for a few weeks, and at times he came across as afraid and nervous. However, the play itself did not feel politically volatile and the rehearsals proceeded as normal.[30] Estonian independence was reinstated in the time that elapsed between the beginning of the Kross play's rehearsals and its opening night. Tension and excitement were palpable in all Estonian visits at the time. Writer Ellen Niit who was in Finland in 1991 with Kross on a lecture tour explained how 'people's mentality right now is that now is the final chance to move ahead with independence, we can't back down'. Kross also saw the future as potentially unstable and raised the possibility of Finland welcoming Estonian asylum seekers.[31]

On the other side of the spectrum, the challenges of translating theatrical form and dramatic expression from one theatrical culture to the next were clearly felt when Estonian Unt visited the National Theatre as a stage director for the second time in the spring of 1991. Polish Sławomir Mrozek's *Portrait* interpreted by Unt became an example of the 'Estonian avantgarde' according to a Finnish theatre critic, where things were made obscure by burying meaning in a variety of ways. Jukka Kajava appreciated the play but did not like the production, he felt Unt's interpretation ruined the text and made the clear unnecessarily unclear.[32] The practice of hiding meaning was no longer necessary when things could be said openly.

The production took on a different dimension when examined from an opposing point of view. Jouko Grönholm felt that the play was a spunky portrayal of post-war Europe and the recent history of Europeanness. The play is set in Poland in 1964 and it depicts a political denunciation and the subsequent unravelling of events. Grönholm felt that the performance style distanced itself from the context of Finnish society, but highlighted the European elements in the play's themes. He felt that the aggregate message of the play raised itself above the personal to the depiction of people who had found themselves victims of Stalin's iron-grip. 'Mrozek and Unt let nobody off the hook, neither the guilty nor the bystanders, nor the people who are aware of their fate, nor the people who are indifferent to it'.[33]

Both points of view were fundamentally ideological, even though they came to opposite conclusions. In Kajava's criticism you can sense a demand for a theatre that deeply touches people and resonates with its audience; he wanted to see turncoats the likes of which he felt were found around him. Kajava felt that creating distance through a political geography that relegated the play to recent history kept the audience apart, effectively reducing them to voyeurs.

Jan Blomstedt looked at the *Portrait* from a third point of view by placing the production in the context of Unt's biography. 'It's about how totalitarianism affects the psyche, a very relevant theme in Eastern Europe right now'.[34] Unt did not see himself as a political agitator, but he had experienced the fight from many angles, both as a signatory of the so-called 'forty letter' for which he was punished in 1980, as well as a signatory for a later text that had a slightly different slant. The 'forty letter' was an open letter written by cultural figures in October 1980 that, among other things, protested against the criminal charges brought against the young Estonians who had protested recently.[35]

Notes

1. Seppälä 2020, 312–314.
2. *The U.S.S.R. and Finland in Dramatic*, 1982, 6–7, 9, 11, 14.
3. Koski 2019, 343; Database Ilona; e.wikipedia.org/wiki/alexander_vampilov. Last visited 18.3.2020.
4. Aleksandr Vampilov, Duck Hunting. [Playbill]; Playtext. The Finnish National Theatre Archives.
5. Timo Tiusanen, *Helsingin Sanomat*, 18.1.1985.
6. Vrt. Rokem 2000, 6–8. Maróti's play becomes a hybrid made up of different histories.
7. Sole Uexküll, *Helsingin Sanomat*, 21.4.1976; Harry Sundqvist, *Aamulehti*, 23.4.1976.
8. Originally an article by Béla Mátrai-Beteghin in the *Magyar Nemzet* newspaper, 6.11.1972.
9. Nieminen 1985, 170–171.
10. Heikki Eteläpää, *Uusi Suomi*, 14.5.1976.
11. en.wikipedia.org/wiki/marin_sorescu. Last visited 25.11.2020.
12. For information on the performances and reception of Havel's plays in the Nordics, see Koski 2016; Kai Savola interview, 27.2.2014.
13. Leena Kulovaara, *Teatteri*, 4/1979, 7, 9.
14. Pekka Autiovuori, interview, 29.4.2014.
15. Valkonen 2008, 298.
16. Ibid.
17. Esslin 1968, 24–25, 314–16, 422–23; extracts from Martin Esslin's article in the *Theater Heute* magazine were translated into Finnish and included in the play programme for the staged production of *The Garden Party* at Tampere's TTT. Kellariteatteri. Tampere 1966.
18. "Kotimaista Kansallisteatterissa." *Uusi Suomi*, 1.9.1977; G. Br., *Hufvudstadsbladet*, 1.9.1977.
19. Kai Savola interview, 27.2.2014; Kai Savola's letter to Pirkko Koski, 17.11.2016.
20. Suomi 2012, 139.
21. Katri Veltheim, *Uusi Suomi*, 10.2.1978.
22. Woods 2012, X. Michelle Woods has studied the English translations of Havel's plays and their relationship with censorship, theatre, and politics. According to Woods Havel's plays have been accepted into the theatre based on local needs, and these motivations were often political: people wanted to confirm their own biases by looking into the life of a radical living on the other side of the Iron Curtain. Havel's interest in language and its power politics did not meet the needs of these audiences. According to Woods this reduced and narrowed the plays' public image and led to them being forgotten when the political landscape shifted.
23. Koski 2019, 238–239.
24. Ks. Zetterberg 2007, 703; Rausmaa 2013, 24, 31–32. Rausmaa lifted this quote by President Mauno Koivisto's as the subtitle of his work 'You can do a lot of things in the name of culture', which is also an accurate description of the theatre activity going on in Finland during the years leading up to the restoration of Estonian independence.
25. Niemi 2015.
26. Lea Tormis, *Teatteriväki*, 2/1989.
27. Koski 2019, 296.
28. Gluhovic 2013, 7.
29. "Kirjailija Jaan Kross: 'Virossa hermopelin aika'."*Kansan Tahto*, 29.1.1991.
30. Juhani Laitala's email to Pirkko Koski, 20.1.2017.
31. "Kirjailija Jaan Kross: 'Virossa hermopelin aika'."*Kansan Tahto*, 29.1.1991.

32 Jukka Kajava, *Helsingin Sanomat*, 29.9.1990.
33 Jouko Grönholm, *Turun Sanomat*, 29.9.1990.
34 Jan Blomstedt, *Kaleva*, 27.5.1990.
35 Ks. Kiin, Ruutsoo and Tarand 1990, 7–15.

12 New plays from the West

In the 1980s public debates surrounding the Finnish National Theatre, complaints of an overabundance of British drama kept resurfacing. However, the plays staged at the Theatre came from a wide range of countries and the actual number of British plays was roughly commensurate with the national average, the figure being broadly in-line with other theatres in Finland. Statistics from 1988 show that British and American plays accounted for about a fifth of all premieres at Finnish theatres.[1] At the National Theatre the proportion was slightly higher which can be explained by the fact that the Finnish National Theatre was mandated to stage dramatic classics and many of these plays originated from Britain or the United States. When you look at the number of actual *new* plays from Britain or the United States that were staged at the time, the figure for the Finnish National Theatre was actually *lower* than the national average. New German, Italian, and French plays were even less well represented, and only a handful of new Nordic dramas were staged at the Theatre.

The lion's share of the Finnish National Theatre's new international programming came from the West. A significant number of plays were seen on the Finnish (or Nordic) stage at the Finnish National Theatre for the first time, helping it fulfil its traditional mandate of promoting internationally important drama. Some of these plays could be classed as artistic "finds", but most of the new plays shown at the Theatre had already made names for themselves outside of Finland. They were united by a common theme: the exploration of the human condition. Overall, the National Theatre's repertoire of new drama reflected Western dramatic conventions. Occasionally the plays' themes touched on national idiosyncrasies that were only partly recognised in Finland. During this period even the most socially critical productions tended to not be overtly political.

The plays that were chosen for Main Stage productions were ideologically sophisticated and largely plucked from the theatres of Continental Europe. In contrast, Anglo-American plays had very concentrated plots and themes, and they tended to be staged on the Theatre's smaller stages. Having a repertoire centred around Western drama reinforced the National Theatre's reputation for being an actor-friendly theatre as the plays staged offered actors plenty of nuanced and starring roles.

DOI: 10.4324/9781003047667-14

Trying to fill the Main Stage auditorium

Only a few Finnish premieres of international dramas were staged on the Main Stage. New international dramas tended to examine the changes and ideologies sweeping Europe at the time; they also played around with scale as alongside individual fates they grappled with socially recognisable groups of national populations.

Pierre Laville's *The Red River* staged at the National Theatre in 1983 is an imaginative narrative about the Russian author Mikhail Bulgakov and the characters of his celebrated novel *The Master and Margarita* mixed in with depictions of Soviet personages. The name of the play is a reference to time and its passing, to artistic lifeblood, and at least in the Finnish context, social revolution. Bulgakov's novel had been published in Finnish translation at the end of the 1960s, and the novel itself was dramatised by KOM Theatre a month after the National Theatre premiere.

The play's familiar context was not enough to guarantee dramatic success, even though the characters in the play from Bulgakov's novel, notably Doctor Woland and the Cat, were widely associated with text. Stage director Eugen Terttula's vision for the production was half-finished and uneven. Individual roles such as Heikki Nousiainen as Woland, Juha Mäkelä as the Cat, or Esa Saario as the Theatre Director were judged to be triumphs, but the actors did not mesh well as a group. One of the other possible contributing factors to the production's lukewarm success was the level of cultural knowledge assumed by the script. This production might have filled more seats if staged on the more culturally elite smaller stages.

Two years later the Finnish National Theatre staged Ariane Mnouchkine's adaptation of Klaus Mann's novel *Mefisto*. The play was already widely known in theatrical circles thanks to the reputation of its French premiere, other televised productions, and the stage and film adaptations of the original novel itself. The novel had been published in a Finnish translation the previous year, and the play itself had already been staged in Finland in Swedish at the Åbo Svenska Teater (Turku Swedish Theatre). The play shows how artists either became victims or agents of Hitler's cultural political agenda, resembling Klaus Mann's biography. The play's protagonist, actor Hendrik Höfgen, ends up as an agent of Nazism, similar to the historic actor Gustav Gründgens who belonged to Mann's social circle. Höfgen's (and Gründgens') most famous theatrical role was Mephisto from *Doctor Faustus*. The play is set in the artistic circles surrounding Hamburg's Art Theatre, depicting a post-World War I Germany in vivid tableaux.

The production conformed to the spatial demands set by the Main Stage. Olli Tola's directing style took its cue from the popular French production and the set design by Kari Junnikkala captured the spirit of the play's era. The costumes conformed to the conventions of its setting: Nazi soldiers in their uniforms, Höfgen's coat-and-tails and Mephisto cape during his star moments, and the nightclub decadence of the early scenes. The wide stage worked well with Tola's visually impressive artistic direction. The stage was stripped bare across its entire breadth and the tiled walls on the side were left visible. The mise-en-scène thrived off the dynamism of the national movements explored, and though the performance tried to be as natural and synchronised as possible, the overall impression was rather fragmented. In the more intense scenes Tola depicted how national socialism cornered individuals and made them feel trapped. The set-like scenery was suddenly replaced by a tangible sense of threat.

The critical reception was mixed with many critics holding opposing views and the production was also reviewed in the context of general attitudes towards the National Theatre. Anneli Kanto complained about the fact that in typical Finnish National Theatre style, the community was edited down to an individual narrative, contemporary references were pushed aside, and ideologies were actively avoided. Kirsikka Moring avoided directly criticising the director: 'Olli Tola has succeeded in a way that is almost maximal at the Finnish National Theatre. And he has failed because of a trap created by circumstances'.[2] Hilkka Eklund felt that the directorial machine contented itself with illustrating history without achieving a critical parallel with the text itself. Finnish audiences were probably unfamiliar with Goethe's *Faust* so the lines that hinged on Faust quotations remained unclear. The actors were generally praised. 'Across the board the delivery was good, very engaging. And the actors cut fine figures,' wrote Timo Tiusanen, who heaped praise on the entire cast, culminating in Nousiainen who was playing the lead: 'Höfgen: draped in red and black, a bat on its way to a blinding light with long strokes of his bat wings'.[3]

Italian Eduardo De Filippo's *The Great Magic* was not a new play, but it had been recently staged in Italy directed by Giorgio Strehler and its reputation ensured topicality. The critical reception of the play highlights the challenges of conveying culture, but also how crucial culture is to audience experience. Compared to the two previous plays, the subject matter of this play did not resonate in Finland and the production itself betrayed some of the challenges of staging international new drama on the Main Stage. The central magic of the play was not captured, in direct contrast with Strehler's Italian production that had originally inspired the programming choice. In Strehler's production, he had successfully transported Neapolitan folk theatre to northern Milan and made a fruitful parallel between the play's distrust of magic and the country's recent history of dictatorship. In Finland the theme of magic was not subject to a strong directorial vision. Magic became merely an interpersonal problem that did not widen into a structural comment on society. In Finland the actors triumphed and ensured the production's appeal by carrying the story forward, but the ideological impact of the production was reduced to a mere fairytale for grown-ups.[4]

Relationships and cultural caricatures

Small-scale family dramas and new plays that focused on intimate encounters between people were usually successful at the Theatre, with some productions becoming runaway successes. The productions themselves were usually received as narratives about individuals, and their larger social themes did not tend to cross cultural borders. As time went on, the stages at the Finnish National Theatre diversified, and the themes of the plays themselves radicalised; it appeared that the Theatre was beginning to cater to a more segmented audience. The dramatic themes explored did not become genuinely radical until the 1980s, when the Willensauna stage and the Omapohja studio took over the mantle of experimentation from the Small Stage.

Directing David Storey's *In Celebration* in 1975, Edvin Laine combined a masterful approach with a softening of the play's political message. The result was a piece of competent and solid theatre without reproach, but also without a huge sense of excitement. Ernest Thompson's *On Golden Pond* in December 1979 was a slow-moving show that benefited from the actors' warm-hearted delivery, especially the performance of actor Hannes Häyrinen. His depiction of an aging man grew into a deep and nuanced character portrait. The playwright was present at the opening night; a clear sign that the Finnish National Theatre predicted a success, which the show turned out to be.

A more controversial play was Simon Gray's *Close of Play* that created a stir in the spring of 1980 with its depiction of academic Jasper Spencer's family's spiteful grudges. Risto Aaltonen gave a suggestive performance that was loaded with passion: a high-strung portrait of alcoholism, inferiority, delusions, fears, and repression. The chemistry between Siimes who played the other brother and Aaltonen was impressive. The production also resonated with its audiences.

Close of Play was also part of Finland's biggest drama festival, Tampere's Theatre Festival, where the best theatre from the preceding year was celebrated and evaluated. Ansa Hartel's review of the Tampere performance in *Aamulehti* (the paper's first review had been a favourable one) was titled 'The anaemic set in a cruel game' and poured scorn on almost every aspect of the production. She was especially critical about the actors' sophisticated delivery that she found anaemic; not even fine stage directing by Lisbeth Landefort was able to drag the play back to the land of the living. The festival panel praised the actors' professionalism and singled out Siimes and Pia Hattara for special praise, but the panel also felt that the play's way of dealing with issues felt superficial and pedestrian.[5] A few days later in *Uusi Suomi* Katri Veltheim challenged this narrow critical view and in turn criticised some of the festival prizes; she would have liked to see at least one of these three *Close of Play* actors acknowledged: Maija Karhi, Hattara, and Aaltonen.[6] The production's critical reception in Tampere is a stark reminder of the inherent contradictions of contemporary theatrical discourse. Perhaps National Theatre plays were inextricably tied to their performance space, "the motherhouse", and outside of that sphere an entirely new form of dramatic expression was expected and required?

In the autumn of 1982, stage director Hannu Heikinheimo's take on Sam Shepard's play *True West* emphasised the play's psychological and naturalist elements, rather than the absurdism that underpinned the text. The production shone a light on the mythologised "American Wild West" but as it was staged abroad devoid of its original national context the Wild West became just a superficial backdrop for the play's dramatic events. Antti Litja played the role of the old-school survivor who pushes back against the societal norms, whereas Mäkelä is the townie who has acquired some polish through education. Litja's performance highlighted physical menace, whereas Mäkelä's performance was built up through tiny and precise gestures that carried him through to the final inebriation and showdown. Audiences generally liked the play, but one of the issues that surfaced with this production was the audience's thematic distance from the subject matter. The play did not have any contemporary links with audience realities. Its success was largely thanks to its comedic elements and the reputation of its actors. Theatre critic Greta Brotherus dismissed it as a farce.

Seen at the National Theatre a few years later, Sam Shephard's *Forever Yours* set in the American South similarly failed to rouse audiences. The play's central passionate affair between two half-siblings did not resonate with Finnish audiences as an analogy for the birth of the American nation and what it means to be American. Incest is an unsavoury topic and the roots of the American nation were distant to most Finnish people so it was particularly hard for audiences to connect with the play on an emotional level. The success of this production hinged on its actors. Mäkelä did a great job at playing the tough old American hero Eddie and Karin Pacius as Eddie's half-sister May was 'faster and more passionate than ever' among her different characters.[7]

A rarity for the Finnish National Theatre was the new German play *Bass Viola* by Patrick Süskind, a funny, ironic, self-ironic, and even airy play. The play was a success largely thanks to the power of monologue actor Leif Wager and his charisma. The play's critical success was influenced by an earlier production of the play at the Swedish musical theatre Oktober that had emphasised the nastier sides of the play's bass player's character. The Finnish production was slated for being too superficial when the script itself clearly had tragic hallmarks and ample opportunities for honing in on the unhappiness of an inconsequential person, but the production eschewed tragedy in its dramatic and casting choices.

Wager was known as a gentle and animated figure. 'But thankfully he is also an actor, with all the accompanying charisma; a talented comic actor above all else. The humour in Süskind's text blossoms and the audience member is persuaded to go on a journey by Wager,' writes Jukka Kajava.[8] Wager himself found this role to be one of his more interesting contemporary ones, allowing him to momentarily step away from playing great men and develop his performance style in close proximity with the audience. He especially praised the special nature of the Willensauna stage where audiences could practically see his thoughts, but he himself could also sense what the audiences were thinking. This was especially evident in the scenes where he was playing his bass onstage, even though the playing was mainly for show, the audience was close and could observe his technique.[9]

Just like *Bass Viola* Herb Gardner's *I'm Not Rappaport* in the autumn of 1989 was a success thanks to the work put in by its cast. Kauko Helovirta explained in an interview that he saw straight away that he'd been given a dream role with this text. Old and poor Nat was a real down-and-out, sitting on a bench in New York's Central Park. The show revolved around Nat and Snad, an old African American man who sits beside Nat, played by Tommi Rinne. The acting and the obvious joy of the performances captivated the audience. Terttu Savola's directing relied on naturalness and realism, and the intimate style created a charged atmosphere. Yet under the playful surface there was some melancholy and a concern for the state of the world.

The whole human message of the play was wrapped up in the figure of Nat; a message that grew out of imagination, morality, and the dreams we have for a better society. Snad was a comic and touching figure, though the cultural differences between New York and Finland were at times alienating. A Finnish audience member was easily swayed by the cliched characters found in contemporary literature and cinema about New York rather than the actual experiences of poor Blacks in New York at the time. The play's Jewishness also failed to elicit special note. The most topical cultural readings of the text did not transfer to the Finnish context. However, the audience clearly liked the production, and thanks to its audience success, the play was transferred from the Willensauna stage to the bigger Small Stage.

Swedish Lars Norén, known for his brutal depictions of family life, was already a renowned playwright in many countries, Finland included, when his play *Autumn and Winter* was staged on the Willensauna stage in 1990. Directed by Heini Tola the production was praised for its controlled energy and the way it enabled actors to thrive on stage. *Autumn and Winter* was a play about women: the play offered its strongest roles to Kyllikki Forsell who played the mother, and Pacius who played her aggressive and problematic daughter Anni. Kajava described the uncompromising nature of Forsell's performance: 'Under the facade of a mother stretching to everything, a disappointed woman's face starts to emerge through the cracks. [–] The external transformation is almost invisible, but the truth that radiates from a heart that's about to break is palpable and emotive'.[10] The portrait of the daughter was especially cruel: 'a portrait of a damaged person, a person who in some strange way uses pain and unhappiness as their lifeforce,' wrote Riitta Wikström.[11] Heikki Eteläpää described the play's ambience: 'Cruel, pitiless? That too. But first and foremost, live, alive with real recognisable characters from our welfare age. And through them, a theatre that is alive'.[12]

Norén's play was one of the few Swedish premieres in the National Theatre's repertoire at the time. Norén was often compared to August Strindberg and his plays were frequently staged, including in Finland. The National Theatre's programming choices often followed a slightly different path to other theatres but in this context the production was part of its national duty to stage drama that was significant in the Nordics.

Dramatic and stage celebrity

Some of the National Theatre's actors had been made stars by the Finnish film industry and the impact of television on actors' celebrity grew significantly, especially from the 1980s onwards. However, celebrities were being formed outside of the media in theatrical circles too, especially at the National Theatre. An actor's public image was invariably impacted by the coverage of their private life in the press, but their image was also influenced by their starring roles at the Theatre. Kajava's critical reviews included a reference to a 'Finnish National Theatre-style' of directing, where the attention was concentrated on key actors[13] and traditional mise-en-scène. Alongside mise-en-scène, intertextuality, and the context of the production, a significant success factor was an actor's personal way of working and their performance mode.[14] Western drama with its emphasis on the actor provided opportunities for individual actors to shine and the stage director's or even an individual actor's performance key played a big role in how a production was ultimately received.

The most famous actor-star of the National Theatre, and perhaps the most famous in Finland, was the great tragedienne Ella Eronen. Among the middle-aged generation of actors who became adults in wartime there were also many other actors, both men and women, who possessed a similar stage-charisma honed in the playhouse, though when it came to the male actors, they were less likely to be designated stars or celebrities. One way that actors got more publicity was through their work at the National Theatre, even in those cases where the dramatic focus was squarely on the individual and the acting style strongly self-expressive.

Monologues formed a good jumping off point for an actor's star power. Italian Dario Fo is one of the key playwrights whose plays strongly emphasise the actor's individual performance. Both his own personality as an actor and the Italian dramatic tradition influenced his texts and his work tended to be popular on Finland's small stages. At the National Theatre, Fo was in a slightly alien setting when Forssell prepared four monologues from his and Franca Rame's text *Donna* in the autumn of 1980. 'The National Theatre is dipping into a highly relevant topic. And in Forsell it has a strong actor with a strong personality', wrote Irmeli Niemi, who not only praised the production, but also the information regarding women's rights that was included in the play's programme.[15]

Out of the four monologues the first one depicts the unravelling of a working class mother's busy morning into grotesque farce, whereas the second is a mature woman's evaluation of herself and her current state of mind. The third monologue is a more openly sexual parody. Critical opinion was divided over the fourth monologue, seemingly an unironic pseudoclassical retelling of *Medea*. Others felt that it was a fitting ending to the evening and elevated the messages from the preceding monologues, whereas others like Niemi felt that it was 'a concession to the Gods of Theatre as a deadening compromise – or maybe aimed at the conventional National Theatre audience who would rather listen to melodramatic vocal acrobatics rather than really *think* about the things that are being said'.[16] The production was very different to the brutal social commentary of the Italian performances.

In Finland, Fo's role as a political critic was often overshadowed by his comedy. Nevertheless, when his plays were staged at the National Theatre and

Figure 12.1 Donna 1980. Kyllikki Forssell
Photography by Johnny Korkman

performed by Forssell with her slightly upper-class public image, a tantalising sense that this production might be "too radical" was created. This impression was reinforced by the fact that people who had a ticket to the Small Stage opening night were sent a 'warning' about the show's language. Even though this stunt mainly elicited mirth, the Theatre did manage to enrage at least one citizen who felt compelled to go on a moral crusade, demanding that the Attorney General raise a civil case against the Finnish National Theatre because the show went against traditional family values.[17] According to the complainant, the worst cases of moral outrage were found in contemporary theatre, on Yleisradio (General Radio), and especially in productions like *Donna*.[18] Audience members were either generally curious about the reported lack of morality or the issue was not even on their radar. The complaint was not heeded and the show stayed in the Theatre's repertoire for several years.

John Murrell's *Memoir* staged in the spring of 1988 recounts the story of the famous diva Sarah Bernhard and her secretary who is writing Bernhard's memoirs. The play had been seen in Helsinki before in Swedish with Eronen playing the starring role. This National Theatre production of the play was directed by Sakari Puurunen who was known for his work on dramas with grave subject matters and the main parts were played by old friends Eeva-Kaarina Volanen and Matti Ranin. Volanen depicted Bernhardt's life by erasing her own personality from behind the glamorous figure. Ranin was a fellow actor, not an accompanist. 'The connection between the two actors is alive and breathing,' wrote Moring. She felt the show had humour, irony, and was capable of laughing at human foibles. Cheap melodrama or the sentimental emphasis on ageing were thankfully absent.[19]

However, there was still a desire to see the majesty of Sarah Bernhardt appear on stage. The Sarah Bernhardt myth and perhaps the ghost of Eronen stalked the play's reviews. Both Bernhardt and Eronen fundamentally 'played themselves' as Bert O. States described it, and when Bernhardt was played by a star like Eronen the brilliance had only doubled. In contrast, to quote States, Volanen – 'every night, she performed only the miracle of her own disappearance'.[20] Emphasising her own personality at the expense of a role was not how Volanen operated. Volanen's Bernhardt was inevitably different to Eronen's, though no worse for being so. Most of the critics were on the side of this (new) interactive form of expression and watched with interest as Volanen's acting career developed and her exploration of the people behind the characters she played deepened.

Volanen was an audience favourite. She carried the badge of celebrity thanks to multiple film roles from her youth. On stage she was an ensemble actor whose reputation had been solidified by the post-war Eino Kalima Chekhov productions. There is a sense that Volanen's celebrity was marked by an impressive career at the National Theatre, as well as her other theatrical activity: her participation in the Raivoisat Ruusut (Raging Roses) group that was founded that very same year. This theatrical collective of women actors from around Finland would go on to run for 12 years; they staged an adaptation of Shakespeare's *Henry the Sixth* entitled *Raivoisat Ruusut* as their inaugural play.

An actor's star power was a challenge to the stage director's power but even when an actor's celebrity was a differentiating force, it could bring a certain allure to a production; though this allure was something that theatre critics and the popular audience often disagreed on. In Christopher Hampton's play *Dangerous Liaisons* Forssell played the role of Marquess de Meurteuil. 'There is hardly any other play to which Forssell's acting talents, elegant lightness, and talent for macabre wisecracking are better suited,' wrote Juha-Pekka Hotinen. Sexual cheap tricks were not needed, but still 'the Marquess oozes with the confident sexuality of an experienced woman like a red lamp'.[21] The production opened in the autumn of 1986 and remained in the Theatre's repertoire for a number of years.

Fo's *Kidnapping Francesca* directed by Mikko Viherjuuri in the autumn of 1988 was one big celebration of Forssell; the actor was not subsumed by her role, but her skills and power superseded the story and raised her to an exalted position where she could bask in her adulation. According to Eteläpää, Forssell maintained her position throughout numerous trapeze numbers: 'With a failsafe sense of confidence that tonight the stage is all hers, no one else's. We get something we rarely see these days: a *primadonna act*'.[22] In the play Francesca, a financial secretary, is abducted, but she dominates over the band of criminals and re-arranges things in her own way. Luckily for the production, this impressive performance was matched by Nousiainen who did not fade into the background, but charmed the audience with his fresh comic acting. Sadly, the themes of the play were obscured by its own stars.

In the production, the play's "Italian" colours were underlined: 'Everything as *alla italiana* as a stiff Finn can imagine and enact,' wrote Eteläpää.[23] The audience were greeted with the play's ambience as soon as they left the coat stands behind and entered the foyer where a singing group of gangsters entertained the crowd on a small stage.

As one of the most influential figures in political theatre at the time, Fo's plays were a success at the Finnish National Theatre. As productions, they highlighted the brilliant human stories that Fo's drama celebrated. When this play was staged, the abduction of people in power was still a very real risk in Central Europe, especially in Italy. Fo was known for his social critique and this play was no exception: it could be seen as a satire about ownership and the power of money. Interpretative models at the National Theatre relegated the drama's political messages to the sidelines.

Global victims: abuses of power

The opening of the smaller Willensauna stage in the beginning of the 1980s encouraged the National Theatre to explore difficult themes more openly and the same pattern repeated itself a decade later when the even smaller Omapohja studio opened. By giving minorities and downtrodden people a voice, the National Theatre broadened its scope as a national institution. The scripts themselves represented a new type of international post-war social drama and the productions highlighted the challenges of reproducing drama that is tied to a specific time and place.

Spanish playwright Antonio Buero Vallejo's *The Foundation* was staged on the Small Stage in early 1981, telling the story of a community of political prisoners condemned to death. The play was based on the playwright's own experience of prison during the Franco era, but the play also reflects on totalitarian abuse of power in general. Vallejo was known and lauded both in his own country and internationally for his symbolic representations of Spanish political history. The logically paced stage direction by Terttula emphasised the individual reactions of the prisoners and their interpersonal relationships. Ismo Kallio's monologue about yearning for a lover was especially impressive, Siimes conveyed the optimism of an intellectual in an imprisoned member of parliament, and Matti Järvinen played a prisoner who was battling with his rage brought on by the injustices. Jouko Keskinen played a young writer recovering from schizophrenia who built himself a pretend world to replace reality. The show was impressive but its social symbolism went undetected by Finnish audiences.

The exact same thing happened a few years later to another Buero Vallejo play, *Cayman*. The play was set in the poor neighbourhoods of Madrid but the story remained unlocated for its Finnish audiences who also failed to grasp the play's metonymic resonance with its theme. In the play life was sustained through belief in an impossible story: the tale of being saved from a caiman's belly.

Buero Vallejo's plays were staged on the Small Stage where audience relations were traditional and it was possible to examine social problems from a distance. Heinar Kipphardt's play *The Life of Alexander März* was staged on the Willensauna stage in spring 1981 at close proximity with its audience. The play tells the story of März who, owing to a birth defect has become a down-and-out and has ended up in a mental hospital. The play also looks at contemporary mental health treatment and recounts the story of März's temporary escape into freedom with his beloved, Hanna Grätz. The story ends unhappily and the institution wins. In the hands of stage director Lasse Lindeman and dramaturge Terttu Savola the vast cast was cut down to just nine people, certain hospital scenes were cut, and a central theme of people not being able to fit in with society emerged from the production. 'We are not looking at somebody who is mentally ill, but an enemy of a society that is mentally unstable', Lindeman describes the approach in a pre-show interview.[24] The show's appeal not only hinged on its intimate atmosphere but also the sensitive portrayal of its two central characters by actors Mäkelä and Pacius.

The playwright came and saw the show, and though he had complained in advance about the shortening of the text, by the interval he was happy with the show.[25] He spoke about the play's genesis and his relationship with Finland. During the war, he had hidden his Jewishness by pretending to be Finnish, read work by Finland's national author Aleksis Kivi, studied the Finnish national epic *Kalevala*, and taught Finnish. Finland was allied with Germany in its fight against the Soviet Union and his trick might have worked. However, Kipphardt was caught, but he managed to stay alive and after the war lived first in East, then West-Germany. The fact that the play's themes resonated with contemporary society was evident in the way that plenty of Finnish plays at the time explored similar themes. For example, one of the recurring themes of Claes Andersson's dramatic work was society's impact on and its responsibility for an ailing mind. The Finnish audiences were primed to interpret the play's central message behind its story.

American Martin Sherman's *Bent* continued the exploration of challenging themes on-stage at Willensauna by depicting a topic that was still taboo: the extermination of gay people at German concentration camps. The show was staged at eye-level with no ramps, bringing the shocking events very close to the audience. According to pre-show materials, the play's central theme was the blossoming of love that is then accompanied with the need to take responsibility for another human being.

The critical reviews of the opening night underlined the play's handling of the universal rules of human interaction. Critics felt that the production had steered clear of sensationalism and had avoided chasing exceptionalism. It seemed that the topic was still a difficult one to broach. The play was compared to other depictions of cruelty and Athol Fugard's *Island* that told the story of South Africa's political prisoners during apartheid, or traditional classic drama about individual enlightenment. Out of all the theatre critics, only Kajava tackled the topic directly. He would have wanted the production to start off with an even stronger message as we were not talking about a Sunday school drama or a 'cautious queer show'. After the sticky beginning, he felt that the cast finally got to act in the *Bent*.[26]

The group of actors excelled and Pekka Autiovuori and Olli Ikonen as the two prisoners and lovers delivered an especially impressive performance. A lot of issues came fruitfully together in the *Pink Triangle*. According to Autiovuori the play's theme was challenging as homosexuality was not openly spoken about at the time. Despite this, the play's subject matter did not cause a commotion and there was no backlash. He felt that the idea behind the production was that homosexuals were the lowest caste in the concentration camp.[27]

The National Theatre also embraced the subject of violence that was sweeping across Europe at the time. Margarethe von Trotta's and Hannelene Limbach's *Lead Time,* directed by Lasse Lindeman, was already known in Finland from an earlier cinematic version. The opening play of the Small Stage's 1984 autumn season told the story of how young people drift into terrorism. In light of the preceding decade the theme was resonant, and the play was based on real events, but the production paled in comparison with its theme. The emotional, even sentimental, delivery obscured what could have been an incisive experience for the audience that resonated with their worldview.

Historic moments of stardom

Plays that were set in the past were seen as interpretations of a shared past when the audience had an understanding of the real events and people behind the dramatic narrative. However, a shared understanding was not a guarantee that the audience would find the events compelling.[28] History could also remain void of meaning if the drama only unfolded as a fictional story. In the ideal scenario the dramatic and the historical dovetailed and the audience was able to transcend cultural and historic boundaries.

Peter Shaffer's *Amadeus* directed by Terttula was an anticipated dramatic success that eventually ran to 203 performances. Around the time of its opening night in the autumn of 1981, the National Theatre had just been subjected to an especially impassioned public conversation in the press about the 'lightness' of its entertainment programming, so the show's success was paramount. The production was universally praised, though some of the critics' choice of wording betrayed an anxiety that being overly positive might look like a retraction of earlier criticism. Behind the production's success was the play's rapidly advancing international reputation and prestige, and the play itself that resonated with audiences to varying degrees. The name of the play referenced the beloved composer but the actual protagonist of the play was Salieri. Audiences were titillated by the dramatic tension created by the clever scheming of two historical figures. The brilliant performance of Salieri's role was another guarantee of success as far as this production was concerned.

Figure 12.2 Amadeus 1981. Jussi Jurkka
Photograph by Johnny Korkman

Jussi Jurkka, an actor who had spent many decades excelling at the National Theatre, especially in its modern plays, controlled the play through his skilled charisma as Salieri. His nasal voice had been previously seen as a problem, but his voice and dry humour were ideal for playing Salieri. Jurkka built his portrait of Salieri intellectually and with sharp outlines. As Mozart, Ikonen was not on par with Jurkka, though 'there is something alive and fearless in this leaping Mozart' wrote Kajava.[29] Ikonen had only started his tenure at the National Theatre that same autumn and was put up against the Theatre's star player in his first big role. 'I watched his [Jurkka's] acting with admiration, the way in which he threw everything he could at Salieri, probably his illness too', Ikonen remembers.[30] Jurkka died of cancer at the age of 51 in April 1982; his final great role had been a feat of willpower.

Jurkka's acting highlighted the play's psychological themes, eschewing its role as historical narrative and transforming the play into 'a morality about the deadly sin of envy and covetousness', as Richard Allen Cave describes the play.[31] Christopher Innes sees an exploration of the relationship between God and man and a test of the values espoused by the society in which the play was written.[32] Jurkka's final role was proof that he was able to deliver on layered role requirements.

During the years that the operetta debates swirled around the National Theatre, Kajava had been an especially strong critical voice. Now he titled his review of the play with 'Amadeus-conversations at the gentlemen's club' and approached the production with a condescending attitude mixed with irony. He compared the directing of this National Theatre play with a previous *Amadeus* production at Tampere's Theatre and was clearly on the side of Tampere. Kajava felt that the acting cast left some room for improvement and Anneli Qveflander's visual world seemed like a direct replica of the staging used for a Main Stage production of the light operetta *Parisian Life,* although Kajava came to the conclusion that that was patently not the case, as the two shows happened concurrently.[33] Losing out to the Tampere production was awkward from the National Theatre's viewpoint as it was directed by ex-National Theatre director Jack Witikka who had just moved into freelance stage directing.

The role of Salieri had been planned as a two-man effort from day one, probably owing to Jurkka's illness, and in May 1982 Kallio stepped into the role: a much more down-to-earth and rooted actor than his predecessor, but not without his own charms. Instead of virtuoso acting, the play had a collected and self-ironic Salieri. Instead of brilliance, human emotions took centre stage.

Also in the spring of 1982, the Theatre put on *About the Lives of Earthworms* by Swedish playwright Per Olof Enquist, another depiction of an artist and a similar dramatic representation of the private life of a known personage. Alongside Norén, Enquist was perhaps the most famous and internationally recognised contemporary writer in Sweden at the time. The play told the story of Danish fairytale writer Hans Christian Anderson and how the country's most famous actress Johanne Luise Heiberg fitted into this tableau. In the critical reception of the play, rather than its history, it was the role of the artist and Tea Ista's celebratory performance as Heiberg that garnered critical attention.

History without any recognisable historical figures tended to not fare well with audiences. In the Autumn of 1982 Edward Bond's play, *Summer*, told the story of an encounter between two women and their adult children at an old summer house in an unnamed Balkan country a few decades after the end of World War II. The play had an interesting premise in the retrospective analysis of past events, but despite its merits, the production did not find its audience. Stephen Poliakoff's *Breaking the Silence* from the spring of 1986 told the story of an aristocratic Russian family travelling by train during the first chaotic phases of the Russian Revolution, their train carriage taking them across Siberia, ending up on the Polish border. Eero Kankkunen's staging included a parlour car that opened from the side, prompting Soila Lehtonen to end her criticism of the play with this sarcastic summary: 'Nothing moves between the auditorium and the stage. The train might as well have had a fourth wall'.[34] The play came across as a piece of exoticism that did not reach its mark in Finland that had followed the Russian Revolution from close quarters.

One of the most successful productions on the small Willensauna stage turned out to be David Pownall's *Masterclass* that was staged in the spring of 1986. Even though the text was American, its topic was close to home in a neighbouring country of the Soviet Union and the play's approach dovetailed well with the prevailing Finnish attitude. *Masterclass* centred on a nightly scene at Stalin's house. Formally the play was a traditional, realist, well-made play and it offered fantastic roles for its actors.

The play's stage director Kurt Nuotio masterfully combined comedy and gallows humour in this absurd comedy where its characters knew that death might always be an option. Nuotio was also capable of lightening the mood without any distracting moralising. Siimes played Stalin and Aaltonen played Ždanov who was the operative power behind Stalin's game of cat and mouse, Wager and Jarno Hiilloskorpi played the two composers, Prokofiev and Shostakovitch, who had both entered dangerous territory. Stage manager Paavo Pirttimaa had decked out the Willensauna stage with red velvet and mahogany furniture.

In this case of dream casting, Siimes was a dictatorial and paranoid Stalin-figure who threw capricious fits, but he was not just a tyrant, he was also a romantic nationalist and a Russian-hating Georgian, deceptively heartfelt and attractive. Nuotio described how Siimes's take on Stalin developed: 'In this unusual role choice for him, Siimes, the very embodiment of friendliness, found new levels to himself and his range as a performer. We have seen Satan pushing through'.[35] Siimes's Stalin was convincing as the historic Stalin and Siimes's performance was the perfect example of a convincing linear character study.

The casting choices for Stalin's entourage upped the dramatic tension. Aaltonen's interpretation of Ždanov was, compared to Stalin, 'the portrait of a slightly smaller, but more rowdy tyrant in a constant state of being on high alert and having to eat humble pie', doing it all 'with the sturdiness and angularity of a trained soldier who through the power of booze would occasionally erupt into a bucolic spontaneous dance, even trying to get a "rise" from Stalin himself'.[36] Wager and Hiilloskorvi had to learn difficult pieces for the piano,

Figure 12.3 Masterclass 1986. Risto Aaltonen, Jarno Hiilloskorpi, Pentti Siimes and Leif Wager Photograph by Johnny Korkman

and though they were just marking them, the finger work had to look genuine in order to work on the Willensauna stage. Master pianist Olli Mustonen, who sat in the audience, applauded them for their convincing acting while pianist Erkki Kallio sat behind playing complex piano music.[37] The music critic from *Helsingin Sanomat*, Seppo Heikinheimo, encouraged music fans to go and watch the show. He praised the Theatre for its excellent programme, but recommended that people also read a few chapters of Shostakovitch's memoir. He also marvelled at the actors' skill at playing musicians: 'Ingenious marriage between theatre and music!'[38]

Notes

1 *Teatteritilasto 1988*, 1989. Published by the Suomen Teatterijärjestöjen Keskusliitto.
2 Kirsikka Moring, *Helsingin Sanomat*, 26.4.1985.
3 Timo Tiusanen, *Uusi Suomi*, 26.4.1985.
4 Koski 2019, 274–275.
5 "Näin perusteli raati valintoja." *Aamulehti*, 26.8.1980.
6 Katri Veltheim, *Uusi Suomi*, 31.8.1980.
7 Jukka Kajava, *Helsingin Sanomat*, 14.4.1985.
8 Jukka Kajava, *Helsingin Sanomat*, 10.11.1983.
9 Wager 2000, 260.

10 Jukka Kajava, *Helsingin Sanomat*, 23.11.1990.
11 Riitta Wikström, *Etelä-Suomen Sanomat*, 8.1.1991.
12 Heikki Eteläpää, *Uusi Suomi*, 23.11.1990.
13 Jukka Kajava, *Helsingin Sanomat*, 8.9.1989.
14 States 1995, 24–28; Carlson 2001; Quinn 1990. States mentions three modes: the self-expressive, the collaborative, and the representational mode. Quinn looks at the actor in the context of a semiotic framework and builds a model that analyses the relationship between celebrity and a role. Carlson develops intertextual analysis further and coins the concept of *ghosting*.
15 Irmeli Niemi, *Helsingin Sanomat*, 26.9.1980.
16 Ibid.
17 "Kyllikki Forssell oli pyytänyt poliisilta apua." *Seura*, 23.1.1981.
18 "Tasavallan presidentti Urho K. Kekkonen." *Porvoon mitta*, 8.2.1981. The mention of Yleisradio connects morality policing with the condemnation of left-wing politics; at the time there was an ongoing public debate about Yleisradio's left-wing politics.
19 Kirsikka Moring, *Helsingin Sanomat*, 29.4.1988.
20 Cf. States 1995, 26–27.
21 Juha-Pekka Hotinen, *Turun Sanomat*, 7.8.1986.
22 Heikki Eteläpää, *Uusi Suomi*, 23.9.1988.
23 Ibid.
24 Lidia Iranso, *Uusi Suomi*, 26.2.1981.
25 Kai Savola's letter to Pirkko Koski, 4.1.2017.
26 Jukka Kajava, *Helsingin Sanomat*, 5.2.1982.
27 Autiovuori, interview, 29.4.2014.
28 Cf. Rokem 2000, 14.
29 Jukka Kajava, *Helsingin Sanomat*, 23.10.1981.
30 Olli Ikonen's email to Pirkko Koski, 4.12.1912.
31 Cave 1987, 252.
32 Innes 1992, 411–415.
33 Jukka Kajava, *Helsingin Sanomat*, 23.10.1981.
34 Soila Lehtonen, *Kansan Uutiset*, 22.4.1986.
35 Simopekka Virkkula, *Aamulehti*, 27.3.1986.
36 Heikki Eteläpää, *Uusi Suomi*, 15.4.1986.
37 Wager 2000, 263.
38 Seppo Heikinheimo, *Helsingin Sanomat*, 16.4.1986.

13 Social upheaval on the national stage

The Finnish National Theatre put on relatively few productions that harboured a strong desire to change society, but the Theatre's programming nevertheless reflected the global politics of the time. In the 1970s, the Vietnam War dominated contemporary politics, and many of the productions put on at the Finnish National Theatre hinted at the Vietnam War issue and more generally displayed anti-war sentiments. The radicalism associated with the 1960s generation started to die down as the 1970s changed into the 1980s, and intergenerational tensions became a source of dramatic exploration instead. In the 1990s the Finnish National Theatre also participated in conversations about the environmental threat.

Generally, the National Theatre's take on productions was not seen as radical and any social messages or political commentary was often sidelined for a variety of reasons. Ironically, the National Theatre's programming was often more radical than the general critical consensus recognised. Messages or themes might be lost in dramatic storytelling, or the unexpected and the new remained unrecognised behind a cultural or temporal veil. The way a production was staged and performed could either reinforce a play's message or create distance, and plays that are now firmly consigned to history might have actually resonated with audience members more than the theatre critics led us to believe: the remaining textual evidence does not capture all experiences of the performances.

Pacifism in its different modes

The Vietnam War that ended in the mid-1970s was a great catalyst for anti-war feelings, especially among the young. A small group of Vietnamese refugees alighted on the Finnish coast in the late 1970s, bringing world events home in a tangible way. World War II was already three decades ago, but the true extent of its horrors had not been unearthed until after the war, and those conversations were still raw. Anti-war sentiments kept resurfacing in the Finnish National Theatre 1970s programming. In contrast, public interest in Finland's wars could be found in historical analysis or memoirs, not pacifism.

The most direct and impressive anti-war play staged at the National was *Johnny Johnson* by Paul Green and Kurt Weill that had its Nordic premiere on

DOI: 10.4324/9781003047667-15

the Finnish National Theatre's Main Stage in the spring of 1975. In this 1930s American play, a pacifist, Johnny Johnson, heads off to World War I, the war that was meant to end all wars, and returns home even more of a pacifist, only to find he has lost his fiancee to a rival suitor who had become rich by profiting from the War. The play's genuine naivety and its unabashed theatricality appealed directly to its audiences' emotions: 'When a small man with a guarded expression finished his singing, the Finnish National Theatre's opening-night audience erupted into uproarious clapping. Lots of banging on the floor', is how the opening night was described.[1] The sincerity of the play kept it from appearing too predictable and its familiar subject matter felt alive and compelling. In the play, humour was very much a byproduct of the tragic. Pentti Siimes's portrayal of the play's eponymous character elicited audience empathy and a sense that they were witnessing an innocent victim of his times.

The production got its energy from Vili Auvinen's directing style that did not shy away from tackling large group scenes. Auvinen's vision was supported by Siimes's brilliant portrayal of the play's namesake. Auvinen was a versatile actor and stage director who had worked with Kai Savola during his previous role as the Director at Tampere's Työväen Teatteri (Tampere Workers' Theatre). Auvinen's previous successes included a production of the Finnish musical play *Tukkijoella* (*On the Log River*) that had a decidedly fresh approach. Auvinen

Figure 13.1 Johnny Johnson 1975. Pentti Siimes and the ensemble
Photography by Kari Hakli

was part of the highly select elite of Finnish contemporary stage directors.[2] Siimes was also one of the most loved comic actors on television at the time, something that people in the audience were loath to dismiss, though critics felt that his on-stage role allowed him to break away from the limits imposed by television and do a better acting job.

Pekka Heiskanen's set design consisted of naivist placards depicting different scenes: the theatricality of the scenery was underlined by the show's opening scene on an empty stage. The style was similar to Brechtian methods, but the stage tableaux were accepted as part of historical reality, without references to contemporary realities and ideologies. Events unfolded at a rapid and colourful pace from highly-charged border wars to comic interludes. The cast worked well together, and many of the smaller roles added colourful details to the overall narrative.

The significance of this theatrical event for the National Theatre, and perhaps for the playwright himself, is lived out by Green's visit to Finland in November 1977. The visit was extensively covered in various magazines; magazine articles told how Green extolled the warmth of the production and felt that the play's themes were even more relevant now than when it was first written. Out of all the productions he had seen, Siimes was the best Johnny. Green himself had been enthused by the idealism of US President Woodrow Wilson depicted in the play. He had fought in World War I, seen Brecht's *Threepenny Opera* in late 1920s Germany (where he also got to know Weill) and later, he would get to know other German refugee artists. According to the programme, the Moscow Art Theatre had been planning to put on the play in the late 1930s, but the project fell through, partly because Green had not consented to the ending being changed to a declaration for the socialist cause. For Green the play had its own morality and the protagonist represented the everyman.[3]

In Finland the World War and pacifism depicted in *Johnny Johnson* were familiar historic themes, even if the setting was in the United States. The play had an easily digestible moral message. Music also played a significant role in the production. The show was praised across the theatrical spectrum of its time, each camp proclaiming the play a success based on their interpretation of what made good theatre. Taisto-Bertil Orsmaa had been expecting a clearer swing to the left when Savola was appointed, and he felt that the Finnish National Theatre's programming was becoming more relevant, but it was only now that the new era was becoming more apparent. 'To have such an ethically and socially poignant and open-minded show as part of the National Theatre's repertoire was surprising and new'. He felt that the play openly discussed the economic and political reasons behind the war, exposed the economic gains made by the establishment, and highlighted the double standard of militarism espoused by capitalist democracies. People do not want wars.[4] The shift was also registered on the right, where Olavi Veistäjä felt that *Johnny Johnson* was proof that the National Theatre had changed its tune and that a new era had begun. The autumn's programming had been explorative, but *Johnny Johnson* was a breakthrough.

In the theatres of the day, political references were usually tangible, and the National Theatre's production did not lead to any practical conclusions. In the end, the most impactful thing was the story. Actor Aila Arajuuri put it well when she described the reasons behind the success of *Johnny Johnson*: the play made a plea for pacifism in a way that resonated with most people — it was entertaining, just sentimental enough, and plentiful in many ways. Weill's beautiful music just added to the play's charms.[5] Savola has discussed how he saw a contemporary link with the Vietnam War in the text,[6] and though a conscious connection might have been there, the link was not picked up on by audiences or critics. The emotional intensity of the production obscured its ties to the contemporary historical moment.

The following year, an adaptation of Shakespeare's *King John* suffered a similar fate despite its strong dramatic expression and Friedrich Dürrenmatt's efforts to simulate the wars of the 20th century. Anti-war sentiments were more readily recognised in Bertolt Brecht's play *Drums in the Night* put on in 1977, perhaps owing partly to the expectations attached to the playwright.

Drums in the Night was the Finnish premiere of the play. Its Romanian director, Radu Penciulescu, and its staging manager, Dan Nemteanu, both worked in Sweden. Brecht condenses the play into one night, set sometime after World War I. The streets of Berlin have erupted in a Spartan rebellion. The play's protagonist, gunner Kragler, is presumed dead but returns back from beyond the grave to interrupt the engagement party of his pregnant bride, ultimately refusing to join the rebels and choosing his bride and the future Germans she will give birth to over doing battle again.[7]

Even though the play itself preceded the Brechtian epic mode, the Finnish critical reception inevitably situated the play among other Brecthian plays and methods that were well-known in Finland. The play left many viewers baffled. The critical reviews that touched on the play's mode were splintered, even contradictory. Critics felt that the production was trying to distance itself from the expressionism that had dominated drama when the play had been first written. The production was seen as an amalgamation between the Brecht-tradition and its own dramatic moment in time: a stylised and sharp satire of bourgeois morality, yet also imprisoned by Brechtian conventions. Not all critics felt that the Brechtian element of the play was essential to its interpretation, and it was seen as a positive that the production had so brilliantly captured the era's impassioned and chaotic spirit.

Despite the focus on dramatic methodology, it was the actors and their performances that particularly affected the reviews of the play. Katri Veltheim was probably the critic who was most enthusiastic about the production. She felt that the acting was tantalisingly good across the board, especially singling out Esa Saario's affecting rendition of the song *Legend of a Dead Soldier*. Others were more measured. One critic praised the actors for avoiding mannerisms, another critic criticised the actors for overdoing them. Antti Litja who played Kragler was deemed good across the board, and his acting likely influenced the entire show. Litja portrayed his character's shift in mood bravely, but at the same time with a subtle consciousness of his own character's position as well as his position as a performer. Litja evidently represented the new Brechtian expression. None of the critical reviews made a connection between the production and the time in which it was staged.

In its programming choices, the Finnish National Theatre communicated its sense of its target audience, "the nation". When it came to the Main Stage, *Johnny Johnson* was proof that national folk drama within the framework of the Finnish tradition was acceptable, something also borne out by the choice of director. Pacifism was explored from a temporal and spatial distance. The examples also show how dramatic intertextuality, *ghosting*, can transfer attention from a play's content to its methodology, in this case to the demands of Brechtian performance that was developed after the play and was slightly alien to the Finnish National Theatre.

Generational rebellion on stage

Even though the Finnish National Theatre had staged plays that reflected contemporary social problems throughout the 1970, it was not until the end of the decade that these thematic connections were publicly acknowledged and deemed robust enough. This change in attitude was influenced by a host of different factors such as the general ideological shift in the theatre world, the expectations attached to the National Theatre's Willensauna stage, and the ability of directors to address contemporary issues in dramas battling with age-old questions of the human condition.

A shift happened with the staging of Albert Camus's *Caligula* directed by Jotaarkka Pennanen and performed by Hannu Lauri who played the title role in one of his best performances. The intense show filled out the entire small Willensauna space with its force and its loud music, positioning the actors in a new kind of relationship with the audience. The effect was strengthened by the production's radical visualisation that brought it to bear on contemporary issues; contemporary dress directed criticism at recognisable social groups and the stage was reminiscent of the most famous occupied building of the time, Lepakko-luola (Bat Cave)[8], that was filled with people from the time's youth movement. Even though Lauri's eponymous role made him a strong focal point in the play, what was so unique about the production was the fact that the entire cast maintained a certain amount of intensity, whilst also jelling together to create a coherent ensemble.[9] The production represented a new form of dramatic expression that emphasised physical presence, a mode that Pennanen had also been experimenting with in his previous work in Turku. The reviews made a connection between this production and the KOM Theatre's production of Shakespeare's *The Tempest* directed by Laura Jäntti that had received a lot of attention for its experiential use of space.[10]

Pennanen has described his own relationship with the playtext. A few years before, the Theatre School's student production of *Pete Q* had broken the spell of dramatic social realism with its absurdity. Politicised social or socially critical theatre had reached a crisis point. For Pennanen, the central point of Camus's text was the question about what it meant to be human and the foundational dichotomy of 'why have a sense of justice in a world that is patently unjust'. In the production social hierarchies were reinforced visually: the patricians represented the establishment in their pinstripe suits and briefcases, and when Caligula entered the stage from behind the audience and settled in front of a mirror, he could see his face and the audience behind it. Caligula and Scipio dressed up in the clothes of an urban street gang told the story of a rebellion with no clear purpose. Caligula felt free only when he was destroying things – something he shared with other similar characters like Kullervo from the Finnish national epic *Kalevala*, disenfranchised youths kicking tires, and Sisyfos from Antiquity. The only difference was an awareness of his own fate.[11]

Caligula was Willensauna's first clear directorial experiment that broke free from the text's prevailing mode by emphasising the importance of performance space when it came to building a relationship with an audience. However, background discussions show that initially the Finnish National Theatre had not considered spatial experimentation in connection with this production. The Finnish National Theatre had suggested the play be staged on the Main Stage. Pennanen insisted on directing *Caligula* on the Willensauna stage, because he wanted to, in his own words, break the 'fourth wall'.[12]

Stanislavski's concept of the invisible wall dividing actor from audience member had of course been broken a long time ago, particularly in the 1970s when Brecht's ideas became prevalent in Finnish theatres. The same breaking effect could also be achieved on a more traditional stage, but Pennanen wanted to go one step further and this required a new kind of space. The entire stage and part of the auditorium were part of the performance.[13] The director found a shared language with set designer Heiskanen. Willensauna's walls were covered in corrugated iron that were daubed with the word 'work', the space was filled with junk and buckets, and some of the chairs were covered in grey plastic. The show began with a song, and rock music was composed especially for the production. The ushers were dressed up as police, and they shoved the audience into their seats. After the interval, the set included a huge copy of Norwegian artist, Bertel Thorvaldsen's, famous Christ-picture. Caligula made his entrance in a white convertible dressed as Marilyn and declared himself a God as the patricians rocked out to rock music.[14]

This was not the first time these themes had been discussed in Finland, but the style had now distinctively changed. Traditionally, Finnish National Theatre productions had stayed within the limits of good taste and moderation, sometimes at the expense of the message or the content itself, but *Caligula* was not guilty on either accounts. The walls bulged with the explosive power of sound and light, and the audience had to watch out as events exploded ahead. Seediness was not covered up with stylisation. The production's mode, combined with its theme, formed a direct bridge with the actual society outside the Theatre's walls. The critical reviews referenced the impending local elections, 'like the patricians, people who are somehow lagging behind their own social

Social upheaval on the national stage 183

Figure 13.2 Caligula 1980. Hannu Lauri and Risto Mäkelä.
Photography by Ensio Ilmonen

moment, repeat empty phrases about morality, the importance of family, the respectability of work'. The caesar kicking back lager contrasted with Cherea enjoying red wine set up a distinction between politician and writer – the power and the intellectual.[15]

Based on the critical consensus, the play succeeded thanks to the way in which it rebuilt theatrical and dramatic space; the way in which it pushed the boundaries of drama by not allowing the audience to isolate itself. The distance between an audience member and the performance was broken in many different ways. The jagged set reached all the way to the back wall and pulled the viewer inside the performance, and actors also used the auditorium's back door for their entrances and exits. Loud rock music and sound effects completely engulfed the small space, there were more actors on stage than in a traditional chamber play, and the actors' dramatic expression was very physical. The production's provocative nature attacked both prevailing theatrical "form" and bourgeois polite society. The result was a strong criticism of authority and power.

In the history of the Finnish National Theatre *Caligula* is a milestone when it comes to a shift in public opinion. The artistic daring that this production represented transferred into more traditional performance methods. During the years that followed, radical directors often demanded more visible spaces for their dramatic experiments, preferably the National Theatre's Main Stage.

In its own pre-show publicity, the Finnish National Theatre hoped to reach new young audience members with this show. This was especially the wish of the play's director.[16] It seems as if this was to remain wishful thinking as the opening night audience was not unduly provoked, and rave critical reviews led to sold out auditoriums, leaving no space for the previously unengaged youths to get a slice of the action. The reason behind the show's run prematurely ending while it was still filling up the auditorium every night must have been in the fact that simply too many of the Theatre's talented actors were involved in the production. Charismatic actors were needed on the bigger stages where more tickets were sold (and tickets cost more). When it came to later successes on the Willensauna stage, there were usually a lot less actors involved. What this production certainly achieved was that people in the theatrical world who had previously given the Finnish National Theatre a wide berth had to rethink their attitudes, and that the demographic of the Theatre audiences changed, getting slightly younger in the process.

The environmental threat

In the 1970s the thinning of the ozone layer was revealed for the first time, and the rate of thinning became alarming in the mid-1980s. The 1987 international agreement to stop using chemicals that destroyed the ozone layer and to limit emissions led to ozone recovery (studies from 2018 show that the thinning has started again). Pentti Holapa's play *Adieu!* in 1991 was staged amid this ozone threat and the accompanying environmental discussion, though by then people felt that the worst threat was behind them. The play's other themes were also topical: political power struggles, the conversations about European integration, and AIDS. The play and the production itself received lots of praise. The play was a political satire, a sensual relationship drama, and a depiction of an eco-disaster. It examines the decisions made by the men at the top of global governments when the threat to Earth is already irreversible and the choice being made is on finding a controlled final solution.

In the play, even when facing total destruction, unscrupulous political activity is still going on. There are also hidden human motivators behind the play's power struggles. The play's name *Adieu!* sums up the play's themes in many ways. The eco-disaster becomes irreversible, and the decision on how the nation must approach its end is taken away from national governments and given to an international secret society. In the end, AIDS provides the final solution to the personal and political power struggles between the play's characters. The final goodbyes are controlled and elegant: 'For now, we still exist. You cannot ask for more. [...] We have existed. [...] This brightness hurts my eyes. [...] Now is the time to don your black sunglasses. [...] These have the same issue that sleeping pills have. You get used to them, you can't live without them'. These lines come from the play's protagonist, Valtioneuvos, and his wife. Before this scene Valtineuvos's secretary suffering from AIDS has travelled to South America to die on his own terms.[17]

Adieu! was Holappa's first and only play. He was known as a diverse writer, a Finnish translator, the owner of an antiques shop, a politician, and at the time a rarity: an openly gay man living in a homosexual partnership. Literary critic Pekka Tarkka analysed the play in the context of the rest of Holappa's output and felt it was 'a new kind of Holappa'. It was a 'condensed drama full of living characters. Romance still plays a role here, like in the topic of an exotic escape'. Holappa's intelligent salon play was a welcome counterbalance to the noisy theatre of the time, felt Tarkka. Tarkka titled his piece 'The Indian Summer of Pentti Holappa. Injecting passion into life on all stages'.[18]

The critical reviews for *Adieu!* tried to find equivalents to the play's fictitious events in Finnish politics. With the benefit of hindsight, it's surprising that the production was barely examined in the context of climate change and discussions around the impending climate disaster. The play's name *Adieu!* was also sidelined in contemporary reviews. As a political statement, the play can be called a 'state-of-the-nation play' a play 'on the state of the nation as it wrestles with changing circumstances'.[19] The production was called a 'jackpot' in its reviews, but it remains unclear what elements of the production particularly stood out and resonated with its audiences. The *Adieu!* production was taken as a play with a social and political message, but the justifications for it were mixed. Background factors influenced the expectations attached to the Finnish National Theatre and perhaps the politicised public reputation of the writer.

By the spring of 1991 the Finnish National Theatre had shaken off its stuffy public image and asserted itself at the forefront of contemporary dramatic circles. *Adieu!* reinforced a new kind of image of the Theatre's approach to domestic Finnish drama. The previous autumn, the Theatre had put on three

Finnish premiere plays, one of them being *Valheita* (Lies) from sensationalist director Jouko Turkka. The Theatre had started to have its finger on the pulse. In *Adieu!*, the luxury lady played by Tiina Rinne had a 'look that could kill or release' and 'gestures that told more than an army of words could'. Seppo Pääkkönen played Valtioneuvos's secretary, and the power struggles between the two were cruelly personal.[20] Valtioneuvos, the central figure of a presidential candidate attempting to lead citizens to their inevitable destruction in a controlled manner, was played by Ismo Kallio. He was known for imitating the Finnish President at the time, Mauno Koivisto, and his 'real-presidential charisma as an entertainer' brought an unexpected depth to the play.[21] Kallio had spent many years imitating the popular President in different media and at a variety of events. The critical reception connected some of the play's characters with political personages of the day, and some of them embodied real contradictions.

In the play the Earth's destruction is inevitable. What was at stake was foretelling the threat and being forewarned. But what caught people's attention were the social issues that were readily recognisable: the social climbing among politicians, the transfer of national sovereignty to a supranational body, or even in this case the potential homoerotic love triangle that was assigned to the playwright. The critical reception focused on elements that would have only personally touched a small proportion of the audience. The critical discussion also emphasised theatrical form and examined politics in a very generalised way, despite ongoing discussions about Finland joining the European Community.

Notes

1. Ilse Rautio, *Ilta-Sanomat*, 6.2.1975.
2. Parras, *Aamulehti*, 16.2.1975.
3. *Johnny Johnson*. [Programme] The Finnish National Theatre Archives.
4. Taisto-Bertil Orsmaa, *Demari*, 8.2.1974.
5. (H.K.), *Iltaset*, 5.2.1975.
6. Kai Savola's letter to Pirkko Koski, 15.2.2017.
7. Stage Director's Point of View: Ritva Heikkilä, *Teatteri*, 3/1977, 8.
8. The empty warehouse building, named the Bat Cave, served as a night shelter for alcoholics in 1967–79, but after that a group of young people squatted the building, transforming it into a diverse anti-mainstream cultural space.
9. Nevala 2006,12.
10. Kirsikka Siikala, *Helsingin Sanomat*, 12.9.1980.
11. Pennanen 2010, 153, 156, 158–159, 164.
12. E.g. Pennanen 2010, 162, 164.
13. Jouko Keskinen's email to Pirkko Koski, 22.2.2016.
14. Pennanen 2010, 162, 164.
15. Heikki Kataja, *Ilta-Sanomat*, 11.9.1980.
16. E. g. Katri Veltheim, *Uusi Suomi*, 9.9.1980.
17. *Adieu!* Main production book. The Finnish National Theatre.
18. Pekka Tarkka, *Helsingin Sanomat*, 1 7.3.1991.
19. See Holdsworth 2010, 39.
20. Kirsikka Moring, *Helsingin Sanomat*, 1.3.1991.
21. Marketta Mattila, *Uusi Suomi*, 1.3.1991. Ismo Kallio was behind the popular Mauno Koivisto tribute act 'Vara-Manu' (Spare-Manu).

14 Popular and commercial elements and National Theatre press debates

Finland has had its fair share of theatrical crises, usually revolving around the real or imagined left-wing sympathies of theatres, as well as the way that drama undermined religious morals and "family values". These two things were often deemed to go hand in hand. However, these specific issues did not often surface in debates about the Finnish National Theatre as it was not profiled as or assumed to be a left-wing institution. The concerns about the National Theatre's entertainment programming did however create a press "sensations" that expanded into different directions.

The Finnish National Theatre found many of its biggest audience successes among the classic international farces and well-made dramas of yesteryear. The reasoning Kai Savola used to justify these popular dramatic choices was that this type of entertainment often functioned as a way for people to access higher forms of culture. However, balancing commercially successful popular drama with drama of high artistic merit in the National Theatre's repertoire caused some of the most controversial public debates ever to engulf the Theatre. The issue was rooted in a desire to separate nationally acceptable drama from commercial or entertainment theatre programming, though definitions for these terms were often inadequate and subject to change. Many critics found farce drama supremely suspect, regardless of its cultural value and possible ironic stance. And operetta as a genre was considered altogether too puerile and unsuitable for the National Theatre.

Despite the censure these genres attracted, most of the shows criticised for being too light-weight attained their commercial aims. The entertainment category of the National Theatre's repertoire is also marked by the vastly different attitudes of the general public and the professional critical audience. Public critical condemnation did not generally diminish the level of interest the general public exhibited towards a play. The National Theatre had to navigate the implications this tension placed on its artistic reputation, and the Theatre frequently had to compromise.

From classic farce to folk theatre

The first production at the Finnish National Theatre that attracted widespread censure was the classical farce *Charley's Aunt,* a play by Brandon Thomas, that

DOI: 10.4324/9781003047667-16

had been a staunch stage favourite for decades. The production was executed to "National Theatre standards" by choosing engaging actors and by heavily investing in the production's visuals. After its opening night in early May 1978 on the Theatre's Main Stage the play was all set to be a run-away hit, but Theatre Director Savola attempted to dampen the enthusiasm by shrinking the number of shows to less than what the audience demand warranted.[1] The play's reputation as a cash cow was well-known outside of Finland as well. Rumours are that it drove a visiting Soviet director Georgi Tovstonogov to wonder whether the Finnish National Theatre was really doing that badly – for him the play was only marched out as a last resort when nothing else could be found to draw audiences.[2]

A few theatre critics at least partly agreed with the general audience on this production. Anneli Kajanto from the "bourgeois" camp felt the production was a good way to wash away the worries of the audience, and left-wing Maija Savutie felt that 'around May Day, as a well-made entertainment drama like *Charley's Aunt* holds its own, though even with the best intentions it is hard to think of anything particular to take home from this production'.[3] The May Day celebrations did not soften other critics. Hilkka Eklund felt that the Theatre's most powerful talent had been made to bounce around the stage acting out a meaningless text. 'Powerful talent' in this context referred to actor Jukka-Pekka Palo, and actors Antti Litja and Esko Roine who played a pair of Oxford students. Palo played the obligatory old dear chaperone, his first big role at the Finnish National Theatre. At the time a man dressing as a woman was guaranteed to elicit comedy, but Palo's ace up his sleeve was his 'genuine youthful prankster spirit', as Savutie wrote. 'The comedy of his old woman is original, not too over-the-top in its scale, but consciously barbed and subtly directing the entire stage business'.[4]

The May Day timing worked out in the production's favour, and despite the splintering of critical opinion the public debate was relatively temperate. *Charley's Aunt* fulfilled the Theatre's entertainment programming quota for many years, and the next new show that caused widespread critical condemnation was not produced until three years later. Jean Girandoux's *The Wicked Duchess* entered the Theatre's repertoire at the request of retired legendary diva Ella Eronen in 1981. She wanted to perform the play for her 50-year anniversary show to celebrate her acting career and did not agree to Savola's suggestion that she instead pick up her role in *Blood Wedding* that she had been forced to interrupt, owing to illness.[5]

The Wicked Duchess directed by Esko Elstelä got off to a good start as an audience hit, but it was quickly upstaged by the stage favourites of the following season, perhaps purposefully sidelined by the Theatre's Director. The play was seen as much too frivolous for the National Theatre, as is evident from its opening night's review headlines: 'Good night, National', and 'Depressing', or 'The incoherent streak at the National strikes again'. Still, the production attracted a few apologists: Eronen was praised for her wonderful performance in the starring role, and the show was also described as 'a sparkling story'. *Helsingin Sanomat* critic Jukka Kajava's review was acerbic to the extent that *Turun Sanomat* re-published parts of it with ironic marginal comments, dubbing the writing style as 'kajaving'. The environmental themes that Eronen had highlighted in her interviews did not convince Kajava who felt that 'you could just as well call Red Riding Hood a dramatic event for motivating the winter feeding of wolves'.[6] The play tells the story of an eccentric Parisienne, a "duchess" played by Eronen who teams up with other aged grand dames to fight against subterranean oil drilling in Paris.

The starring role in *The Wicked Duchess* dominated the play, which suited Eronen down to a tee. She distanced herself from everybody else in the production and her on-stage charm was unstoppable, even impressing Kajava who saw 'self-ironic slithers of coquetry' in her performance. Age was no issue for Eronen who was almost half a century older than the actor Pekka Autiovuori who played her boyfriend. The Theatre had heavily invested in the production's visual form by hiring a dancer from the National Opera, Eva Hemming, as the play's choreographer, and Mago who had worked in Sweden as the set and costume designer – with interesting results: 'If I was the Director at the Finnish National Theatre, I would be deeply concerned if the audience at my opening night would be clapping as new costumes arrived on stage, one more incredible than the next', wrote Kajava.[7]

The National Theatre dared to return to classic French farce a few years later, though Georges Feudeau's *Monsieur Is Hunting!* was staged on the Small Stage rather than the Main Stage in the autumn of 1983. Romanian Lucian Giurchescu directed the production, and despite unenthusiastic reviews, the show was a hit and it was staged an impressive 140 times over four years. The experienced Finnish National Theatre quartet of Kyllikki Forssell, Kauko Helovirta, Tommi Rinne, and Pia Hattara formed the production's cast. All four were skilled at performing farce, which is something that the Theatre's younger actors had considerably less experience in. Evidently, the audience did not mind the characters being played by slightly older actors.

The choice of Feaudeau's play mirrored international dramatic trends: the writer's works had recently become popular in both post-war France and England. Feuadeau's elegant dramatic structure was in-line with the National Theatre's programming criteria, but there was clearly some caution in the air. Tellingly, the production was not transferred to the Main Stage unlike some other productions that had been a hit with audiences.

The National Theatre did return to classic farce on the Main Stage later, but this time the production was not a hit with audiences. Noel Coward's old play *Blithe Spirit* staged in the late autumn in 1988 inspired theatre critics, Kajava especially, to write witty articles laced with irony that were funny but merciless. Often, they did not even see the play as worthy of proper analysis. Kajava sent 'Greetings from the National Funhouse' where 'the party never stops'.[8] The production did not win fans elsewhere either, but Soila Lehtonen from *Kansan Uutiset* at least condescended to analyse the reasons for the show's issues and look at its missed opportunities. Most importantly she felt that British irony did not translate well on the Finnish stage. Lehtonen understood the rationale behind staging European farce classics, but felt that it would be more important to bring contemporary comedy to the stage.

There were absolutely valid reasons for the negative critical reaction to this production of Coward's play, but drawing conclusions about the Finnish National Theatre as a whole based on one production seems excessive. The repertoire at the Finnish National Theatre had always been varied, and productions ranged from the shoddy to the excellent. During the dramatic season the Theatre also put on major visiting international productions that represented a broad dramatic spectrum.

In some contexts, the farce genre was accepted and tolerated. The Finnish National Theatre had designated Johann Nestroy's play *He Will Go on a Spree* staged in 1984 as a farce. Its positive critical and audience reception was supported by a successful production and the reputation of Tom Stoppard who had adapted the text. The critics felt that the production was serious, in contrast with some of the other productions labelled as farces. The original genre of the play, Viennese folk drama, was unfamiliar to Finnish audiences, but contemporary Stoppard was well-known. Kirsikka Siikala from *Helsingin Sanomat* analysed the production from the point of view of its dramatisation and concluded that Stoppard had transformed the original play into a satire by consciously leveraging farce, but that Stoppard's adaptation did not get to shine in this Finnish National Theatre production. The production was closer to Nestroy than Stoppard. The play was directed by the experienced and multifaceted actor, Pentti Siimes. Siimes put a lot of energy into the play's style and the result was raucous action and humane humour. The play follows a pair of shop assistants who go on a spree; the duo was played by Jouko Keskinen and Autiovuori who excelled with their sympathetic performances and their physicality.

Farces at the Finnish National Theatre did not receive general (critical) approbation despite their status as classics. But the popularity of some of the productions with audiences meant that the genre was a potential route into the world of drama for sections of the population, just as Savola had predicted in his justification for including farce in the Theatre's repertoire in the first place. In Finland the definition of classic drama was quite narrow-minded and only the older generation of critics appreciated the historical genres of some of the Theatre's more "lighter" entertainment programming.

An operetta causes a scandal

Jacques Offenbach's operetta *Parisian Life* had its opening night in September 1981 and it was shown a total of 128 times amid a widespread and raging press debate. In the 1980s the entire operetta genre was dismissed as old-fashioned, and even though Offenbach's work included some irony that distanced it from earlier romantic incarnations of the genre, the production was irretrievably tied up with its operetta label. It was futile to attempt to find a serious message among the Parisian merrymaking of a Swedish noble couple or in the dress-up games servants played to mimic their masters. The production was deemed especially disdainful when coupled with *Wicked Duchess* from the previous spring. It was unthinkable that the Finnish National Theatre should be staging productions like this.

The Finnish National Theatre justified its choice by claiming that it wanted to provide talented singers among its resident actors an opportunity to practise their musical skills in their own theatre. Leif Wager had extensive musical experience from Helsinki's Svenska Teatern's (Swedish Theatre) musicals and from his cinematic singing exploits, and Siimes had sung in operettas and musical dramas in his youth. At the National Theatre, the ability to sing was not a requirement made of its actors, but in the right dramatic context songs had been deemed acceptable, and many actors had performed songs at the Theatre as part of other dramatic programming. The most famous musical drama in the repertoire was Teuvo Pakkala's *On the Log River* and in the play *Johnny Johnson* Kurt Weill's songs had been an important part of the production where Siimes had played a central role.

Music also played a central role in the *Parisian Life* production. Atso Almila, who would become permanently attached to the Finnish National Theatre the following year, and Esa-Pekka Salonen who would go on to accrue international

Figure 14.1 Parisian Life 1981. Ahti Jokinen, Jarno Hiilloskorpi, Karin Pacius, Maija Karhi and Jouko Keskinen
Photography by Johnny Korkman

fame, shared conductor duties. To support the production's singing, opera singer Eeva-Liisa Naumanen was also drafted in. The two conductors' differing temperaments could be traced in the production's music; Salonen's parts tended to be a lot shorter than Almila's, in keeping with Salonen's briskness.[9] The production's ornate set design and customers were designed by the Finnish National Opera set designer Seppo Nurmimaa and choreographer Flemming Flindt. The production's execution did little to stem the criticism of the production itself.

The play's critical reception revolved around *Helsingin Sanomat* critic Kajava's passionately negative review that barely mentioned the actual production. Many other critics came out condemning the production and the fact that it was staged at all. A few also suggested that members of the audience were actually encouraged by Kajava's derision towards the production. At the time, even the more positive reviews reminded their readers that *Parisian Life* was not "art" even though the theatre critic might have enjoyed their time at the theatre. Nobody thought the production was an all-round success, and even Kajava had been charmed by the production's brisk can-can dancing. Critic Katri Veltheim who had been writing theatre reviews since the original heyday of the operetta, attempted to approach the production within the context of its own genre. She was disappointed by the production's lack of energy after a promising beginning. Veltheim felt that musical theatrics, ostentatious costumes, and scenes of Paris obscured the story's tone. As a stage director, Lisbeth Landefort was unable to maintain an ironic grip of the play. Veltheim also felt that the play's highs were lacking in jubilance and exuberance. As the public discussion quickly became polarised, the actual balancing of the good and bad elements of the production mentioned in these critical reviews were quickly sidelined.

The original subject of criticism, the Finnish National Theatre's operetta production, faded into the background in the heated public exchanges of opinions that ensued. The production itself fared well: *Parisian Life* continued to be a hit with its audiences for a number of years. However, a disproportionately large public debate negatively impacted the Finnish National Theatre's reputation, even though the Theatre attracted some of the country's best musicians for its musical programming. Experimentation with this entertainment genre did not last long; a kind of turning point was reached in the early 1980s in the National Theatre's "entertainment programming". From then on audience success was courted from a new angle. The Theatre found new material to stage in order to draw people to the Theatre's Main Stage.

Criticism and crisis at the centre of public attention

Kajava's 1981 review of the Finnish National Theatre's *Parisian Life* operetta production was the catalyst for heated debate. Opinions were exchanged on the accuracy of Kajava's review, the mission of the Finnish National Theatre, and the state of Finnish theatres overall. Problems were found right across the Finnish theatrical world.

As Kajava laid into the *Parisian Life* production, he used equally strong language to condemn the entire Finnish National Theatre: the country's main stage 'trailed behind' without 'the Theatre and its numerous boards and committees' caring for the problem as long as the audience kept coming to see 'the ex heroes and heroines of Finland's film industry'. Kajava stated that 'things are as well as they are in a funeral procession'. He felt that the house lacked soul and that it failed to inspire or fire itself up. 'It's rare that the National will put on work where you can actually smell the sweat, the sweat that comes from uncompromisingly following your aims and putting yourself on the line'. Young people's voices were not being heard. Kajava conceded that a few of the plays on the National's smaller stages had spark, and that some of them had even courted controversy, but the Main Stage was 'stalling and idling from year to year'.[10]

The debate fanned out into the rest of the press and ballooned into a discussion about 'a theatrical crisis', though many commentators felt that the expression itself was a bit excessive. Some commentators felt that the commotion was a convenient way for people to get new material for their television chat shows and causeries. Throughout, the Finnish National Theatre was often discussed in terms that were based on impressions, rather than the actual functions of the working Theatre. Over the years, there had been other dramatic failures, but there had also been plenty of impressive productions staged on the Theatre's Main Stage. However, the Theatre's best – consecutive – audience hits were actually light classic farce or boulevard comedies that were not generally held to a high artistic regard. Regardless, Kajava was particularly vitriolic in his choice of words, and he effectively extended a critique of an individual production into a full-blown attack on the institution. This was not common practice in theatrical criticism.

Anneli Kanto from *Kansan Uutiset* felt that the theatrical debate had morphed into something amorphous. This is what had been actually drenched up as evidence of a full-blown 'crisis': the financial difficulties of Helsinki's City Theatre, the politics of programming at the Finnish National Theatre, and Kajava. Kajava had been "denounced" on television by old-school theatre director Edvin Laine and by critic Heikki Eteläpää from the *Helsingin Sanomat* sister newspaper *Uusi Suomi*. According to Kanto the lack of Finnish drama at the National Theatre, the Theatre's lack of resident directors, or even the stupidity of the roles handed out to its actors, did not add up to a theatrical crisis. She recognised the challenges presented by larger stages at bigger theatres, but she felt that it was hard to find evidence of a widespread serious theatrical crisis. Instead, Kanto was looking forward to many of the upcoming National Theatre productions such as *Amadeus*.[11]

Tampere-based Olavi Veistäjä weighed in on the crisis in his theatrical causerie column (Parraksen pakina) in *Aamulehti*. He drew his own conclusions from the heated televised discussion about the 'crisis' between Laine and director Kalle Holmberg. The conversation on the television show drifted into whether communists held power at theatres and influenced dramatic education, something on which Laine and Holmberg heavily disagreed on. Veistäjä's conclusion was that Finnish theatre was clearly influenced by the left, though 'political posturing had recently calmed down'. The other subject of Veistäjä's column was Kajava's scalding review. Veistäjä did not offer his opinion on the production (that he had not seen), but he took umbrage with Kajava's review. According to Veistäjä the text was 'slander with its roots God-knows-where', not a critical review. He also quoted Heikki Eteläpää's article that speculated that Kajava was angling for a Theatre Director post for himself.[12]

Among the Finnish National Theatre staff there was a variety of reactions and opinions to the commotion. Maija Karhi who worked on the *Parisian Life* production remembered Kajava fondly in her memoirs. She said that Kajava clearly leant over to the left, but that he was sharp and had a good sense of humour.[13] Kajava was generally considered to be a well-informed expert. Autiovuori remembers the *Helsingin Sanomat* articles not as slander, but as belittlement and denigration that seemed to be more about the Finnish National Theatre itself and not its productions.[14] Marjukka Halttunen felt that *Parisian Life* in 1981 was the final straw that finally brought the brewing political debate to a head on the Main Stage.[15] On the other hand the play *Parisian Life* can also be seen as a positive turning point for the Main Stage and its productions.

Pentti Paavolainen wrote about the relationship between the Theatre and the press in the *Teatteri*-magazine in the Autumn of 1981 and in that context brought up Kajava's call to contemporary theatre to renew itself: ' [- -] it's a privilege and a huge help that a sharp-penned critic is out here demanding for continued innovation and renewal'. The Finnish National Theatre was not being asked to do any more than other theatres were. 'It was not long until the groups of Teatterikeskus (Centre for Independent Group Theatres) organised a collective mud slinging match about Jukka Kajava'.[16] Kajava was also critical of theatrical groups that were at a distance from the Finnish National Theatre. A decade later, when Kajava had become the country's undisputed premier theatre critic, Raija Pelttari argued that his blind spots were heaping praise on the theatre groups and rarely giving it out to Helsinki's larger theatres. 'Kajava cannot be bribed. He has really stayed true to his vision, which when thinking of his critical targets is sometimes maybe a tad too uncompromising. But I respect his bravery in speaking out [...]'.[17]

Undeniably, the Main Stage was problematic for the Finnish National Theatre. First, Main Stage productions heavily profiled the Theatre and swayed its public reputation and, second, its hit shows were quickly forgotten. Savola himself mentioned folk theatre as the Main Stage's genre in a variety of different contexts, and perhaps the debate that arose around *Parisian Life* was part of the reason why audience success on the Main Stage for the next few years was courted with folk plays and the popularisation of history rather than operettas and classic farces. The timing of the public debate that was sparked by one single production casts things in rather a strange light as the year preceding the 'crisis talks' had actually been an exceptionally good one for the National Theatre. It had been especially hard to get tickets to some of the Small Stage and Willensauna stage shows, partly thanks to rave critical reviews.

Public "crises" had the tendency to flare up and die down very quickly. Although some of the articles had almost reached witch hunt proportions, and despite frequent repetition, they were actually mainly isolated one-offs. The Finnish National Theatre was deserving of some of the criticism directed its way, but no critic was consistently negative in their reviews of the National Theatre. The end of the 1970s and the beginning of the 1980s were just as turbulent at the Finnish National Theatre as they were in the wider Finnish theatrical circles. The Finnish National Theatre was often approached with a slight apprehension, which was reflected in the reviews of its productions. However, both negative and positive reviews are both evidence of the fact that the National Theatre held a unique position in the Finnish theatrical world, even though the precise nature of that position still remained amorphous.

Notes

1 Mäkinen and Grahn 2014, 104. Actor Esko Roine who was part of the show said that the production was only staged once a week, despite tickets selling like hot cakes.
2 Cf. Mäkinen and Grahn 2014, 104.
3 Maija Savutie, *Kansan Uutiset*, 10.5.1978.
4 Ibid.
5 Kai Savola's letter to Pirkko Koski, 17.11.2016.
6 Jukka Kajava, *Helsingin Sanomat*, 16.4.1981.
7 Ibid.
8 Jukka Kajava, *Helsingin Sanomat*, 2.12.1988.
9 An interview with Seppo Pääkkönen, 4.4.2017.
10 Jukka Kajava, *Helsingin Sanomat*, 1.10.1981.
11 Anneli Kanto, *Kansan Uutiset*, 10.10.1981.
12 Parras [Olavi Veistäjä], *Aamulehti*, 11.10.1981.
13 Valkonen 2008, 265.
14 Pekka Autiovuori, interview, 29.4.2014.
15 Simonen 2010, 117, 122.
16 Pentti Paavolainen, *Teatteri*, 10/1981, 24.
17 Raija Pelttari, *Keski-Pohjanmaa*, 23.3.1990.

15 The advent of the small and the young

By the early 1990s the Finnish National Theatre had solidified its artistic standing in Finland by keeping pace with both social change and the latest dramatic movements. What had also partly helped the Theatre reach its artistic aims was its new layout as the Theatre expanded its performance territory with the addition of new stages and smaller performance spaces. Theatre practitioners could set the tone by choosing a large or a small stage, choosing between an intimate or distant audience relationship. Consequently, the way in which the Theatre's repertoire represented the concept of 'the nation' diversified and became more segmented as well, which resulted in an improved public reputation.

On the smaller stages, specialist audiences could be catered for and these smaller performance spaces attracted new audiences, especially young people who were instrumental in the Theatre's continued success. The smaller stages also enabled a new kind of collaborative approach, fostering close working ties between the Theatre and the Theatre Academy. The stages emerged as the natural arena where young Finnish playwrights built their reputations around contemporary issues, although it must be noted that exploring such issues was not limited to domestic Finnish drama. The National Theatre's small stage productions are a great example of the Theatre's strengths in tradition, timing, and intergenerational collaboration.

While the Finnish economic downturn of the early 1990s negatively impacted the Theatre's Main Stage takings, the Theatre's smaller stages had audiences clambering to get in. Thanks to their contemporary subject matter and provocative artistry, the smaller stage productions added significant value to the Theatre's wider public reputation.

The opening of the Omapohja studio performance space

'Exit, a new Finnish play, could hardly have come at a more opportune time: the day of the structural changes seminar'. Kirsikka Moring from *Helsingin Sanomat* was referring to a large-scale governmental day of talks that took place in Finland in November 1987, coinciding with the play's opening night. Moring hinted that, ironically, the theatrical production was a more productive way to interrogate social change than the political seminar itself.[1] *Exit*, written by Ilpo Tuomarila and directed by Katariina Lahti, did not shy away from depicting Finland's people at a low ebb. As a space, the new Omapohja studio successfully dealt with the challenges of the contemporary theatrical milieu. The production style itself was seen as an evolution of Jouko Turkka's controversial work and Jussi Parvianen's attitude. Parvianen had shocked the theatrical circles of the time with his plays, and Turkka was a known agitator. 'It's anxiety-inducing, nauseating theatre that seems to practically spew its problems onto the ears and eyes of the audience', writes Pentti Ritolahti. 'But these really are the experiences and voices of Finnish people, those people we cross on the streets and squares, as we slowly skulk by and turn our noses up'.[2] Tiina Rinne, one of the actors whose performance dominated the production felt that the play's 'characters were so searing that they offered us all a distinctive opportunity to witness real, live human beings'.[3]

Different generations of actors encountered each other in this performance. Jukka Puotila played the protagonist, Tom, a young man incapacitated by his father's war heroism. His (Soviet) Estonian wife, Hella (played by Pirjo Luoma-aho), was the only sane character in the entire play and the character of the punk little brother was played by Petteri Sallinen. Rinne excelled in the role of the mother: her exhilaratingly awful depiction of a third-rate bar singer desperately clinging to life and performing old tunes accompanied by a four-person orchestra was particularly memorable. On occasion the basement where the play was set was also visited by a struck-off doctor, Eero, played by Seppo Laine. 'Everyone had been left behind by the yuppy Finland train,' as Soila Lehtonen wrote.[4] The production won the prestigious Thalia-prize at the Tampere Theatre Festival the following year and won praise for its ability to step outside of narrow societal limits and its adept staging, as well as for the ways in which the play intermingled strength and coarseness with freshness and used music to support its cast.[5]

Finland and Estonia had traditionally been connected by a shipping route, and as well as trade, shared cultural ties between the two countries were activated during glasnost. In addition, many Finnish construction workers explored Estonia while working on a new hotel in the capital, Tallinn, resulting in many intercultural marriages. While depicting the Estonian Hella in her first National Theatre role, actor Luoma-aho was encouraged by both the playwright and the director to use an Estonian accent to improve cultural realism. And she prepared for this by studying Estonian television programmes. In reality, the virtual connection tended to go the other way and Estonians often learned Finnish by listening to Finnish television. The production overturned the prevailing cultural power dynamic between Finland and Estonia.

The characters in the production were recognisable, yet also caricatures to the extent that the audience was able to laugh at the more unseemly sides of their surroundings. By then, the trope of children brought up by men traumatised by war indulging in a form of rebellion against their fathers had almost become a cliche, but nevertheless it resonated with its contemporary setting. The production was a moving mixture of nostalgia and a timely tale of human fallibility. The new basement-like performance studio was the ideal performance space, and the National Theatre offered a depiction of contemporary Finland that did not flatter, but also displayed genuine warmth.

Translated plays also reached new resonance in the intimate Omapohja studio space. US playwright Lyle Kessner's *Orphans* became a big hit the following Spring. Thanks to its runaway success the production was eventually moved to the slightly bigger Willensauna stage to make way for new dramatic experiments at Omapohja. The *Orphans* production was judged an all-round success: good directing, thoughtful acting from a good cast, Juhani Pirskanen's staging, Sara Popovits's costumes seamlessly ranging from rags to linen elegance, rounded off by Terttu Savola's life-affirming translation of the playtext. Jukka Kajava felt that as a stage director Kurt Nuotio offered up one of the most coherent and compelling feats of stage direction that he had seen in a while; 'a sign of new and youthful thinking at the National Theatre'.[6] Heikki Eteläpää compared Kessner's play to Athol Fugard's *"Master Harold"...and the Boys* and felt that it was a great dramatic find for the small studio space.

The play is set in a basement where two young orphaned men are joined by an elegant gentleman (Harold) on the run from his gangster friends. Harold quickly takes the boys under his wings. The Athol Fugard connection was explicit and written into the play's theme, and the connection was also picked up by Pentti Ritolahti who noted the pervading sense of distrust and being on edge written all over the abusive authority-figure played by Tapani Perttu. The older brother played by Markku Maalismaa was 'a portrayal of a street thug that gets under your skin'. Petteri Sallinen's interpretation of the younger brother laid bare the lack of security, fear, and loneliness inherent to orphans, as well as the sudden ecstasy of believing you can survive on your own.[7]

The Omapohja studio was designed to be an experimental performance space where younger and more inexperienced dramatic artists could test their own powers without the pressures of an opening night at a big theatre. Alongside the Willensauna stage, the Omapohja studio quickly became a stage especially favoured by young playwrights, directors, and actors. But it was also a place for more experienced actors to break boundaries and explore new ground in socially provocative drama. Economic recession, the topic of Jim Cartwright's *Street*, had become commonplace for its Finnish audience yet the production still hit a nerve. The play was new, but it was framed within the tradition of British society dramas. In Finland this meant continuity with the world of prominent post-war British drama. In the play, actor Tea Ista distinguished herself by exploring 'a new, unfettered style of acting as she explored five female characters whose range went from vacant staring to joie-de-vie and from submissive to fiery seduction'.[8]

A new generation of playwrights

The National Theatre dramaturge, Terttu Savola, played an important role in the activation of the Theatre's ties with the Theatre Academy during the early

The advent of the small and the young 199

Figure 15.1 Orphans 1988. Tapani Perttu, Petteri Sallinen and Markku Maalismaa
Photography Johnny Johnson

1990s. Finland was seeing the advent of a brand-new generation of dramatists whose theatrical skills were being honed during their studies through joint productions put on by the Academy's different student bodies. At the Finnish National Theatre, actors from the National Theatre and the Theatre Academy performed side-by-side. The main focus of these collaborative dramatic activities were Willensauna and Omapohja.

Nam nam, a play produced on the Willensauna stage in December 1990, was written by Harri Virtanen. Virtanen was patently no longer a student – in fact, by then he had already started teaching at the Theatre Academy. Influenced by his studies in New York, Virtanen's play displayed a distinctively controlled and economical use of the dramatic form. The play itself revolved around property speculation; a contemporary issue that lent itself to the depiction of increasingly impoverished ethics and values. The play mixed tears with laughter and questioned what it really means to be human.

The acting chemistry between actor Heikki Nousiainen, known for his starring roles, and younger actors Risto Kaskilahti and Päivi Akonpelto was seamless and skilful. Nousiainen's portrayal of Petteri Kuuliainen, the old sales maverick on his way down, brought a welcome diffusion to the play that helped break the tension. The bank manager Ken Olin (= 'who am I') played by the expressive Kaskilahti shed his skin many times during the play. Akonpelto's portrayal of a truth-teller in the middle of a house sale was a straightforward role. *Nam nam* was heralded as an ushering in of a new era at both the National Theatre and in the sphere of domestic Finnish drama as a whole.

Michael Baran's *Suruaika* (Mourning) was shown at the Omapohja studio the following spring. The play was directed by Petri Lehtinen as part of his final degree and alongside actors from the Finnish National Theatre, student actors from the Finnish Theatre Academy and Tampere University populated the stage. Collective interviews conducted around the time of the performance provide strong evidence of the extent to which the boundaries between the traditional theatrical establishment and the group theatres had eroded. The play's director even expressed his gratitude for the opportunity to work in a large theatre in the Theatre Academy's student paper. 'It felt like a real luxury to be surrounded by top experts in their field'. Baran himself explained how for the first time he understood the importance of a good prompter and an experienced monitor. This sense of exploration was reflected in the way in which generations approached each other. 'The overwhelming feeling at the Finnish National Theatre was that of curiosity towards young people, not suspicion'.[9]

Baran's play revolves around a blind competitive swimmer, Janne (played by Santeri Kinnunen), and his relationships, and is essentially an individual's introspective journey into himself through analysing one of his recent dreams. The story was about young people, and young people ran the show. The show was such a success that the Omapohja studio had to accommodate extra runs and some of the young people involved, including the playwright, were snapped up for permanent residencies at the Finnish National Theatre.

Laura Ruohonen's *Lintu vai kala* (Fish or Fowl) was staged at Willensauna at almost the same time, and like Baran, Ruohonen became known as one of the most exciting Finnish playwrights of the ensuing decades.[10] Both young playwrights had the unique ability to explore contemporary themes outside the context of purely realist drama. Before switching to performing arts, Ruohonen had studied biology, and a preoccupation with nature and the environment was highly present in her work.

By the time this production was staged, Ruohonen had already written several radio plays, and her plays had been put on in various city theatres. Her plays often had a strong moral and ethical slant. Alongside nature, Ruohonen's output as a playwright showed a keen interest in philosophy, language, and gender.[11] *Lintu vai kala* explored the insignificance of a human life when contrasted with a global threat, similar to Pentti Holappa's play *Adieu!*. Though unlike the world presented in Holappa's work, Ruohonen approached her subject with empathy, making protecting the world a possibility. The play's structure also opened it up to a new direction. 'In *Lintu vai kala* the actual plot is largely an excuse. What is more important is what is behind what people are saying,' Ruohonen explained in an interview she gave around the time of the play's premiere.[12]

Over the next few decades, environmental concerns became a permanent feature of Ruohonen's work. Alongside Baran, she represented the Finnish National Theatre's new ties to the emerging generation of dramatists trained by the Theatre Academy. This Theatre Academy offered a view of drama that had moved beyond the simplified sense of community and its tendency to enforce theatrical norms. Instead, drama was still seen as a social force, but its role was understood to be much more multifaceted.

Figure 15.2 Lintu vai kala 1990. Anna-Leena Härkönen and Mari Rantasila
Photography by Leena Klemelä

The Omapohja studio was also the venue for an interesting acoustic study, Hannu Raittila's play *Leningradin yö* (Leningrad Night), a joint venture between the National Theatre and the Finnish Radioteatteri (Radio Theatre). The play's title retained St Petersburg's former name, Leningrad, though it was eventually changed to St Petersburg during rehearsals. The experimental element of the play centred on its aural world, and for the Radioteatteri theatre company it was a new kind of venture where they hoped to build a deeper connection with their audience. The production was finalised in the autumn of 1991 and it was also produced as a radio play. The play's soundscape had been collected from a variety of sources, including steel plants and gutters to the sounds for the finale recorded at the Church of Isaac in St Petersburg. The soundscape was amplified with music, and this play also proved that using sounds positively impacted the visual world of a play, making it more engaging.

The play's text and its story converged on a future "Leningrad", in the year 2017. The city had become a no-go zone during the preceding thirty years: a lawless city where only the crime was organised. The changes happening in Russia in the early 1990s were probably the inspiration behind the imaginative world depicted in the play, but Raittila had also studied political history, and in the year leading up to this production, he had written several other radio plays. This play was an intriguing piece of theatrical experimentation, but Raittila eventually became one of Finland's most celebrated prose writers, leaving his dramatist past behind him.

The productions staged on the Willensauna stage and in the Omapohja studio were a tangible marker of how the artistic community at the Finnish National Theatre had become steadily younger throughout the 1980s. These forward-thinking Willensauna and Omapohja productions were proof of the Finnish National Theatre's transformation from the previous two decades. The Finnish National Theatre had finally found an answer to its most staunch critics from the 1970s. Now, the Finnish National Theatre was a theatre with a significantly younger demographic, a theatre where domestic drama had achieved a strong and future-looking position, and a theatre with an established and fruitful working relationship with the radically reformed Theatre Academy. Finding success on the Main Stage was still proving to be challenging, but its role in the balance of determining the Theatre's national position had become less and less significant.

Notes

1 Kirsikka Moring, *Helsingin Sanomat*, 19.11.1987.
2 Pentti Ritolahti, *Kotimaa*, 24.11.1987.
3 Riitta Wikström, *Teatteri*, 7/1990, 25.
4 Soila Lehtonen, *Kansan Uutiset*, 19.11.1987.
5 Newspaper articles about the award, 23.8.1988. The Finnish National Theatre Archives.
6 Jukka Kajava, *Helsingin Sanomat*, 28.3.1988.
7 Pentti Ritolahti, *Kotimaa*, 31.3.1988.

8 Koski 2019, 309–310.
9 Pekka Vänttinen, *Theatre Academy*, 2/1991, 12–13.
10 In 1992 Michael Baran was made resident dramaturg at the Finnish National Theatre, and his plays have been regularly staged at both the Finnish National Theatre and around Finland. Laura Ruohonen has worked as a stage director and a playwright, and she is also known for her work on child culture. Her plays have been staged outside of Finland, and in the 2010s Katri Tanskanen looked into Ruohonen's work as part of her doctoral thesis on new Finnish drama.
11 Marketta Mattila, *Uusi Suomi*, 9.2.1991.
12 Kylänpää Riitta, and Riitta Sourander, *Me naiset*, 30.8.1991.

16 Theatre company visits from East and West

After the Second World War Finland had to navigate its position between the two political power blocs of Eastern and Western Europe. After he accepted the position of Theatre Director of the Finnish National Theatre in 1949, Arvi Kivimaa's mission was to ensure Finland's close ties with the West. As a theatre company the Finnish National Theatre visited Paris, Stockholm, Copenhagen, Vienna, West Berlin, Moscow, Leningrad (St Petersburg), Lubeck, Oslo, Tallinn, Budapest, and during the last spring of Kivimaa's directorship in 1974, the company visited Leningrad again, as well as Warsaw. These countries were treated to both national Finnish drama as well as one-off plays by dramatists such as Euripides, Lope de Vega, Sławomir Mrożek, and Samuel Beckett. Eino Kalima's Chekhov productions also made their way to the East, but they were mostly shown in the West. In addition, during the two Kivimaa decades the Finnish National Theatre welcomed, on average, two visiting theatre companies a year from all over the world and only a total of six of those came from behind the Iron Curtain. Notable productions included plays put on by the Royal Shakespeare Company and the Berliner Ensemble.[1]

When Kai Savola took over from Kivimaa as Theatre Director of the Finnish National Theatre in 1974, not only was he almost twenty years younger than his predecessor, he was also operating in a very different political climate. Savola's generation had a more complex and ambiguous relationship with Eastern Europe and its drama. Visiting theatrical productions from the Eastern Bloc functioned as a form of bridge between the West and the countries who were behind the Iron Curtain. British drama still occupied a prominent position at the Finnish National Theatre, and the National Theatre also welcomed multiple theatre companies from China and Japan. When it came to the Nordics, only one visiting theatre company from Sweden was seen at the National Theatre during this period. Overall, the total number of visits and residencies fell, but many of them were all the more impressive. The National Theatre was still frequently being asked to tour other countries as well, but the funding for the trips was not forthcoming, which particularly impacted the Theatre's Nordic connections.[2] Visits by the National Theatre to other countries had to wait until the 1980s to really get started, and there were less and less of them as time went on.

DOI: 10.4324/9781003047667-18

The National Theatre's policy on visiting theatre companies was not impacted by left-wing ideology when its Director changed. Rather than angling for national-cultural commentary, the main criteria for staging visiting drama remained predominantly artistic. If any politicisation was implicit, it was usually deflected as a criticism against the country of origin.

Visits from British and German theatres were supported by the British Council and the Goethe-Institut and theatrical visits from the Far East were often supported by the embassies of the countries involved. Some of the costs of these visits were allocated to various existing transnational cultural agreements. The British productions had often been designed with touring in mind and production costs had been calculated accordingly, in comparison, the expense of a large-scale original permanent theatre production was much higher. All the practical challenges associated with visiting companies were by no means financial. When the Gorki Theatre did a three-day tour with the play *Hanuma*, the visit lasted a whole week and consisted of 70 people and when the Taganka Theatre came to town, their productions required over twenty weapons from the 19th century and a special pass was needed to transport the guns over the border.[3]

Gorki Theatre, Taganka Theatre, and other Eastern European triumphs

Savola was a keen follower of Soviet theatre, but he kept a tight grip on Finnish-Soviet theatre collaborations. The relationship with the Soviets was challenging yet progressive, and internationally renowned Soviet productions were staged in Finland. A telling example of the challenges of the Soviet-Finnish collaboration is the fact that the Taganka Theatre's *Three Sisters* was deemed unsuitable by the Soviets for staging in Finland because Yuri Lyubimov's interpretation of the play did not align with the reigning artistic view of the work. Conversely, the National Theatre's *Diary of a Madman* was deemed unsuitable for Russian consumption for the same reason.[4] The visiting contract with Taganka Theatre had already been the result of painstaking negotiations, with the Soviets repeatedly trying to offer another alternative theatre.[5]

The collaboration with Leningrad's Gorki Theatre had been ongoing since the 1960s, and it continued in the years 1975, 1976, and 1977. Regardless of genre or style, the productions that visited Finland directed by the Theatre's Director, Georgi Tovstonogov, all had lively storytelling along with well thought-out details tied to a solid artistic vision in common.

In 1975 the Gorki Theatre visited with *Hanuma*, a Georgian classic from A. Tsagarett. *Hanuma* was a high farce where the courtship exploits of an impoverished ruler are interspersed with intricate folk dances and music. Nikolai Gogol's *The Government Inspector* came to the Theatre in 1976 and was praised for its ability to seamlessly marry detail-oriented drama with a larger story arc, as well as the way it took comedy right up to the edge of tragedy. In 1977 the Gorki Theatre created shockwaves in Finland with M. G. Rozovsky's dramatisation of a Tolstoy novella called *The Story of the Horse*. All three nights were sold out, applause went on for almost ten minutes, and inside the Theatre the banging and shouts of bravo were deafening. The most striking element of the production was the imaginative interpretation of the Holstomer horse by E. A. Lebedev. Lebedev was part of a collective whole where everything was impressive: the depiction of horses and people, the visual world, and the music.

The Gorki Theatre was replaced by the Taganka Theatre in the 1980s. Its week-long visit in May 1982 kicked off a long-term collaboration during which both theatres visited each other, culminating in the world-famous Soviet director Yuri Lyubimov directing plays at the Finnish National Theatre.

During the first Taganka Theatre visit to Helsinki, three plays were staged. Dostoevsky's *Crime and Punishment* was a pared-back production that coupled a spartan exterior with an intense and precise performance from its actors. The production directed by Lyubimov hinged on striking imagery. In another Taganka Theatre production of Molière's *Tartuffe* the actors stepped out of full body portraits of their characters dressed up in Sunday-best, only slowly peeling back their true natures. In a dramatisation of John Reed's *Ten Days That Shook the World* the stage was overtaken by the events of revolutionary St Petersburg where the audience were both physically and dramatically surrounded. Crowds that clashed in a partly symbolic way were substituted for satirical portraits of individual characters, and the production itself leveraged both pantomime and shadow play. The old weapons that had been brought over for the production were fired on-stage and in the auditorium itself. The political message was multifaceted.[6]

During the 1988–1989 season three elite Soviet theatres visited the Finnish National Theatre. The exchange of culture became accelerated as the Soviet cultural landscape opened up, and in that same year Finland welcomed a total of seven visiting Soviet theatre companies.[7]

The arrival of the *Cerceau* production by A. Vasiliev's theatre company to Finland had been the result of an ongoing process.[8] Vasiliev had rapidly become a European household name, largely thanks to his 1985 production of Viktor Šlavkin's *Cerceau*. According to a Russian article published in the *Teatteri* magazine, the play's main theme is the dream of human togetherness and the eventual destruction of that dream. The production was steeped in tradition and a 'typically beloved Russian preoccupation with the deeper meaning of existence, a desire to find spiritual brotherhood and teachers'.[9] According to Savola, Vasiljev maintained that the production was not related to the perestroika, but that the perestroika had merely enabled him to make theatre in his own way.[10]

Cerceau derived its name from a French game, and although the hoop-throwing game was also featured on stage, the name was also a metaphor for the production itself: people sitting on the porch of a ruined villa and talking about life. The old house with all its objects invoked the past. '*Cerceau* is a drama of disunity, dissonance, and discord; in the final scenes the villa's windows are nailed shut as the temple of unity collapses. Closing windows with doors is a powerful image,' wrote Soila Lehtonen.[11] For Finnish audiences, this visiting residency signalled a new type of Soviet theatre. The message was interpreted as universal.

The Georgian Rustaveli Theatre's *King Lear* directed by Robert Sturua was pessimistic. At the end of the production the staging collapsed and salvation seemed impossible. The journey towards the climax of the tragedy was done in typical Georgian spirit: 'Above all thunders the chilling story of Shakespeare's *King Lear* with its message about the thirst for power, about evil that gets its comeuppance,' wrote Jukka Kajava.[12] The structure of the production shone through with clarity and the play's messages came through as layered.

A lot had changed in the Taganka Theatre circles between their spring 1982 residency at the Finnish National Theatre and their 1988 *Boris Godunov* production. Lyubimov had stayed in the West in 1984, for which he had lost his Soviet citizenship, but he had been able to eventually return to Russia and finish rehearsals for *Boris Godunov* that had been banned five years previously. The play had been the original reason for him heading to the West. The play's namesake was played by Taganka's new Director, the future Minister of Culture, Nikolai Gubenko. The most impressive feature of the production was the emerging portrait of a national people. The play's power struggle and the way it portrayed citizens demanding law and order were elements that marked it out as dangerous and that had led to its repression in the first place.

During its third visit in the Spring of 1990, the Taganka Theatre brought one of its most impressive productions to the Finnish National Theatre: *The House on the Embankment*, coupled with a poetry and song night dedicated to the beloved actor Vladimir Vysotsky. Both productions were directed by Yuri Lyubimov. Lyubimov was back on the Taganka Theatre's management board, largely thanks to the efforts of Nikolai Gubenko, who also played a big role in the Vysotsky night.[13]

Yuri Trifonov's *The House on the Embankment* was a critical, sympathetic, and humane political exploration of value nihilism. In the world inhabited by the production, not a lot is needed for total destruction: 'Modern Raskolnikovs do not murder with axes, they just lightly push you to immediately create a vacant space'.[14] David Borovski's set design was a significant element of the production. On stage, Glebov, guilty of denouncing his friends, was squeezed between a stage-width sheet of glass and the audience, reduced to watching events unfold from the other side of the glass for 50 years.

Finnish people had a special relationship with their distant linguistic cousins in Hungary, and the relations between the two nations were especially close during the 1980s. Budapest's Katona József Theatre was a kindred spirit of Moscow's Taganka Theatre, although its position did not cause as much tension as Taganka's did in Moscow. Hungarian cultural politics were also generally much freer than those of the Soviet Union. In 1989 the Finnish National Theatre hosted *The Three Sisters* directed by Tamás Ascher. Kajava felt that the production deserved a place among some of the most reputable productions in European theatre: 'Ascher reaches us over the din of a tragic avalanche and talks to us directly about the opportunities presented to us all today.'[15] The production picked up pace towards the end and ended on a particularly impressive note when Olga's rousing monologue about her hope for a better future was drowned out by increasingly loud military music.

The return of the Estonia-connection

In the late 1980s the Finnish-Estonian connection was activated through theatrical collaborations, allowing the two neighbouring nations to work evermore closely in the wide sense of the word. Very quickly the decision-making on the Estonian side became increasingly national: no longer did all decisions involve Moscow. Finland had previously been able to attract notable Estonian dramatists and visiting theatres through the Soviet channels[16], but usually a deal with Moscow was about Russian drama or putting on Russian plays, not about Estonia. The activation of the Finnish-Estonian connection coincided with Mikhail Gorbachev's political reforms in the Soviet Union, the perestroika and glasnost, as well as a new national awakening in Estonia.

The increasingly open atmosphere in Estonian theatres encouraged people to take an interest in their own history, activating a collective need to process and deal with the past. 'As the perestroika and the openness of the 1980s contributed to a more liberal atmosphere, the theatres were first on the scene to reclaim territory from the censors', writes Seppo Zetterberg in *Viron historia* (The History of Estonia).[17] The Finnish National Theatre's Estonian connection became established in the years 1986, 1988, and 1990. In the beginning, the visiting Estonian productions were predominantly small-scale culturally historical affairs, but as time went on, large-scale successful plays from both Finland and Estonia started to grace the Estonian stage. The Finnish National Theatre's Willensauna stage became the ideal place to put on Estonian productions, even when the Finnish National Theatre was not directly involved in the production. The Finnish National Theatre was not the only theatre in Finland to make the most of these new collaborative opportunities with Estonia.

In the spring of 1986 theatrical visits emulated the spirit of genial, neighbouring nations. Sweden had many Estonian refugees, and Sweden's Baltic Institute asked Pärnu's Dramatic Theatre on a tour that extended from Stockholm to Gothenburg. The Dramatic Theatre arranged to perform at the Finnish National Theatre on the way, and Mati Unt's *An Hour of Ghosts on Jansen Street* was performed on the Willensauna stage in May of that same year.

The play's premiere had already taken place in Estonia in 1984 at the Lydia Koidula Home Museum in Pärnu where the 50-seat auditorium sold out for many years. The play has three historical characters: a Museum tour guide, Valvoja, who is visited first by the Finnish writer Aino Kallas, and then by an Estonian writer Lydia Koidula. She was a significant Estonian poet and cultural figure, while Aino Kallas had married an Estonian scientist, later ambassador, and used Estonian folk tradition in her writing. The Theatre's visit was a cultural event that went beyond the staging of the play where the Estonian actors toured Helsinki, visiting sites significant to the lives of both Kallas and Koidula. Koidula and Kallas were the personification of the friendship and kinship between the two neighbouring nations.

The Finnish reviews emphasised this cultural significance and the production was judged to be well-executed, if slightly traditional: an understandable critique in Finland in 1986 when the focus was very much on Jouko Turkka's and Jussi Parviainen's radical work. The head of the cultural department at *Helsingin Sanomat* Marja Niiniluoto wrote that 'the visit to Willensauna is just the sort of cultural event that is ideally situated to support and enliven Estonian-Finnish relations'.[18] Another culturally significant tour was Pärnu's Drama Theatre's visit to the Finnish National Theatre the following autumn. Their production of *Friedebert Tuglas's Life* was received in Finland as a part of the centenary programme celebrating Tuglas's life, rather than a theatrical event.

Slowly, the focus of visiting Estonian theatre companies shifted to a more theatrical direction. In May 1988 Tallinn's Youth Theatre put on August Strindberg's *Miss Julie* at the Finnish National Theatre directed by Unt. In this version of the play all three characters were seen as victims not in control of their own emotions, eventually overrun by events. Later that same year in the autumn, members of the Ugala Theatre from Viljand performed an evening of Estonian poetry named *The River Flows* which included Hando Rummel poems composed by Väino Uibo and accompanied by Toomas Uibo.

Juhan Viiding's visit in the autumn of 1988 hit home with the Finnish people: he performed poems and songs alongside his accompanist Tõnis Rätsep in an ensemble called *Öötöö* (Night work). Viiding was known in Finland as both an actor and a poet. The show was deemed to act 'as an interpreter for a nation who have been through a lot […] in notes of sharp satire and naked protest'.[19] Viiding ushered in a new era of transparency for Finnish spectators and society when it came to Estonian culture where it was no longer necessary to spend ages hunting down secret meanings in speeches. It was also a sign of a shift towards the German-European spirit, a move towards the south. The production was especially convincing in its content and form, as well as in its depiction of a sensitive artist's position in a politically charged era. Political metaphors were less strident than first expected.

The increasingly free political climate of Estonia was becoming more and more apparent when Tartu's Vanemuine Theatre visited in February 1990 and put on Finnish Tauno Yliruusi's play *Makuuhuoneet* (Bedrooms) from the end of the 1960s. The politically satirical play took on a new significance when interpreted by the Estonians. In the play, Brezhnev and Dubček are in their bedrooms with their wives discussing the impending threat of invasion facing Czechoslovakia. The production's stagecraft centred on the play's action swapping between the two bedrooms. Dramatic tension was built up through the differing opinions of the couples. Kajava intimated that the play would have been politically too risky for the Estonians to stage before, and furthermore alleged that politics had also been behind the reluctance to stage the play in Finland in 1968. Another potential reason for the lack of interest in the play in Finland could have been found in its format. The visiting production did not make a splash from a dramatic perspective, but its political significance in the Estonian context was acknowledged. Kajava also felt that it was high time that both the Finnish and the Estonians 'should start looking at themselves, as well as around'.[20]

The unravelling of the long-term Soviet censorship was evident in how Estonian theatre visits started to resemble traditional theatrical exchanges. For example, in April 1990, Tallinn's Youth Theatre brought both a contemporary play and a national classic to the Finnish National Theatre's stage, as was often the case with theatrical residencies. The Theatre put on Tom Stoppard's *Rosencrantz and Guildenstern Are Dead* and the Estonian classic, Hugo Raudsepp's folk play *The Idler*. Tom Stoppard's absurdist play from the 1960s took on a new relevance in this new context as it was interpreted as a satire of modern-day Estonia. The play was directed by Roman Bask who was praised for being incisive and actors Guido Kangur and Andrus Vaarik shone in a production marked by dark humour and clowning. *The Idler* directed by Unt, although funny, garnered less attention, maybe partly because under the guise of a folk play the show was unable to capture the freshness of the original. However, Guido Kangur stole the show as the star of *The Idler*.

British theatrical culture

Many impressive shows came to the Finnish National Theatre from the West, often as part of a Nordic or Soviet tour. Visiting British companies would often put on Shakespeare plays. British actors were deemed to represent a higher level of the dramatic arts. Helsinki had previously welcomed the likes of The Royal Shakespeare Company and many Peter Brook productions. During this time period there were markedly less sensational productions, but the work of British performers still attracted widespread acclaim.

On its way to Moscow, *Under Milk Wood* toured in Helsinki in the spring of 1976 as part of its Nordic tour supported by the British Council.[21] This production was the only English-language show put on by Wales's unofficial national theatre company, Theatr Cymru, who usually performed in Welsh. The play was known in Finland from an earlier radio play adaptation called *Milkwood*. In this production directed by Malcolm Taylor two narrators controlled the play's events and six other actors each played all the characters in turn. The headline for critic Heikki Eteläpää's review 'When you can even hear the dew drop'[22] describes the intensity of the production. On stage, dead members of a fishing village sit peaceably on a pier adorned by fishing nets and recount their lives and other village stories using the poetic words of Dylan Thomas. The four shows were sold out in a flash.

British theatre company the Actors' Company put on three very different plays the following year, championing a very English controlled diction and expression. The first play was by playwright James Saunders known for his absurd comedies. His *After Liverpool* was a veritable potpourri of duologues where young actors 'cultivated dialogue in a light, controlled, and polished manner'.[23] The second play, John Osborne's *The Entertainer*, was a depiction of music hall artist Archi Richie's family life. The production was criticised for its dense rhythm but despite these reservations, the production's actors and the cast chemistry were seen as convincing. The third play was Arthur Pinello's old comedy *The Amazons* from 1913, the play text praised for the freshness of its irony. The production reinforced the comedic talents of the actors. The visit from the Actors' Company exemplified the challenge of "translating" specific cultural references in drama. Even though Osborne was well-known in Finland for his dramatic works, notably for his play *Look Back in Anger,* this time the depiction of family dynamics in his play did not connect with the wider social context. When the show failed to sell itself as a metonymy for the national psyche, it became just another story about times gone by.[24]

The visit from the Old Vic Company in the autumn of 1982 was highly anticipated, and their production of Shakespeare's *Hamlet* managed to meet these high expectations. The piece of drama was experienced as masterful, controlled, flowing: in all ways the theatrical event of the season. Derek Jacobi's Hamlet and Jane Wymark's sensitive and exquisite Ophelia excited particular praise. The visit was interpreted as a powerful and brilliant example of the British Shakespeare-tradition.

The tickets for the 1985 visit from the British National Theatre were also quickly sold out. This time the Theatre came to Finland with a dramatised version of George Orwell's *Animal Farm* that had been adapted and directed by Peter Hall. The company was praised for their depiction of the symbolic troupe of farm animals, but critics felt that the book's political references to Stalin and totalitarian regimes in general were obscured. Eteläpää titled his review 'Farmyard terror as bouncy storytime entertainment'. He felt that by choosing a child-like voice to perform the role of the child narrator the play's political message was transported to the realm of the fairy tale.[25]

Finnish theatre critics were often stumped by the British productions with their distinctive British dramatic expression and subtle social commentary, which was in direct contrast with the Finnish spirit of an age that called for more direct political statements. This meant that social or political messages in British plays often went undetected. However, the audience appreciated the overall quality of the shows and the talented actors.

The duo behind the British theatre company Cheek by Jowl, Declan Donnellan, and Nick Ormerod, had visited the Finnish National Theatre before as stage directors and set designers. Their own theatre company came to Finland to perform Shakespeare's *Twelfth Night* on the National Theatre's Small Stage in May 1987. Critic Kajava had not warmed to Declan Donnellan's Finnish National Theatre production of *Macbeth*. For Kajava, *Twelfth Night* represented a similar quintessentially English acting style. His review in *Helsingin Sanomat* was titled 'Fake moments of insights jog around in Cheek by Jowl's *Twelfth Night*'. He did not see the point of staging a production that was missing a clear link to the audience's present-day reality. Even the audience members who had shouted 'bravo' at the opening night were targeted by Kajava.'[26] Hannu Harju's review in *Uusi Suomi* was titled 'Jaunty British entertainment', and Harju did not have a problem with the style or energy of the production, despite its lack of message: 'Robust and present acting form the backbone of *Twelfth Night's* stage play. And it is not until after the show is over that a thought about the frothiness of the play enters the mind'.[27] The Finnish Shakespeare tradition was narrow and it generally centred on the most famous plays, particularly Shakespeare's tragedies.

Finnish people's limited Shakespeare knowledge and the ability of classics to reflect the ages were played out in the critical reception of Michael Bogdanov's and Michael Pennington's English Shakespeare Company's *The Winter's Tale* and *Coriolanus* at the Finnish National Theatre in early 1991. These two very different Shakespeare plays were rarely seen in Finland. The Bohemian harvest celebration of *The Winter's Tale* was entertaining, but it did not resonate with its Finnish audience. In contrast, *Coriolanus* struck a nerve. The entrance of individual actors on the stage holding banners with the text 'Demokratie' inevitably transported the January 1991 audience to the situation in the Baltics, and although the show was set in Rome, its contemporaneous themes remained apparent. Overall, the company's visit highlighted the breadth of Shakespeare's dramatic output and the possibility of adapting his plays to new social and political contexts. It also proved that Shakespeare's plays could become reanimated and reactivated with political meaning, as happened when *Coriolanus* was staged in the middle of the political threat to Baltic states as tanks tragically first overran Lithuania, then Latvia.

Western diversity and Far East traditions

Even though the Finnish theatrical circles were sometimes heated and marked by animated debates, Finland had a culture of collaboration and the country's many theatrical organisations provided a natural forum for discussion and cooperation. Many of the visits to the Finnish National Theatre were a result of joint theatrical celebrations, seminars, and congress programming.

In the spring of 1979, the Viennese Performing Arts School put on a Wolfgang Bauer play *Magic Afternoon* in conjunction with the Max-Reinhardt-Seminar. The production was a part of the biannual National Theatre Days celebrated in Helsinki. The play itself had been credited with being the catalyst for a wave of new naturalist contemporary plays in Europe.[28] The students also put on an ensemble performance of various Austrian writers. Theatre professionals appreciated the prestige of the Max-Reinhardt-Seminar, even though Austria was not one of the more popular places to visit in the 1970s.

West Berlin's Grips Theatre visited in October 1979 with their play *Max und Milli* that was part of the national Festival of Children that included a joint children's theatre seminar for theatrical enthusiasts. The Grips Theatre had been founded in 1966 with the idea of reaching its child audiences through realist performance and laughter. *Max und Milli* was aimed at the over-5s, but the show's audience in Finland also included adults who were interested in juvenile culture. The Finnish National Theatre also welcomed the Düsseldorfer Schauspielhaus who brought an adaptation of Franz Xaver Kroetz's *Neither Fish Nor Flesh* in August 1982. The play depicted unemployment and its effects on family relations, topics that had become familiar in Finland as well. On the whole, visits from German practitioners and theatres were smaller in number during the Savola era, even though German plays were consistently, if sparsely, represented in theatre programming. Most of the time, the relationship was focused on West Germany.

In late autumn 1979, the Finnish National Theatre had a visitor from nearby. Stockholm City Theatre's *Doll's House* provided Finnish audiences with a fresh angle and approach to this famous play by Henrik Ibsen. The production's performance was judged to be more stripped-back and lighter than Finnish performance culture at the time. The Finnish National Theatre's Nordic relations had been plagued by a lack of financing, and in this specific case the visit was aided by the production being part of a larger Nordic tour bound for Tallinn.

Puppet theatre Feng Lei's 1981 visit to the Finnish National Theatre with their play *Ruby* was part of the National Theatre Days and a clear sign of Savola's ongoing interest in Asian theatre. 'Traditions, high standards, and opulence: all to be expected from the Shanghai Feng Lei's production. Humour, vivacity, and a playful nonchalance were a surprise,' wrote Riitta Wikström.[29] In the production, modern lighting and projections were married with traditional Chinese dramatic techniques. The puppets themselves were imaginative and constantly shape-shifting as they depicted the battle between good and evil in the classic Chinese tale. The *Jade Lotus Flower* production from 1987 included almost life-size clay puppets, a skilled and deliberate expression style, and age-old aesthetics. Three years later the Finnish National Theatre staged a Chinese kunqu-opera from the Beifang theatre company who put on a three-hundred-year-old classic *The Palace of Eternal Youth*. A lot of the play's meaning was inevitably obscured from its Finnish audiences, and much of the show's merits centred on its exceptionality. 'You realise that you are witnessing sacred, centuries-old secrets,' Kirsikka Moring wrote as part of a series of articles she used to explore this art form.[30]

Japanese theatre also enjoyed multiple outings at the Finnish National Theatre. To end the 1985 Spring season the Finnish National Theatre's Main Stage welcomed Hōshō-school performers from the Hōshō-ry Theatre who performed for one sold-out night as part of their European tour. The Hōshō-school was one of the five strands that upheld the Japanse nō-tradition where training and education were supplemented with performance.[31] The hōshō-school could trace its origins back to the 15th century, and among the troupe's 14 actors, there were actors in the 18th generation. The main act was nō writer and theorist's Zeami's *Feather Cape* (assumed to be written by him). The publication of Kai Nieminen's masterful translations in the programme helped people follow the play as it unfolded according to strict conventions.[32]

The following year the Finnish National Theatre welcomed the Japanese Yukiza Marionette Theatre and their production of *Macbeth*. This was another traditional Japanese theatre company, founded in 1643 and still run by a descendant of its founder Magosaburo Yuki, now in the 11th generation. *Macbeth* was part of the theatre's "modern" programming, and the production made the most of both traditional and more experimental performance methods. Lady

Macbeth was conversely played by either a person or a puppet. Lady Macbeth's breakdown scene was especially impressive: the last lines of the scene were recited by a *Joruri*-teller playing a *samisen*-lute. The beauty of the traditional drama resulted in a thrilling Lady Macbeth in her breakdown scene.[33]

The Finnish National Theatre travels

By the 1980s the Finnish National Theatre was also finally able to start exporting its own productions. One-person shows were put on by Eeva-Kaarina Volanen, Tarmo Manni, Tiina Rinne, and Kyllikki Forssell. Manni visited Czechoslovakia and West-Germany, Forsell visited Stockholm, and Volanen and Rinne both visited Tallinn and Tartu. Taking one-person shows abroad was relatively easy and many of these small-scale productions also toured Finland.

The Finnish National Theatre's visits to Soviet Moscow and Tallinn in 1985 were on a bigger scale. The programme included Aleksis Kivi's *Heath Cobblers*, Peter Schaffer's *Amadeus* and Aleksander Galin's *Retro*. The itinerary was formed through discussions the Finnish National Theatre had with the Soviet Ministry of Culture. Savola had originally proposed two plays for the programme: *On the Yalta* and *Cherry Orchard,* but the latter was not seen as enough in-keeping with Soviet Chekhov conventions (even though it was directed by the Soviet Anatoli Efros and the production was well-received), and the former did not correspond with their official view of Chekhov's character. The hosts were intrigued by *The Heath Cobblers* and *Amadeus* and they also selected *Retro*, where Eero Kankkunen's stagecraft was deemed especially interesting.[34]

In 1989 the Finnish National Theatre made a reciprocal visit to Moscow's Taganka Theatre and put on two impressive productions, Lyle Kessner's *Orphans* and Nikolai Erdman's play *The Suicide,* which would be the first time the uncensored version of Erdman's play text would be performed in the Soviet Union. When performed in Moscow, Erdman's play, directed by Hungarian Ascher, seems to have more successfully drawn out its political themes than when performed in Finland.[35] The way in which the play *Orphans* depicted violence and obscenity in a naturalist way was novel for its Moscow audiences, and it's unlikely that either play would have been given the green light to be shown in the Soviet Union before then. It was the start of a new era for the Taganka Theatre: the visit coincided with Yuri Lyubimov's return from exile the following week, and the Theatre's lobby now included a reinstated picture of Lyubimov that had been removed in 1984.[36]

The Finnish National Theatre took August Strindberg's *Facing Death* to the Vanemuine Theatre in Estonian Tartu in autumn 1988, reciprocating a visit from the Tallinn Theatre who had come to Finland the previous spring with *Miss Julie;* these reciprocal visits can be seen as a generalised cultural exchange where both parties display their knowledge of a classic dramatic text. On the other end of the spectrum, Rein Saluri's *Lähtö* (Going) and David Pownall's *Master Class* in Tallinn in the spring of 1989 brought up a lot of national feeling.

In Estonia Saluri's text was well-known and the public discussion about the deportations to Siberia had already opened up, but the tangible staging of the events shocked the audience, and deeply resonated with the Finnish performers who could sense the audience's emotion. When the show's audience changed from its first audiences in Finland to its eventual Estonian audience, many of the Finnish performers felt a deep sense of reverence as they performed to the people who actually had a collective memory of the events they were depicting on-stage. 'Many actors felt the need to speak quieter when they recounted their experiences', remembers Kaius Niemi who played the son of the deported family. 'Estonia was still part of a supranational super power, and lost in its clutches, individual human fates did not weigh much. This kind of collective experience of systemic violence was alien to us Finns who had been born after the war. It made us return to Helsinki feeling pensive and humbled'.[37] For the Estonians in 1989, the age of censure was not so far behind and there was still a tangible sense of threat.

The Estonian theatre academic Lea Tormis analysed the merits of this Finnish interpretation of Estonian history, posing the question as to whether a suitable dramatic classic would have been a more pertinent choice during such a politically unstable time. 'Even the most creative and empathetic Finnish theatre practitioner cannot on some deep level fathom what kind of position these plays place them in'. Tormis had previously seen Unt's *Lähtö* in Helsinki before its Tallinn production. He felt that in *Lähtö* Unt had almost attained the tragic absurdity of the Estonian survival strategy, and that the visiting production showed a clear development from the Finnish opening night. 'The production was alive. And, I might be mistaken, but the performers somehow had a more personal and more painful relationship with the play than when they performed it on their home stage', Tormis mused.[38]

Pownall's depiction of Stalin's nocturnal games with composers and their lives was judged to be an interesting piece of theatre and factual fiction in Finland, but for an Estonian audience, this play was steeped in reality. (In fact, the play had already been seen in Tallinn, staged by the city's Youth Theatre). Tormis felt that it was harder to analyse *Master Class* than *Lähtö*, as it was hard to avoid the direct comparison with the play's recent interpretation by Tallinn's actors: their tension-filled approach to depicting Stalin corresponded more closely to the sense of threat pervading Estonia at the time.[39]

The Finnish National Theatre was invited back to Tallinn by their Youth Theatre in 1989, putting on the play *I'm Not Rappaport,* with the Estonian element being provided by Erkki-Sven Tüür's music. The following year the Finnish National Theatre performed in Estonia twice: *The Orphans* at Tartu's Vanemuise Theatre and *Portrait* at Tallinn's Youth Theatre.

Notes

1 Heikkilä 1972, 245, 258–61; Mehto 1999, 252.
2 Kai Savola's letter to Pirkko Koski, April 2016.

216 Finland's National Theatre

3 The Finnish National Theatre Archives: archival material pertaining to theatre visits.
4 Wikström, Riitta, *Etelä-Suomen Sanomat*, 9.2.1992.
5 The Finnish National Theatre Archives: financial board meeting memo 25.2.1982; the folder pertaining to the Taganka visit; Kai Savola's letter to Pirkko Koski, 13.3.2017.
6 Folder pertaining to the Taganka Theatre visit. The Finnish National Theatre Archives.
7 Liisa Byckling, *Seuratieto*, 8/1988.
8 Kaarina Naski, *Karjalainen*, 21.10.1988.
9 'Kellarin sävel.' *Teatteri*, 9/1988, 26–27.
10 Kai Savola's letter to Pirkko Koski 13.3.2017.
11 Soila Lehtonen, *Kansan Uutiset*, 7.10.1988.
12 Jukka Kajava, *Helsingin Sanomat*, 10.5.1989.
13 Kirsikka Moring, *Helsingin Sanomat*, 8.3.1990.
14 Kirsikka Moring, *Helsingin Sanomat*, 11.3.1990.
15 Jukka Kajava, *Helsingin Sanomat*, 14.4.1984.
16 For example, the Theatre Academy's *Seven Brothers* in the 1970s or *The Three Sisters* directed by Adolf Shapiro.
17 Zetterberg 2007, 703, 717–719.
18 Marja Niiniluoto, *Helsingin Sanomat*, 27.5.1986.
19 Heikki Eteläpää, *Uusi Suomi*, 9.11.1988.
20 Jukka Kajava, *Helsingin Sanomat*, 23.2.1990.
21 Finnish National Theatre, Board meeting notes, 3.3.1976. Finnish National Theatre Archives.
22 Heikki Eteläpää, *Uusi Suomi*, 14.4.1976.
23 Heikki Eteläpää, *Uusi Suomi*, 12.4.1977.
24 Cf. Holdsworth 2010, 56–62.
25 Heikki Eteläpää, *Uusi Suomi*, 29.8.1985.
26 Jukka Kajava, *Helsingin Sanomat*, 6.5.1987.
27 Hannu Harju, *Uusi Suomi*, 6.5.1987.
28 LSP, *Etelä-Suomi*, 31.3.1979.
29 Riitta Wikström, *Uusi Suomi*, 15.4.1981.
30 Kirsikka Moring, *Helsingin Sanomat*, 30.10.1990; Kirsikka Moring, *Helsingin Sanomat*, 1.11.1990.
31 Miettinen 1987, 215.
32 Jukka O. Miettinen, *Helsingin Sanomat*, 30.5.1985.
33 Jukka O. Miettinen, *Helsingin Sanomat*, 15.9.1986.
34 Kai Savola's letter to Pirkko Koski 13.3.2017.
35 Heikki Eteläpää, *Uusi Suomi*, 15.11.1989. 'Here [in Finland] I am unable to make political theatre, I don't know Finland and its conditions well enough. And here people do not understand the betrayal of communism on a personal level, its repression of human rights, as people in socialist countries do', Ascher told an interviewer around the opening night.
36 Also: Sally Laakso, *Neuvosto-Karjala*, 15.12.1989.
37 Niemi 2015, 78–81.
38 Lea Tormis, *Teatteriväki*, 2/1989, 38–39.
39 Ibid.

17 Conclusion

The National Theatre during a time of transition

During the decades under review, the National Theatre changed its structural foundations. For one, the average age of its acting cast declined significantly (albeit not until the 1980s). The number of other permanent artistic staff at the Theatre was small and varied widely. Owing to the large number of visiting directors, no special artistic vision emerged for the National Theatre from a stage directing point of view, though the Theatre's extensive international connections ensured that it stood out among other contemporary Finnish theatres. The most visible changes at the Theatre pertained to its performance spaces, and the construction of smaller stages impacted audience segmentation, theatre programming selection, and the dramatic vision of the productions themselves. The Theatre also expanded its administrative connections with key national decision-makers, but retained its independence and held on to its private ownership model.

In the run-up to the end of the Cold War, Finland's location on the western edge of the Iron Curtain between the two power blocs of a divided Europe, as well as its language and social atmosphere, formed an important context for the National Theatre's activities, which was reflected in the formation of its own cultural status in Finland and in its international relations. The National Theatre was free to decide on its own artistic policy, but it was judged and evaluated in function of shifting cultural and social mores.

The temporal and geographical delineation of this study illustrates how international currents, in many ways and on many levels, overlapped with the national characteristic of the Theatre. The local became part of a multifaceted international network. The maturing of the 1960s generation was an international phenomenon, leading to a struggle for influence and a battle about the perceptions of drama between different generations. These international events were also reflected, and to some extent, adapted to the Finnish national context. This is evident in Finnish theatre in general, and my aim has been to show how the National Theatre stood out from other dramatic institutions in shaping national identity amid the diametric demands of tradition and change.

DOI: 10.4324/9781003047667-19

Changing times and the National Theatre's policy

When analysing European national theatres, Bruce McConachie defines general features and structures, many of which, though not all, also describe the Finnish National Theatre.[1] In my own analysis, which is framed by time and space, features and operating models that are specific to Finland stand out, although they also have the potential to be generalised on the wider international stage.

The national representativeness of the Finnish National Theatre was never questioned, not even in the 1970s when the fiercest cultural debates were raging. The Theatre was always predominantly a Finnish-language theatre, just like 90 percent of the country's citizens; Finland has two national languages, Finnish and Swedish, and Sámi is also spoken in Lapland.[2] The Swedish-speaking minority (6.5 percent) had a significant number of theatres in their own language (especially when analysed in relation to their population). Some of these theatres did occasionally also perform in Finnish. Therefore, there was no particular need for Swedish-speaking programming at the National Theatre, and especially in the Helsinki metropolitan area, Swedish-speakers also generally mastered Finnish.[3] However, language did not always define nationality, portraits of national character were not limited to Finnish-language ones, and plays and productions were not selected on the basis of specific language groups.

When defining the "nation" that made up its repertoire's target audience, the National Theatre showed social sensitivity and paid attention to various disadvantaged social groups and dissident thinkers, though Finnish society was rarely depicted as multicultural. Occasional descriptions of Finnish-Jewish families and theatre critics' references to Somali refugees are stark reminders of the fact that the dramatic homogeneity did not accurately reflect the reality of the country.[4] Citizens were not judged on cultural grounds and everyone was supposedly treated as equals, although a distinct lack of visibility and diversity was also restrictive. This phenomenon was sign of the times. Later, multiculturalism and its visibility significantly increased in Finland, and the Finnish National Theatre's programming reflected that fact.

Looking at European national theatres, Bruce McConachie distinguishes between two important time periods and justifies the division by emphasising – without underestimating political factors – key forms of communication such as print culture and the later development of mass media such as photography, radio, and film.[5] The latter of the eras, 1950–1980, only partly applies to the Finnish National Theatre. The most important media that maintained, examined, and partly upheld the Theatre's position was Finland's press that extensively wrote about culture. Even when the press was being critical about the Theatre, it justified its position on the National Theatre in the context of the special demands placed on the Theatre itself. Television entertainment benefited from, rather than undermined, the prestige of the National Theatre's actors.

The choice of the 1970s and 1980s as the subject of my study is based on national specificities and broader societal change. The general background is the close ties between Finnish theatrical culture and civil society. The position of the Finnish National Theatre was strongly challenged by the political and social activism of the 1960s generation and the general politicisation of society that began in the 1960s and 1970s. The battle waged at the National Theatre focused on people's involvement and ability to define and influence its content and programming, rather than a fundamental questioning of its national status. The 1980s marked a strengthening of the Finnish National Theatre's position, but despite the stability of the position, its way of operating as a national institution was the subject of ongoing and relentless critical scrutiny. This periodisation corresponds with the accepted idea that 1968 was an important watershed moment for theatre history, as post-war theatre conventions gave way to contemporary mores. However, slightly differing from the rest of the Finnish theatre field, the Finnish National Theatre chose its own path, though its transformation still gestured towards a new, especially international, vision of drama.

Different generations did not have an equal share when it came to participating in the life of the Finnish National Theatre. In the 1970s the Theatre's artistic management and resident stage directors came from the generation of adults who had matured during the war and who had entered the labour market during the rise of modernism in the 1950s and the international social currents of the 1960s. The artistic staff included only a few members from the 1960s generation, and among them only a very few represented the leftist factions that became dogmatised in the 1970s. From the beginning of the 1980s, the average age of National Theatre artists went down, and the reforms of the late 1980s were largely undertaken by the generation who followed the 1960s generation.

Nordic and Finnish premieres were central to the creation of a coherent artistic policy at the National Theatre. In the 1970s, the middle class was not in vogue, but the audience at the National Theatre was distinctively middle class. Loren Kruger references the debate sparked by Pierre Bourdieu's work that argues that the leisure of the ruling classes is becoming universally accepted as art, whereas lower class amusements are invariably defined as entertainment.[6] The National Theatre had to reach the general public, but it could not be branded as an entertainment venue. The solution was found in socially conscious Finnish folk theatre which was supported by and fostered by the growing appreciation of popular art in the 1980s. The definition for dramatic classics remained narrow and only the oldest critics appreciated the historical genres of entertainment drama. At the same time inside the National Theatre on its new smaller stages a new "artistic theatre" was born, repeating what happened in the 1950s, but in the spirit of the new age: a type of parallel phenomenon to the wave of modernism that hit the Small Stage in the 1950s.

The international Finnish National Theatre

In many respects, the "national" nature of the Finnish National Theatre was a concept that relied on other countries. The ideological impetus behind the founding of the Theatre was found in Germany, and one of its general goals was to raise Finland to the status of other European nations with long-standing cultural identities. Dramatic theories and methods, as well as trends and performance conventions, frequently crossed geographical and linguistic boundaries. The National Theatre continued to include international productions as part of its programming and embrace influences from abroad in its productions.

During the period under review it is evident that caught in various cross-border currents, the Theatre was able to engage with international contexts not in order to push Finnish national identity aside, but conversely to shape Finnish identity through 'cultural practices arising out of collaboration and interaction'.[7] Alongside the inevitable development of the Finnish theatre, the National Theatre also aspired to be an internationally recognised cultural institution. When writing about the birth of national theatres Kruger argues 'that national theatre has always existed in a *transnational* field'. According to Kruger, 'the transnational character of the national theatre, whether acknowledged or not, has affected conceptions of repertoire, location, and audience and thus conditions of its legitimation or, better, its *naturalization*, from the earliest movements'.[8] The Finnish National Theatre did not deviate from this model, but adapted transnationalism to Finland's unique national context. Transnationalism emphasised the high arts, where even entertainment needed to be "artistic", or at the very least educational.

Finland's location enabled the National Theatre to establish functional working relationships, foster connections, and reap artistic influences from both sides of the Cold War border that divided Europe. Finland became a meeting place for different European cultures, a position that required careful navigation, but also brought fruitful benefits and creative solutions to artistic problems.[9] The way in which the Finnish National Theatre expressed itself artistically emphasised its cultural independence, often differing from Finland's prudent official policy, especially when it came to Eastern Europe. In addition to theatrical connections, towards the end of the Cold War, the critical reception of Eastern European plays became increasingly politicised with more than one review referencing the 1975 treaty on free movement that contemporary Eastern European national movements often invoked. The National Theatre's official party line vis-a-vis Eastern Europe can be summed up in the spirit of that agreement.

The National Theatre did not have an identical approach when it came to dealing with the East and the West. There were more artist visits from the East, but many of these visitors, especially the stage directors, were also well-known and established in the West. The exchange of productions also emphasised the Theatre's Eastern European connections. In the Western context, politics were rarely invoked. Asian dramatic visits centred on cultural heritage and cultural exchange. Most of the National Theatre's new international repertoire was from the West. Eastern European drama at the Theatre tended to veer away from new drama and premieres, though many of the productions attracted attention and sparked debate. A common uniting feature was the examination of individuals in a problematic social environment.

The European dividing line was seen differently at the National Theatre than in other Finnish theatres. The Finnish dramatic scene had traditionally always looked to German theatres and Finnish theatres continued to visit a divided Germany. In contrast with the strong influence East Germany exerted over Finnish other theatres, the National Theatre's ties with East Germany were insignificant. In fact, the National Theatre's approach was more reminiscent of West Germany, where opposition to state-run theatre was strong and interest in German culture was not taken as a form of nationalism.[10] This attitude was reflected in the National Theatre's limited German programming, but also in its on-stage depictions of Finnish history.

Despite a shared cultural tradition, the National Theatre's Nordic connections were limited. In the case of theatrical visits, this was often due to a lack of funding. Finland's Swedish-language theatres, especially Svenska Teatern and Lilla Teatern in Helsinki, naturally took the mantle of Nordic artistic visits. Outside of these two theatres there were plenty of other Nordic points of contact and many theatre companies organised tours in Sweden, especially among Finnish expat communities. There is no obvious reason for the lack of Nordic connections at the National Theatre.

National drama, national character, and collective memory

According to the 1975 *Taide- ja teatteripoliittinen ohjelma* (*Art and Theatre Politic Programme*), the National Theatre's mandate included taking responsibility for the advancement and conservation of 'Finnish drama and the Finnish language'.[11] The performance of Finnish classics was traditionally central to the Theatre's policy, but they did not necessarily help the Theatre stand out in the contemporary theatrical scene, especially when the Theatre failed to bring life to forgotten dramatic classics or popular classics were produced to little fanfare. The National Theatre succeeded with dramatic classics when it explored socially conscious folk drama that had been previously overlooked in its theatre programming. The Theatre thus helped narrow the gap between popular and high art, mirroring a wider phenomenon in 1980s art research.

Promoting dramatic literature required the support of the writing community which suited the National Theatre, as it strongly favoured premieres for its productions. However, the Theatre was not able to directly quantify its requirement to stage domestic Finnish drama. During the period under review, permanent connections with Finnish dramatists remained few and far between. Instead, the Theatre promoted dramatic literature by encouraging well-known writers to write plays and by bringing new versions of old plays to the stage. Only a few of the plays moved to other theatres after their premiere at the National Theatre. The Theatre only really fulfilled its destiny as a staunch promoter of Finnish drama with the advent of a new generation of writers as the 1990s approached.

The National Theatre's traditional preoccupation with national myths and Finland's romantic national past did not align with the ideological goals of the

1970s–1990s. Instead, political history, popular movements, and 20th-century social history proved to be significant guarantors of public attention and interest. A special "Finnish" feature were dramas depicting nationally rejected or controversial phenomena, especially depictions of 20th century history and political crises. These productions were strongly related to the idea of re-evaluating recent history that had been activated in the 1960s, both in art and scholarship. Creating a dramatic juxtaposition between the people and the elite also proved to be a successful guarantor of audience success. The National Theatre participated in the construction of a Finnish national identity, especially when it came to analysing the nation's past, but the Theatre actively avoided nationalist tendencies.

Marvin Carlson states that theatre is 'a site of memory, both personal and cultural', and memory is equally associated with story, performers, and places. Memory provides the recipient of a performance with the right codes and strategies that form the basis of their perception. Memory for an audience is also triggered by real-life things on-stage.[12] The *memory machine* described by Carson is most evident in the successful domestic dramas of the National Theatre, some of them appealing to audiences in an openly affective manner. For example, the play *Kolmekymmentä hopearahaa* triggered an unusual audience reaction: when at the end of the performance the fictional congregation left the stage singing, the National Theatre audience repeatedly joined in and started singing the hymn. The affectivity of drama could also become a cross-border experience and build empathy for another culture, as happened with the play *Lähtö* that depicts Stalin-era deportations in Estonia.

During these years, Finnish military history was extensively evaluated in historical studies and in Finnish literature, films, and theatres. In the collective memory of the Finnish people, war wounds were still raw. War was also a battleground for Finnish national identity as the 1960s generation distanced themselves from their parents who had fought in the 1939–1944 war and re-evaluated the events of the Finnish Civil War of 1918. At the National Theatre plays about Finnish history, and especially about the wars, were highly susceptible to reinterpretations. These reinterpretations played a central role in creating dramaturgical tensions that were frequently fuelled by public debate. By staging these plays, the Finnish National Theatre participated in the discourse about national Finnish identity, including its own position as a national institution.

Alongside themes, timelines, and contents, Nadine Holdsworth draws attention to the importance of aesthetic strategies in national drama.[13] Although the Finnish National Theatre produced plays that reflected societal problems throughout the 1970s, tangible statements about practical problems were themselves obscured by the productions' Brechtian-style performance elements. (They were not "Brechtian" enough). The most significant aesthetic choice the Theatre made during this time was successfully leveraging forms of Finnish folk theatre to great audience success on the Main Stage. Carnivalism was explored to the extreme in Jouko Turkka's play *Valheita*, whose aesthetic form of depicting national themes incorporated features from international drama. Social criticism was embedded into the renewed form of Finnish folk theatre that was associated with numerous international dramatic currents, though the idiosyncratic Finnish style was still in evidence, the national and international in perfect balance. Through formal experimentation, the National Theatre had broken the chains and bonds of modernity. The Finnish National Theatre was embarking on a new era.

Notes

1 McConachie 2008, 49–51.
2 They were designated by law as 'national languages', not 'official languages'. The status of the Sámi language was strengthened in the 1990s.
3 Swedish-speakers, for example, had parallel theatres, schools, newspapers, and universities. They "represented" the needs of their own language group. Helsinki's Svenska Teatern gained special financial status in the 1990s, but the representativeness of its language group was inherited as early as the late 1910s.
4 Small groups of refugees had entered the country in 1973 from Chile, in 1979 from Vietnam, and in the 1980s from Somalia; the Roma population also began to assert their position in society.
5 McConachie 2008, 49, 55–56.
6 Cf. Kruger 1992, 10.
7 Holdsworth 2010, 71.
8 Kruger 2008, 35.
9 Miklossý 2018, 32. However, according to Katalin Miklossý, interaction across the Iron Curtain cannot be prevented by strict demarcations. She looks at the Baltic region and the countries of Central and Eastern Europe as 'an in-between space', differing from the West but also with a special status in the East. As a meeting place, Finland had contacts to East, West, and this in-between space'.
10 Cf. Irmer 2008, 173–179.
11 *Taide- ja teatteripoliittinen ohjelma*, 1975, 12.
12 Carlson 2001, 3–5.
13 Holdsworth 2014, 5.

Bibliography

Archives

The Finnish National Theatre Archives: including institutional archives, newspaper clippings and photos (if not mentioned otherwise)
The Theatre Museum Archive
The Finnish Literary Society Archive
The Dramatists' Union (Writers' Guild in Finland) Archive

Interviews

Memos, recordings, emails, and letters in Pirkko Koski's archive

References

Akonpelto, Päivi and Komi, Soila. 2011. *Ilta Soilan kanssa*. Kirja kerrallaan ja Suomen Kansallisteatteri: Helsinki.
Alter, Robert. 2000. *Canon and Creativity. Modern Writing and the Authority of Scripture*. Yale University Press: New Haven and London.
Anderson, Benedict. 1981. [1992, 1995]. *Imagined Communities. Reflections on the Origin and Spread of Nationalism*. Revised ed. Verso: London and New York.
Anttonen, Pertti J. 2005. *Tradition through Modernity. Postmodernism and the Nation-State in Folklore Scholarship*. SKS: Helsinki.
Balme, Christopher. 2008. *The Cambridge Introduction to Theatre Studies*. Cambridge University Press: Cambridge.
Bigsby, C. W. E. 1985. *A Critical Introduction to Twenteeth-Century American Drama*. Volume Three. Beyond Broadway. Cambridge University Press: Cambridge, New York, and Melbourne.
Bratton, Jacky. 2003. *New Readings in Theatre History*. Cambridge University Press: Cambridge.
Brecht, Bertolt. 1967. *Schriften aus Theater*. Suhrkamp Verlag: Frankfurt am Main.
Cándide Smith, Richard. 2002. "Introduction: Performing the Archive." In *Art and the Performance and Memory*. Ed. Richard Cándide Smith. Routledge: London and New York, 1–2.
Canning, Charlotte M. and Postlewait, Thomas (Eds). 2010. *Representing the Past. Studies in Theatre History and Culture*. University of Iowa Press: Iowa City.
Carlson, Marvin. 1989. *Places of Performance. The Semiotics of Theatre Architecture*. Cornell University Press: Ithaca.

Carlson, Marvin. 2001. *The Haunted Stage. The Theatre as a Memory Machine*. University of Iowa Press: Ann Arbor.
Carlson, Marvin. 2008. "National Theatres: Then and Now." In *National Theatres in a Changing Europe*. Ed. S. E. Wilmer. Palgrave Macmillan, Houndmills and New York, 21–33.
Carlson, Marvin. 2010. "Space and Theatre History." In *Theorizing Practice. Redefining Theatre History*. Eds. W. B. Worthen and Peter Holland. Palgrave and Macmillan: Houndmills and New York, 195–214.
Cave, Richard Allen. 1989. *New British Drama in Performance on the London Stage 1970–1985*. Colin Smythe: Gerrards Cross.
de Certeau, Michel. 1984. *The Practice of Everyday Life*. University of California Press: Berkeley, Los Angeles and London.
Cochrane, Claire and Robinson, Joanna. 2016. Eds. *Theatre, History and Historiography Ethics, Evidence and Truth*. Palgrave Macmillan: Houndmills and New York.
Conquergood, Dwight. 2004. "Performance studies: interventions and radical research." In *The Performance Studies Reader*. Ed. Henry Bial. Routledge: London and New York, 311–322.
Esslin, Martin. 1978, 1985. *The Theatre of the Absurd*, 3rd Edition. Penguin Books: Harmondsworth and New York.
Eteläpää, Heikki (Ed.). 1986. *Minä, Manni*, 2nd ed. Kirjayhtymä: Helsinki.
Fischer-Lichte, Erika. 1997. *The Show and the Gaze of Theatre. A European Perspective*. University of Iowa Press: Iowa City.
Fischer-Lichte, Erika. 2002. *History of European Drama and Theatre*, Translated by Jo Riley. Routledge: London and New York.
Fiske, John. 1989. *Understanding Popular Theatre*. Unwin Hyman: Boston.
Forssell, Kyllikki and Kinnunen, Raila. 2007. *Suurella näyttämöllä*. WSOY: Helsinki.
Freshwater, Helen. 2009. *Theatre & Audience*. Palgrave Macmillan, Houndmills and New York.
Füllner, Niklas. 2014. *Theater ist eine Volkssauna. Politisches Gegenwartstheater aus Finnland in der Tradition von Bertolt Brecht*. /e/podium: Munich.
Gluhovic, Milija. 2013. *Performing European Memories: Trauma, Ethics, Politics*. Palgrave Macmillan: Basingstoke.
Goodlad, J. S. R. 1971. *A Sosiology of Popular Drama*. Heinemann: London.
Grahn, Annika. 2014. *Tapani Perttu*. Like: Helsinki.
Grosby, Steven. 2005. *Nationalism. A Very Short Introduction*. Oxford University Press: Oxford.
Haapala, Pertti. 2006. "Suomalainen rakennemuutos." In *Historiallinen käänne*. Ed. Juho Saari. Gaudeamus: Helsinki: 91–124.
Haapala, Pertti. 2010. "Vallan rakenteet ja yhteiskunnan muutos: Mielikuvaharjoitus 1800–2000-lukujen Suomesta." In *Valta Suomessa*. Ed. Petteri Pietikäinen. Gaudeamus and Helsinki University Press: Helsinki, 101–117.
Hallberg, Pekka. 2019. *Oikeusvaltio maailman tuulissa*. Docendo: Helsinki.
Häyrynen, Simo. 2015. *Kulttuuripolitiikan liikkuvat rajat. Kulttuuri suomalaisessa yhteiskuntapolitiikassa*. SKS: Helsinki.
Heikkilä, Ritva (Ed.). 1972. *Suomen Kansallisteatteri. The Finnish National Theatre*, 2nd ed. WSOY: Helsinki.
Heiskanen, Juha and Nevala, Maria-Liisa (Eds). 2004. *Suomen Kansallisteatteri. Pieni näyttämö 50 vuotta*. Kansallisteatteri: Helsinki.
Heiskanen, Juha and Nevala, Maria-Liisa (Eds). 2006. *Suomen Kansallisteatteri. Willensauna 30 vuotta*. Kansallisteatteri: Helsinki.

226 Bibliography

Hodgdon, Barbara. 2003. "Photography, Theater, Mneumonics: or, Thirteen Ways of Looking a Still." In *Theorizing Practice. Redefining Theatre History.* Eds. W. B. Worthen and Peter Holland. Palgrave Macmillan: Houndmills and New York: 88–119.

Holdsworth, Nadine (Ed.). 2014. *Theatre and National Identity. Re-Imagining Conceptions of Nation.* Routledge, New York and Abingdon.

Holdsworth, Nadine. 2010. *Theatre & Nation.* Palgrave Macmillan: Houndmills and New York.

Huovinen, Maarit (Ed.). 1986. *Rauni Luoma. Ilon ja murheen näyttämöllä.* WSOY: Helsinki.

Hurley, Erin. 2011. *National Performance. Representing Quibec from Expo 67 to Céline Dion.* University of Toronto Press: Toronto, Buffalo and London.

Innes, Christopher. 1992. *Modern British Drama 1980–1990.* Cambridge University Press: Cambridge.

Irmer, Thomas. 2008. "Aspects of National Theatres in Germany after 1945." In *National Theatres in a Changing Europe.* Ed. S. E. Wilmer. Palgrave Macmillan: Houndmills and New York, 173–179.

Kajas, Iiro. 2013. "Suomen Lausujain Liitto ja lausuntataide." In *Näyttelijänä Suomessa.* Ed. Pirkko Koski. WSOY: Helsinki, 301–303.

Kallinen, Timo. 2001. *Näyttämötaiteilijasta teatterityöntekijäksi. Miten moderni tavoitti suomalaisen teatterikoulutuksen.* Teatterikorkeakoulu: Helsinki.

Kallinen, Timo. 2004. *Teatterikorkeakoulun synty. Ammattikoulusta akatemiaksi 1971–1991.* Like: Helsinki.

Keinänen, Hely (Ed.). 2010. *Shakespeare Suomessa.* WSOY: Helsinki.

Kievari, Solja (Ed.). 2005. *Ismo Kallio. Kaikkea alaan kuuluvaa.* Tammi: Helsinki.

Kiin, Sirje and Ruutsoo, Rein, and Tarand, Andres. 1990. *Neljänkymmenen kirje. Kokemuksia neuvostotodellisuudesta.* Suom. Jaakko Anhava et.al. Otava: Helsinki.

Koho, Timo. 1991. *Teatteriarkkitehtuurin merkitysarvot. Teatterirakentamisen suhde yhteiskunnan arvomaailmaan kaupungistuvassa Suomessa.* Muinaismuistoyhdistyksen aikakauskirja 97: Helsinki.

Koho, Timo. 2003. "Suomalaisesta teatterista Suomen Kansallisteatteriksi." In *Suomen Kansallisteatteri. Teatteritalo ennen ja nyt.* Ed. Maria-Liisa Nevala. Suomen Kansallisteatteri and Otava, Helsinki.

Kolbas, E. Dean. 2001. *Critical Theory and the Literary Canon.* Westview, Boulder and Oxford.

Korsberg, Hanna. 1999. "Jättiläisten kilpajuoksu Pienen näyttämön rakentamisen taustalla." In *Niin muuttuu mailma, Eskoni. Tulkintoja kansallisnäyttämöstä.* Helsinki University Press: Helsinki, 209–228.

Korsberg, Hanna. 2004. *Politiikan ja valtataistelun pyörteissä. Suomen Kansallisteatteri ja epävarmuuden aika.* Like: Helsinki.

Korsberg, Hanna. 2014. "Maailman modernein kansallisteatteri." In *Pieni näyttämö 60 vuotta.* Eds Markku Laine, Auli Turtiainen, and Aina Bergroth. Kansallisteatteri: Helsinki, 31–39.

Koski, Pirkko. 1992. *Teatterinjohtaja ja aika. Eino Salmelaisen toiminta Helsingin Kansanteatterissa 1934–1939.* Helsinki.

Koski, Pirkko. 1997. "Draama näyttämöllä." In *Tie tulkintaan. Juhlakirja akatemiaprofessori Heikki Ylikankaalle.* WSOY: Helsinki, 270–278.

Koski, Pirkko. 2000. *Kaikessa mukana. Hella Wuolijoki ja hänen näytelmänsä.* Otava: Helsinki.

Koski, Pirkko. 2005a. "Traditio ja murros. Eino Salmelainen Nummisuutarien tulkkina." In *Näyttämö ja tutkimus 1: Esitys katsoo meitä.* Eds, Pia Houni et al. TeaTS: Helsinki, 115–131.

Koski, Pirkko. 2005b. *Strindberg ja suomalainen teatteri*. Like: Helsinki.

Koski, Pirkko. 2008a. "Control vs. Subversion: Popular Theatre on the Move." In *Amfiteater. Journal of Performing Arts Theory*, Ljubljana, 115–131.

Koski, Pirkko. 2008b. "Justification as National Throughout Changing Times: The National Theatre of Finland." In *National Theatres in a Changing Europe*. Ed. S. E. Wilmer, 99–110.

Koski, Pirkko. 2010a. "Ideology vs. History: The Night after the Last One." In *Art History & Criticism 6: Performing History from 1945 to Present*. Vytautas Magnus University, Faculty of Arts: Kaunas, 148–153.

Koski, Pirkko. 2010b. "Puntila and Geography." *Nordic Theatre Studies*, 22/2010, 68–85.

Koski, Pirkko. 2013. *Näyttelijänä Suomessa*. WSOY: Helsinki.

Koski, Pirkko. 2016. "Tekijyys ja poliittiset suhdanteet: Vaclav Havelin näytelmät Pohjoismaissa." In *Näyttämö & Tutkimus 6*. TeaTS: Helsinki, 157–180.

Koski, Pirkko. 2019. *Suomen Kansallisteatteri ristipaineissa. Kai Savolan pääjohtajakausi 1974–1991*. SKS: Helsinki.

Koski, Pirkko. 2021. "National Trauma on a Foreign Stage." *Nordic Theatre Studies*, vol. 32(2), 26–39.

Koski, Pirkko and Palander, Misa (Eds). 2007. *Kansaa teatterissa. Helsingin Kaupunginteatterin historia*. Like: Helsinki.

Koskimies, Rafael. 1972. *Suomen Kansallisteatteri II*. Otava: Helsinki.

Kott, Jan. 1965. *Shakespeare tänään*. Translated by Salla Hirvinen. WSOY: Porvoo and Helsinki.

Kruger, Loren. 1992. *The National Stage: Theatre and Cultural Legitimation in England, France and America*. University of Chicago Press: Chicago.

Kruger, Loren. 2008. "The National Stage and the Naturalized House: (Trans)National Legitimation in Modern Europe." In *National Theatres in a Changing Europe*. Ed. S. E. Wilmer. Palgrave Macmillan: Houndmills and New York, 34–48.

KUPOLI. Kulttuuripolitiikan linjat. 1992. *Komiteanmietintö* (Committee report) 1992(36). Valtion painatuskeskus: Helsinki.

Kyrö, Pakka. 1984. "Teatterimme taiteellinen tase." In *Tietoa teatterista*. Suomen Teatterijärjestöjen Keskusliitto: Helsinki, 38–52.

Lahtinen, Outi. 2012. "Mitä aalto jättää jälkeensä." In *Taidekritiikin perusteet*. Ed. Martta Heikkilä. Gaudeamus: Helsinki, 84–117.

Landefort, Lisbeth. 2004. *Älä osoita sateenkaarta. Kohtauksia elämästäni*. Ed. Barbro Holmberg. Translated by Leena Vallisaari. Tammi: Helsinki.

Leerssen, Joep. 2000. "The Rhetoric of National Character: A Programmatic Survey." *Poetics Today*, 21(2), 267–289.

Leerssen, Joep. 2008. "Introduction. Philology and the European Construction of National Literature." In *Editing the National Memory: Textual Scholarship and Nation-Building in Nineteenth-Century Europe*. Eds. Dirk van Hulle and Joep Leerssen. Rodopi: Amsterdam and New York.

Lehtinen, Sani. (Ed.) 2006. *Muistijälkiä. TTT-Kellariteatteri 1965–2005*. Tampereen Työväen Teatteri Oy: Tampere.

Lehtonen, Mikko. 2013. "Miten tutkia liikkuvaa maailmaa." In *Liikkuva maailma. Liike, raja, tieto*. Ed. Mikko Lehtonen. Vastapaino: Tampere, 7–29.

Lehtonen, Mikko and Koivunen, Anu. 2010. "Kansalainen minä: Median ihannesubjektit ja suostumuksen tuottaminen. In *Valta Suomessa*. Ed. Petteri Pietikäinen. Gaudeamus and Helsinki University Press: Helsinki, 229–250.

Bibliography

Lehtonen, Mikko and Löytty, Olli. 2007. *Kolonialismin jäljet: Keskustat, periferiat ja Suomi*. Gaudeamus: Helsinki.

Linko, Maaria. 1990. *Teatteriesitykset ja julkisuus*. Jyväskylän yliopisto, Nykykulttuurin tutkimusyksikkö: Jyväskylä.

Lounela, Pekka and Tainio, Ilona. 1988. *Mauno Manninen ja hänen intiimi teatterinsa*. Tammi: Helsinki.

McConachie, Bruce. 2003. *American Theater in the Culture of the Cold War. Producing and Contesting. Containment, 1947–1962*. University of Iowa Press: Iowa City.

McConachie, Bruce. 2008. "Towards a History of National Theatres in Europe." In *National Theatres in a Changing Europe*. Ed. S. E. Wilmer. Palgrave Macmillan: Houndmills and New York, 49–60.

Mäkelä-Eskola, Raija. 2001. *Pang – siinä se on! Teatterikatsojan tunneresonanssi*. Tampereen yliopisto (väitöskirja): Tampere.

Mäkinen, Eija and Grahn, Annika. 2014. *Esko Roine*. Like: Helsinki.

Malkin, Jeannette R. 1999. *Memory-Theater and Postmodern Drama*. UMP: Ann Arbor.

Massey, Doreen. 2008. *Samanaikainen tila*. Eds. Mikko Lehtonen, Pekka Rantanen, and Jarno Valkonen. Translated by Janne Rovio. Vastapaino: Tampere.

Mayer, David. 1977. "Towards the Definition of Popular Theatre." In *Western Popular Theatre*. Eds. David Mayer and Kenneth Richards. Methuen: *London and New York*.

Mehto, Katri . 1999. "Ifigeneia ja Seitsemän veljestä maailmalla." In *Niin muuttuu mailma, Eskoni*. Ed. Pirkko Koski. Helsinki University Press: Helsinki, 230–252.

Meinander, Henrik. 2017. *Gustaf Mannerheim. Aristokraatti sarkatakissa*. Translated from a Swedish manuscript by Kari Koski. Otava: Helsinki.

Meinander, Henrik. 2019. *Samaan aikaan: Suomi ja maailma 1968*. Siltala: Helsinki.

Meri, Lauri. 2002. *Pentti Siimes. Näyttämöllä, kotonaan*. Otava: Helsinki.

Miettinen, Jukka O. 1987. *Jumalia, sankareita, demoneja. Johdanto aasialaiseen teatteriin*. Teatterikorkeakoulu: Helsinki.

Miklossý, Katalin. 2018. "Alueellisuuden merkitys: Kehityksen ongelmat ja voimavarat." In *Demokratian karikot. Itäinen Eurooppa suuntaa etsimässä*. Gaudeamus: Helsinki, 30–51.

Neuvostoliitto ja Suomi teatteriyhteistyössä. 1982. (Text in Finnish, English, and Russian.) ITI:n Neuvostoliiton ja Suomen Keskus: Helsinki.

Nevala, Maria-Liisa (Ed.) 2003. *Suomen Kansallisteatteri. Teatteritalo ennen ja nyt*. Otava and Suomen Kansallisteatteri: Helsinki.

Nevala, Maria-Liisa. 2006. "Willensauna 1976–2006." In *Suomen Kansallisteatteri. Willensauna 30 vuotta. The Finnish National Theatre. 30 Years in the Willensauna*. Eds. Juha Heiskanen and Maria-Liisa Nevala. Suomen Kansallisteatteri: Helsinki, 2–104.

Nevala, Maria-Liisa. 2018. *Jack Witikka. Suomalainen suurmies*. Minerva: Helsinki.

Niemi, Irmeli. 1983. *Pääosassa katsoja*. Tammi: Helsinki.

Niemi, Irmeli and Lotti, Leila. 1977. *Kiinteiden ammattiteattereiden katsojakunta keväällä 1977*. Suomen Teatterijärjestöjen Keskusliitto: Helsinki.

Niemi, Juhani. 1991. *Kirjallisuus instituutiona. Johdatus sosiologiseen kirjallisuudentutkimukseen*. SKS: Helsinki.

Niemi, Juhani. 2000. *Kirjallinen elämä. Kirjallisuuden yhteiskuntasuhteiden kartoitusta*. SKS: Helsinki.

Niemi, Kaius. 2015. "Sain kukkakimpun ja paljon muuta." *Teema*, 4/2015, 78–81.

Nieminen, Reetta. 1985. *Eeva-Kaarina Volanen: Tämä rooli*. Weilin+Göös: Espoo.

Paavolainen, Pentti. 1987. *Turkan pitkä juoksu*. Gaudeamus: Helsinki.

Paavolainen, Pentti. 1992. *Teatteri ja suuri muutto. Ohjelmistot sosiaalisen murroksen osana 1959–1971*. Kustannus Oy Teatteri: Helsinki.

Pennanen, Jotaarkka. 2010. *Elämää pienempi näytelmä*. Like: Helsinki.
Pietikäinen, Petteri. 2010. (Ed.) *Valta Suomessa*. Gaudeamus and Helsinki University Press: Helsinki.
Postlewait, Thomas. 2009. *The Cambridge Introduction to Theatre Historiography*. Cambridge University Press: Cambridge and New York.
Quinn, Michael L. 1990. "Celebrity and the Semiotics of Acting." *New Theatre Quarterly*, vol. VI(22), 154–161.
Rajala, Panu. 1995. *Titaanien teatteri. Tampereen Työväen Teatteri 1918–1964*. Tampereen Työväen Teatteri: Tampere.
Rajala, Panu. 2001. *Tasavallan toinen teatteri. Tampereen Työväen Teatteri 1964–2001*. Tampereen Työväen Teatteri: Tampere.
Rajala, Panu. 2004. *Tunteen tulet, taiteen tasot. Tampereen Teatteri 1904–2004*. Tampereen Teatteri: Tampere.
Rausmaa, Heikki. 2013. *"Kyllä kulttuurin nimissä voi harrastella aika paljon." Suomen ja Viron poliittiset suhteet keväästä 1988 diplomaattisuhteiden solmimiseen 1991*. Helsingin yliopisto: Helsinki.
Rebellato, Dan. 2009. *Theatre & Globalization*. Houndmills and New York.
Rinne, Tiina. 2003. *Tanssivan tähden alla*. Otava, Helsinki.
Rinne, Tiina and Steffa, Liisa (Eds). 2003. *Jalmari Rinne. Muistelija*. Otava: Helsinki.
Rokem, Freddie. 2000. *Performing History. Theatrical Representations of the Past in Contemporary Theatre*. University of Iowa Press: Iowa City.
Salmelainen, Eino. 1957. *Hurma ja surma. Muistelmia tavallaan*. Tammi: Helsinki.
Salmelainen, Eino. 1968. *Teatterin naisia. Eilisen ja nykypäivän havaintoja*. Tammi: Helsinki.
Sauter, Willmar. 2000. *The Theatrical Event. Dynamics of Performance and Perception*. University of Iowa Press: Iowa City.
Savolainen, Johanna. 1999. "Timo Sarpanevan ja Oiva Toikan lavastukset näytelmiin Anna Liisa ja Figaro ottaa eron." *In Niin muuttuu mailma, Eskoni*. Ed. Pirkko Koski. Helsinki University Press: Helsinki, 253–268.
Schulman, Sari. 2003. "Arkkitehtina ajassa." In *Suomen Kansallisteatteri. Teatteritalo ennen ja nyt*. Ed. Maria-Liisa Nevala. Suomen Kansallisteatteri and Otava: Helsinki, 120–168.
Seppälä, Mikko-Olavi. 2020. *Parempi ihminen, parempi maailma. Suomalaisen työväenteatterin päättymätön tarina*. Vastapaino: Tampere.
Seppälä, Mikko-Olavi and Tanskanen, Katri. 2010. *Suomen teatteri ja draama*. Like: Helsinki.
Sevänen, Erkki. 1998. *Taide instituutiona ja järjestelmänä. Modernin taide-elämän historiallissosiologiset mallit*. SKS: Helsinki.
Siitonen, Seppo-Ilmari. 2007. *Ohjaaja tarttuu yhteiskuntaa harteista* (MA dissertation), University of Helsinki, Kaisa Library.
Simonen, Elina. 2010. *Teatterin suorasuu. Marjukka Halttunen*. Otava: Helsinki.
Soikkanen, Timo and Vares, Vesa. 1998. "Sukupolvi selittäjänä Suomen historiassa." *Historiallinen aikakauskirja*, 1998(1), 37–53.
States, Bert O. 1995 [1983]. "The Actor's Presence: Three phenomenal modes." In *Acting (Re)considered. Theories and practices*. Ed. Phillip B. Zarrilli. Routledge: London and New York, 22–42.
Suomi, Juhani (Ed). 2012. *Salaisuuksien vartija. Lehtiä valtiosihteeri Matti Tuovisen päiväkirjasta 1972–1985*. Turun ylipisto: Turku.
Suutela, Hanna. 2005. "Joukkojen aika." In *Seitkytluvun moninaiset äänet*, Eds. Hanna Suutela and Misa Palander. Like: Helsinki, 194–214.

Bibliography

Taide- ja teatteripoliittinen ohjelma. 1975. *Suomen Teatterijärjestöjen Keskusliitto*, Helsinki.
Teatteritilastot. *Theatre Statistics*. 1988–1993. Suomen Teatterijärjestöjen Keskusliitto: Helsinki.
Tiusanen, Timo. 1969. *Teatterimme hahmottuu. Näyttämötaiteemme kehitystie kansanrunoudesta itsenäisyyden ajan alkuun*. Kirjayhtymä: Helsinki.
Tiusanen, Timo. 1977. *Dürrenmatt. A Study in Plays, Prose, Theory*. Princeton University Press: Princeton and Guildford.
Tompkins, Joanne. 2006. *Unsettling Space. Contestations in Contemporary Australian Theatre*. Palgrave Macmillan: Houndmills and New York.
Valkonen, Kaija (Ed). 2008. *Maija Karhi. Samppanjaluonne – minäkö?* Tammi: Helsinki.
Virtanen, Matti. 2001. *Fennomanian perilliset. Poliittiset traditiot ja sukupolvien dynamiikka*. SKS: Helsinki.
Wager, Leif. 2000. *Hävyttömän hieno elämä* (2nd ed.). WSOY: Helsinki.
Wiles, David. 2011. *Theatre and Citizenship. The History of a Practice*. Cambridge University Press: Cambridge and New York.
Williams, Raymond. 1973. *Drama from Ibsen to Brecht*. Penguin Books: Harmondsworth.
Wilmer, S. E. (Ed.). 2008. *National Theatres in a Changing Europe*. Palgrave Macmillan: Houndmills and New York.
Wilmer, S. E. and Koski, Pirkko. 2006. *The Dynamic World of Finnish Theatre*. Like: Helsinki.
Woods, Michelle. 2012. *Censoring Translation. Censorship, Theatre, and the Politics of Translation*. Continuum: London and New York.
Worthen, W. B. and Holland, Peter. 2003. *Theorizing Practice. Redefining Theatre History*. Palgrave Macmillan, Houndmills and New York.
Ylikangas, Heikki. 1987. *Käännekohdat Suomen historiassa: pohdiskeluja kehityslinjoista ja niiden muutoksista uudella ajalla*. WSOY: Porvoo.
Ylikangas, Heikki. 1988. "Mielikuvitus kirjailijan ja historiantutkijan työssä." In *Toisen tasavallan kirjallisuus*. Ed. Iris Tenhunen. WSOY: Helsinki, 89–98.
Ylikangas, Heikki. 2001. *Tulkintani talvisodasta*. WSOY: Helsinki.
YLIOPPILASTEATTERI. *Akateeminen näytelmäseura. Matrikkeli*. 1979. YTS: Helsinki.
Zetterberg, Seppo. 2007. *Viron historia*. SKS: Helsinki.

Index

Note: Locators in *italic* refer to figures and locators followed by "n" refer to endnotes.

Aalberg, Ida 56
Aaltonen, Risto 118, 123, 128, 129, 132, 136, 163, 174
Aamulehti newspaper 32, 81, 120, 123, 163, 193
Åbo Svenska Teater 161
About the Lives of Earthworms (play by Enquist) 173
acting methods of Stanislavski 42
Actors' Company 210–211
Adieu! (play by Holappa) 184–185, 201
Adolescent (play by Dostoevsky) 50
After Liverpool (play by Saunders) 210
Agreement of Friendship, Cooperation, and Assistance 3
Ahonen, Ritva 93, 94
Akonpelto, Päivi 200
Albee, Edward 133, 136
Allen, Woody 48
All's Well That Ends Well (play by Shakespeare) 112
Almila, Atso 81, 154, 191
Alter, Robert 71
Amadeus (play by Shaffer) 171–173, *172*, 193, 214
Amazons, The (play by Pinello) 211
American social drama 134
Anderson, Benedict 6, 7
Andersen, Hans Christian 173
Andersson, Claes 170
Anglo-American relationship dramas 132–133, 160; Betrayal 136; Crucible, The 136; Death of a Salesman, The 134, 135; Heartbreak House 133; Long Day's Journey into Night 134; Man And Superman 133–134, 133; More Stately Mansions 133; Mourning Becomes Electra 136; No-Man's Land 136; Who's Afraid of Virginia Woolf 136
Animal Farm (play by Orwell and Hall) 211
Anttonen, Pertti J. 7
apprentice group 52n6
Arajuuri, Aila 180
Arkielämää (Jotuni) 76–77
Art and Theatre Politic Programme see Taide-ja teatteripoliittinen ohjelma
Artaud, Antonin 42, 143
artistic direction, creators of 19–22, 38; international stage directors as 46–51; music conductors as 46; set designers as 45–46; stage directors of Finland as 44–45; theatrical actors as 38–41
artistic merit of Finnish National Theatre 65–68
Arts as an Institution and a System, The see *Taide instituutiona ja järjestelmänä* (Sevänen)
Arvidson, Adolf Ivar 15n21
Ascher, Tamás 50, 132, 138, 141, 207
Asian dramatic visits 220
As You Like It (play by Shakespeare) 112
Ateneum (National Art Gallery) 54
Audience (play by Havel) 15n13, 151, 152
Ausley, Charles 109n28
Autiovuori, Pekka 100, 148, 151, 151, *152*, 171, 189, 190
Autumn and Winter (play by Norén) 165
Auvinen, Vili 44, 77, 137, 178

Bailes, Sinclair 139
Baltic Institute of Sweden 208
Bankruptcy (play by Ostrovsky) 48, 124
Baran, Michael 200, 203n10

232 Index

Barba, Eugenio 50
Barbarians (play by Gorki) 137, 139
Bass Viola (play by Süskind) 164
Bat Cave 181, 186n8
Bauer, Wolfgang 212
Beaumarchais, Pierre-Augustin Caron de 140
Beckett, Samuel 204
Bedrooms *see Makuuhuoneet* (play by Yliruusi)
Beifang theatre company 213
Benedictine Order 148
Bent (play by Sherman) 170–171
Bergman, Ingmar 115, 116
Berliner Ensemble 42, 204
Betrayal (play by Pinter) 136
"big Finnish dramas" 69
Blithe Spirit (play by Coward) 189–190
Blomstedt, Jan 157
Blood Wedding (play by Lorca) 139, 188
Bogdanov, Michael 212
Bond, Edward 174
Boris Godunov (play by Puškin) 207
Bourdieu, Pierre 91, 219
Bratton, Jacky 16n31
Breaking the Silence (play by Poliakoff) 174
Brecht, Bertolt 42, 50, 72, 75n24, 83–84, 87, 179, 148
British drama 160, 198, 204, 211
British National Theatre 211
British theatrical culture 210–212
Brook, Peter 42, 50, 92, 114, 118, 129
Brotherus, Greta 164
Brotherus, Heikki 104
Buero Vallejo, Antonio 169
Bulgakov, Mikhail 161
Bull of the Commercial Council, The *see Kauppaneuvoksen härkä* (Pakkala)

Cajander, Paavo 112, 117
Caligula (play by Camus) 114–115, 181–184, *183*
Cambridge Introduction to Theatre Historiography, The (Postlewait) 9
Camus, Albert 114, 181
Canth, Minna 71, 78, 79
Carlson, Marvin 5, 8, 11, 53, 59, 222
carnivalism 222
Cartwright, Jim 198
Castrén, Elli 118
Cave, Richard Allen 173
Cayman (play by Buero Vallejo) 169
celebrity stars from National Theatre: Eeva-Kaarina Volanen 167–168; Ella Eronen 166; Kyllikki Forssell 166–167, *167*, 168
Central European theatre 67
Cerceau (play by Šlavkin) 206
Charley's Aunt (play by Thomas) 187–188
Charta 77, 153
Cheek by Jowl theatre company 48, 116, 211
Chekhov, Anton 47, 127, 145, 146, 147; *Cherry Orchard, The* 129, 130, *131*, 132, 143n7; *Seagull, The* 132; *Three Sisters, The* 130, 131–132; *Uncle Vanya* 129, 131, 132
Chekhov, Eino Kalima 168
Chekhov on the Yalta (play by Habeck-Adameck) 147
Cherry Orchard, The (play by Chekhov) 47, 51, 129, 130, *131*, 132, 143n7, 214
Chwedczuk, Marian 121
Cid (play by Corncille) 48, 121
City Theatre of Oulu 25
City Theatre of Vaasa 104
civil rights agreement of Helsinki CSCE summit 153
classic farce dramas: Blithe Spirit 189–190; Charley's Aunt 187–188; He Will Go on a Spree 190; Monsieur Is Hunting! 189; Wicked Duchess, The 188–189, 191
Clift, Montgomery 109n28
Close of Play (play by Gray) 163
Comedians *see Komeljanttarit* (play by Ostrovsky and Lyubinov)
Comedy of Errors, The (play by Shakespeare) 50, 112
Conquergood, Dwight 10
contextual factors around theatrical event 10
Continental European dramas: Blood Wedding 139; Figaro Gets a Divorce 140; Figaro's Wedding 140; My Brother Federico 139–140; Tales From The Vienna Wood 141; Vast Domain, The 141–142
Continuation War 15n5
Coriolanus (play by Shakespeare) 113, 212
Corneille, Pierre 48, 121
cosmopolitan conviviality 7
Coward, Noël 189, 190
Crime and Punishment (play by Dostoevsky) 206
Crucible, The (play by Miller) 136
Cuban missile crisis 4
cultural heritage of Continental Europe 118; French classics 118; Molière's

plays in Finnish National Theatre 118–120; old German-language classics 121–122; verse drama 121

Dance of Death, The (play by Strindberg) 128
Dangerous Liaisons (play by Hampton) 168
Death of a Salesman, The (play by Miller) 134, 135
de Certeau, Michel 6
De Filippo, Eduardo 162
Demari see Suomen Sosialidemokraatti newspaper
Denisov, Edison 124
de Vega, Lope 204
Diary of a Madman, The (Gogol and Terttula) 122, 124–125, 205
diversity of Finnish National Theatre 65–68
Dodin, Lev 48, 124
Doll's House (play by Ibsen) 213
domestic Finnish drama, debates about development of 68–70
domestic repertoire of Finnish National Theatre: challenges of updating traditional classics 76–83; Finland of poets 93–94; Finnish people on theatrical stage 83–93
Don Carlos (play by Schiller) 121–122
Donna (play by Fo and Rame) 166, *167*
Donnellan, Declan 48, *49*, 113, 116, 141, 212
Dostoyevsky, Fyodor 47, 50, 123, 124, 125
Drake, Patrick 44, 121
Drama from Ibsen to Brecht (Williams) 127
dramatic classics 67, 219; canonical 79; from Continental European countries 118; domestic and international 71; Finnish 68, 71, 79–80; Russian 67; *see also* modern dramatic classics
Dramaten see Royal Dramatic Theatre, Sweden's
Dramatic Theatre of Pärnu 208, 209
Dream of My Generation see *Sukupolveni unta* (Hämäläinen)
Drums in the Night (play by Brecht) 180
Duck Hunting (play by Vampilov) 146
Dürrenmatt, Friedrich 113, 114, 149, 180
Düsseldorfer Schauspielhaus 212

Eastern European drama 145, 220; classics in Finnish theatres 111; Estonian history 154–157; from metaphor to documentary-style 147–154; rarities from Soviet Union 146–147
Eastern Mitteleuropa 147

Eeva Maria Kustaava (play by Rintala) 93
Efros, Anatoli 47, 130, 132
Ekholm, Rauno 117
Eklund, Hilkka 32, 122, 124, 129, 162, 188
Elstelä, Esko 43, 113, 118, 121, 133, 148, 188
Empty Space (Brook) 118, 129
Enough Stupidity for Every Wise Man (play by Ostrovsky) 46, 122–123
Enquist, Per Olof 173
Entertainer, The (play by Osborne) 210
environmental threat, dramas about 184; *Adieu!* 184–185; *Lintu vai kala* 200–201 *201*
Erdman, Nikolai 50, 137, 138, 146, 214
Erik XIV (play by Strindberg) 128
Eronen, Ella 139, 166, 188, 189
Esslin, Martin 136, 153, 158n17
Estonian avantgarde 157
Estonian historical drama at Finnish National Theatre 145, 154; *Lähtö* 155–156; *Tohtori Karellin vaikea yö* 156–157
Etelä-Suomen Sanomat newspaper 32
Eteläpää, Heikki 33, 51, 129, 151, 165, 168, 169, 193, 194, 198, 210, 211
Euripides 204
European surrealism 143
Exit (play by Tuomarila) 196–197

Facing Death (play by Strindberg) 214
Father, The (play by Strindberg) 128, 129
Faust (play by Goethe) 162
Feather Cape (Zeami) 213
Fehér, Miklós 119
Feng Lei Puppet theatre 213
Feudeau, Georges 189
Figaro Gets a Divorce (play by von Horváth) 140
Figaro's Wedding (play by Beaumarchais) 140
Finland: Austrian refugees in 109n19; democratic society and market economy 2–3; Finnish national agenda 8; Iron Curtain impact in 1; language of elites in 1–2; national culture of 111; national policy in 7; national theatres in 5; past theatrical event in 11–13; of poets 93–94; professional repertoire theatres in 3; relationship with Estonia 197; signed in YYA treaty 15n4; social turbulence in 3–4; Soviet Union's 1939 attack on 15n5; transnationalism of 220; truce peace treaty with Soviet Union 75n24

234   Index

Finnish-Estonian connection 51, 208–210
Finnish Civil War (1918) 102, 104, 222
Finnish dramatic canon 71, 73
Finnish Dramatists' Union 69
Finnish Maaseututeatteri Theatre 143n7
Finnish National Theatre 1, 4–5, 7, 12, 21, 42, 145, 199–200; Actors' Association 60; actors attachment to 40; archives of 12, 16n50; artistic personnel in 38–39; "big Finnish dramas" in 69; changes in structural foundations 217; changing times and policy 218–219; characterisation of building 53–54; classic drama productions 111; collective memory 221–223; conversations about national identity 108; exalted status of 13; examining Finnish history 108; Finnish-Estonian connection 208–210; for Finnish folk theatre 76; and Finnish press 31–33; Foundation 22, 23; for free movement of art 15n13; functioning family 61; and general public 33–36; ideological priorities 84; international connections of 27–28, 219–221; justification for cross-cultural partnerships 47; lack of permanent directors 44–45; Main Stage building *see* Main Stage building; from modern architecture to spatial exploration 56–60; national character 221–223; national drama 221–223; and national operations 25–27; national representativeness 218; national stature and fulfilling national mission 5–9; new artistic direction(s) 19–22; Nordic connections 221; Omapohja studio space *see* Omapohja studio space; permanent costume designer in 46; poetry evenings at 93; policy and position 71; policy on visiting theatre companies 205; popularity of theatrical actors 40–41; preferred "apolitical" theatre 150; private, national, and societal pressures 22–25; private ownership of 22–23; production photographs in 12; reformation process of 19; repertoire 68, 70, 160; reputation 51; researching theatre history 9–11; return to absurdist roots 142–143; during rupture time 13–14; Small Stage building *see* Small Stage building; standards 188; succeeded in ideological movements 89; in tradition and turbulent times 1–5; travels 214–215; unequal distribution of roles in 40; Vietnam War reflections in dramas of 177; visiting foreign directors role in 47–51; visiting theatre companies from East and West 204; Willensauna stage *see* Willensauna stage; *see also* literary works as national interpretations

Finnish people on theatrical stage 83; Bertolt Brecht 83–84, 87; Edvin Laine 86–87, 89–91; Eino Salmelainen 84; Ernst Toller 91; Eugen Terttula 89; Heikki Ylikangas 89; Hella Wuolijoki 83–84, 86–87, 89; Ilmari Turja 91; Joonas Kokkonen 90; Jouko Turkka 91–93; Terttu Savola 86
Finnish "Poor Theatre" 118
Finnish premiere 219
Finnish press 31–33, 150
Finnish Radioteatteri 202
Finnish Reciter's League 93
Finnish theatre: critics 30–33, 211; repertoire theatres 26, 67; stage directing 42; system 8; theatrical culture 33; touring theatre 118
Finnish Theatre *see* Finnish National Theatre
Finnish Theatre School (and Theatre Academy) 24, 26, 39, 42, 53, 62n15, 121, 199–200, 201
Finnish Winter War 105
Fischer-Lichte, Erika 11, 92
Fish or Fowl *seeLintu vai kala* (play by Ruohonen)
Fiske, John 96
Fo, Dario 166–167, 168–169
folk drama 72, 74; Brecht's 'old folk drama' 72–73; national 181; realistic style of 84; Viennese 190
folk theatre: from classic farce to 187–190; farcical 67; Finnish 43, 72–73, 76, 92, 116, 219, 222–223; Neapolitan 162; radical 91
Fontaine, Lynn 109n28
Forever Yours (play by Shepard) 164
Forssell, Kyllikki 41, 134, 165–167, *167*, 168, 189, 214
'forty letter' 157
Foundation, The (play by Buero Vallejo) 169
François, Claude 51, 142
Freshwater, Helen 30
Friedebert Tuglas's Life (play adaption by Normet) 209

Index 235

From Stage Artist to Theatre Worker see Näyttämötaiteilijasta teatterityöntekijäksi (Kallinen)
Fugard, Athol 170, 198

Galin, Aleksander 146, 214
Garden Party, The (play by Havel) 152, 158n17
Gardner, Herb 164–165
General Radio *see* Yleisradio
generational rebellion dramas on Finnish stage 181–184
generation of Masters, A' by Raymond Williams 127; examining Chekhov's plays 127, 129–132; examining Ibsen's plays 127–129; examining Strindberg's plays 127–129
Georgian Rustaveli Theatre 207
German-language classics 121–122
ghosting 181
Ghosts (play by Ibsen) 128, 129
Girandoux, Jean 188
Giurchescu, Lucian 189
Gluhovic, Milija 156
Goethe, Johann Wolfgang von 162
Gogol, Nikolai 122, 124–125, 205
Going *see Lähtö* (play by Saluri)
Golden Calf, The *seeKultainen vasikka* (play by Jotuni)
Gonda, János 119
Gorbachev, Mikhail 208
Gorki, Maxim 137, 139
Gorki Theatre 205–207
Government Inspector, The (play by Gogol) 122, 205
Goya, Francisco 139
Gray, Simon 163
Great Magic, The (play by De Filippo) 162
Green, Paul 177–179
Grips Theatre of West Berlin 212
Grönholm, Jouko 157
Grosby, Steven 5
Grotowski, Jerzy 42, 50
Gründgens, Gustav 161
Gubenko, Nikolai 207

Haapala, Pentti 8
Haavikko, Paavo 93
Habeck-Adameck, Anne 147
Hallberg, Pekka 2
Hällström af, Arto 26, 27, 43, 45, 83, 120, 121, 136, 142, 143
Halttunen, Marjukka 85, 134, 139, 194

Hämäläinen, Helvi 94
Hamlet (play by Shakespeare) 113, 211
Hampton, Christopher 168
Hanski series 52n11
Hanuma (play by Tsagarett) 205
Hanuszkiewicz, Adam 48, 121
Hard Night for Doctor Karell, A *see-Tohtori Karellin vaikea yö* (play by Kross)
Hare, David 105
Harju, Hannu 33, 68, 138, 142, 211
Härkönen, Anna-Leena *201*
Hartel, Ansa 163
Hattara, Pia 129, 141, 163, 189
Haunted Stage, The (Carlson) 11
Havel, Václav 15n13, 151–154, 158n22
Häyrinen, Hannes 41, 45, 52n11, 121, 148, 149, 163
Häyrynen, Simo 8, 70
Heartbreak House (play by Shaw) 133
Heath Cobblers see Nummisuutarit (play by Kivi)
Heiberg, Johanne Luise 173
Heikinheimo, Hannu 163
Heikinheimo, Seppo 175
Heikka, Mikko 137
Heiskanen, Pekka 45, 46, 115, 179, 182
Helasvuo, Esa 114
Helovirta, Kauko 77, 85, 141, 147, 164, 189
Helsingin Sanomat newspaper 31, 32, 69, 81, 103, 114, 115, 175, 189–193, 196, 209, 211
Helsinki City Theatre 21, 25, 34–36, 39, 69, 77, 124; playing *Heath Cobblers* in 80; stage directors of 43
Helsinki television channels 41
Helsinki University 42, 93
Hemming, Eva 189
Hen-Pecked Husband's Wife, The *see Tohvelisankarin rouva* (play by Jotuni)
Henry the Sixth (play by Shakespeare) 168
He Will Go on a Spree (play by Nestroy) 190
Hiilloskorpi, Jarno 88, 123, 174, *175, 191*, 151
historical character's depiction 96–97; *Lapualaisooppera* 101; *Mannerheim Puolassa* drama about Mannerheim 98–99; *Ministeri murhataan* drama about Ritavuori's assassination 97–98; *Yks perkele, yks enkeli* drama about Kivi 100, 101; *Yössä Gehennan* drama about Kivi 100; *see also* war history and contemporary politics
History of Estonia, The *see Viron historia*

236 Index

Hodgdon, Barbara 12
Holappa, Pentti 184, 185, 201
Holdsworth, Nadine 5, 7–8, 222
Holmberg, Kalle 20, 25, 39, 42, 45, 52n6, 80, 193
Horváth, Ödön von 50, 140
Hōshō-ry Theatre 213
Hotinen, Juha-Pekka 68, 92, 123, 168
Hour of Ghosts on Jansen Street, An (play by Unt) 208
House on the Embankment, The (play by Trifonov) 207
How Fish Kiss see *Miten kalat suutelevat* (play by Katz)
Huotari, Olga 50
Hypochondriac, The (play by Molière) 118, 120–121

Ibsen, Henrik 78, 127, 128, 213; *Ghosts* 128, 129; *John Gabriel Borkman* 143n1; *Lady from the Sea, The* 128
idiosyncratic Finnish style 223
Idiot, The (play by Dostoyevsky) 47, 123–124
Idler, The (play by Raudsepp) 210
Ikonen, Ansa *85*, 173
Ikonen, Olli 41, 171
Imagined Communities (Anderson) 6
imagined community, national as 6–7
I'm Not Rappaport (play by Gardner) 164–165, 215
Importance of Being Earnest, The (play by Wilde) 143
In Celebration (play by Storey) 163
Innes, Christopher 173
In The Nights of Gehenna see *Yössä Gehennan* (play by Tuomarila)
Iona (play by Sorescu) 150
Iron Curtain 1, 47; location of Finland and 27, 217; social commentary dramas from behind 137–139
Island (play by Fugard) 170–171
Iso-Heikkilän isäntä ja hänen renkinsä Kalle (play by Brecht and Wuolijoki) 84
Ista, Tea 91, 128–130, 136, 141, 163, 198

Jääkäri Ståhl (play by Turja) 103–105
Jacobi, Derek 211
Jade Lotus Flower 213
Jaeger Ståhl see *Jääkäri Ståhl* (play by Turja)
Jäntti, Laura 181
Järnefelt, Arvid 77
Jartti, Tero *88*, 91

Järvinen, Martti 100, *101*, 138, 169
Järvinen, Yrjö *88*, 91, 134
Jasný, Vojtěch 47, 123
Jaunty British entertainment 211
John Gabriel Borkman (play by Ibsen) 143n1
Johnny Johnson (play by Green and Weill) 177–181, *178*, 191
Jokela, Eila 104
Jokinen, Ahti *191*
Jotuni, Maria 71, 76, 78, 79
journeyman group 52n6
Julius Caesar (play by Shakespeare) 112
Junnikkala, Kari 161
Jurkka, Jussi 41, 52n11, *172*, 173
Justiina (play by Wuolijoki) 86–87
Juurakon Hulda (play by Wuolijoki) 86, 87, *88*, 89
Jylhä, Yrjö 93

Käännekohdat Suomen historiassa (Ylikangas) 106–107
Kajanto, Anneli 188
Kajava, Jukka 31, 32, 83, 100, 114, 115, 69, 81, 139, 157, 164–166, 170, 173, 189, 192–194, 198, 207, 209
Kalevala 182
Kalima, Eino 84, 91, 127, 129, 204
Kallas, Aino 208
Kallinen, Timo 39
Kallio, Erkki 173, 175
Kallio, Ismo 41, 134, 169, 186
Kangasluoma, Tuukka 140
Kangur, Guido 210
Kankkunen, Eero 174
Kanneviskaali Samuel Kröll (play by Järnefelt) 77
Kansan Näyttämö theatre 143n12
Kansan Uutiset newspaper 26, 32, 68, 115, 140, 193
Kanto, Anneli 68, 162, 193
Kantor, Tadeusz 50
Karhi, Maija *85*, 151, 163, *191*, 194
Kaskilahti, Risto 200
Katona József Theatre 207
Katz, Daniel 102
Kauppaneuvoksen härkä (play by Pakkala) 82–83
Kellariteatteri of TTT 58
Kermode, Frank 71
Keskinen, Jouko 169, 190, *191*
Kessner, Lyle 198, 214
Kidnapping Francesca (play by Fo) 168
Kiirastuli (Jylhä) 93

Index 237

King John (play by Shakespeare) 67, 112, 113–114, 180
King Lear (play by Shakespeare) 36, 112, 113, 114, 207
Kinnunen, Santeri 200
Kipphardt, Heinar 170
Kirkkolehti (Church) magazine 137
Kivi, Aleksis 71, 80, 99, 170, 214
Kivimaa, Arvi 2, 3, 4, 19, 20, 25, 84, 127, 204
Klemelä, Leena 12
Knipper, Olga 147
Koho, Timo 55, 57, 59
Kohout, Pavel 151
Kohti maailman sydäntä (play by Peltonen) 108
Koidula, Lydia 208
Koivisto, Mauno 158n24, 186
Koivunen, Anu 6
Kokkonen, Joonas 90
Köllö, Miklós 119
Kolmekymmentä hopearahaa (play by Ylikangas) 73, 89–90, 106, 222
Kolonialismin jäljet: keskustat, periferiat ja Suomi (Lehtonen and Löytty) 111
Komeljanttarit (play by Ostrovsky and Lyubinov) 50
Komi, Soila 52n11, 130
KOM Theatre 39, 62n17, 161
Korhonen, Kaisa 45, 132
Korsberg, Hanna 56
Körttiläiset tuomiolla (Ylikangas) 89
Koski, Pirkko 137
Kott, Jan 114, 115
Kotšergin, E. S. 122
Krejča, Otomar 50–51, 141
Kroetz, Franz Xaver 212
Kross, Jaan 50, 156–157
Kroutžil, Antonín 153
Kruger, Loren 6, 53, 220
Kullervo (play by Kivi) 99
Kulovaara, Leena 44
Kultainen vasikka 78–79
Kurosawa, Akira 115
Kuusisto, Ilkka 77
Kyrö, Pekka 33, 44, 68

Lady from the Sea, The (play by Ibsen) 128
Lahti, Katariina 100, 197
Lahtinen, Outi 30, 32
Lähtö (play by Saluri) 50, 155–156, 214, 215, 222
Laine, Edvin 42, 79, 86–87, 89–91, 102, 105, 163, 193

Laine, Seppo 197, 52n11
Laitala, Juhani 156
Landefort, Lisbeth 44, 102, 140, 151, 163, 192
Landström, Björn 46, 85
Långbacka, Ralf 20, 25, 39, 42, 52n6, 130, 15n12
Lappish War 15n5
Lapualaisooppera (play by Salo) 101
Lapua Opera, The *seeLapualaisooppera* (play by Salo)
Larivaara, Merja *88*, 91
Larsson, Marjukka 46
Last Temptations, The *see Viimeiset kiusaukset* (opera by Kokkonen)
Lauri, Hannu 114, 181, *183*
Laurila, Aarne 32, 77
Laville, Pierre 161
Lead Time (play by von Trotta and Limbach) 171
Lebedev, E. A. 206
Leerssen, Joep 96–97
left-leaning youth movement 4
left-wing ideology 39
Legend of a Dead Soldier (song) 180
legitimacy 6
Lehtinen, Petri 200
Lehtolapsi (play by Leino) 77–78
Lehtonen, Mikko 6, 10, 111
Lehtonen, Rauli 33
Lehtonen, Soila 174, 189
Leino, Kasimir 77
Leningradin yö (play by Raittila) 202
Lepakkoluola *see* Bat Cave
Leventin, Valeri 130
Lies *see Valheita* (play by Turkka)
Life of Alexander März, The (play by Kipphardt) 170
"light entertainment" productions 34
Liitto magazine 107
Lilla Teatern 132
Limbach, Hannelene 171
Lindeman, Lasse 43, 170, 171
Lindholm, Hannu 83
Linko, Maaria 11, 32
Linna, Väinö 102
Lintu vai kala (play by Ruohonen) 200–201 *201*
Liski, Paavo 25
literary works as national interpretations: cultural heritage of Continental Europe 118–122; old Russian classics 122–125; production of Shakespeare's classic drama 111–118

238 Index

Litja, Antti 148, 149, *152*, 164, 180–181, 188
Long Day's Journey into Night (play by O'Neill) 134
Look Back in Anger (play by Osborne) 211
Lorca, Federico García 139–140
Lovechild *see Lehtolapsi* (play by Leino)
Löytty, Olli 111
Lubomirsk, Marie 99
Lunt, Alfred 109n28
Lynch, Kevin 53, 60
Lyubimov, Yuri 48, 49–50, 51, 124, 205, 206, 207, 214

Maalismaa, Markku 50, *117*, 124, 198, 199
Macbeth (play by Shakespeare) 48, 112, 113, 116–117, 211, 213
Machine Wreckers, The (play by Toller) 91
Magic Afternoon (play by Bauer) 212
Main Stage building 27, 34–35, *35*, 54–55, 61, 194; actors on *73*; *Arkielämää* staged at 76; drama for national populations 76; *Erik XIV* staged at 128; *Great Magic, The* staged at 162; *Heath Cobblers* staged at 80–81; *Johnny Johnson* staged at 178; *Juurakon Hulda* staged at 86, 87, *88*, 89; *Mefisto* staged at 161–162; *More Stately Mansions* staged at 133; new Finnish drama at 70; old folk drama' at 73; programming conflicts in 70; *Red River, The* staged at 161; *Tohvelisankarin rouva* staged at 79–80, *80*; *see also* Omapohja studio space; Small Stage building; Willensauna stage
Mäkelä, Juha 114, 161, 164, 170
Mäkelä, Risto 93, 115, 116, 121–122, *183*
Makuuhuoneet (play by Yliruusi) 209
Målarsalen stage 58
Malmberg, Niiles Kustaa 89
Man And Superman (play by Shaw) 133–134, *133*
Mandat (play by Erdman) 137
Mannerheim, Carl Gustav 98–99, 103, 104, 107
Mannerheim in Poland *seeMannerheim Puolassa* (play by Tuuri)
Mannerheim Puolassa (play by Tuuri) 98–99
Manni, Tarmo 41, 124, 125, 214
Mann, Klaus 161
Marat/Sade (play by Weiss) 125
Maróti, Lajos 147, 148
Marton, László 47, 119
Marxist-Leninist student movement 4
Massey, Doreen 10

Master and Margarita, The (Bulgakov) 161
Master Class (play by Pownall) 174–175, 214, 215
Master Harold"...and the Boys (play by Fugard) 198
masters group 52n6
Mattila, Marketta 83
Maunula, Paavo 90
Max und Milli (play by Ludwig) 212
McConachie, Bruce 218
Measure for Measure (play by Shakespeare) 67, 112
Mefisto (play by Klaus Mann and Mnouchkine) 161–162
Meinander, Henrik 99
melodrama 124, 168
Memoir (play by Murrell) 167
Memoirs of a Theatrical Man, The (Lyubimov) 48–49
memory machine 222
Mesikämmen and Mustarouva (play by Lahti) 93
metaphorical dramas 147; *Audience* 151, 152; contemporary Hungarian plays 148, 149–150; *Garden Party, The* 152; *Night After The Last One, The* 147–148; *Protest* 152–153; *Red Line, The* 151; *Source, The* 150; *Theatre of the Absurd, The* 153–154; *Unveiling* 151, 152; *Vastaanotto* 151, *152*
Meyerhold, Vsevolod 42, 50, 137
middle-aged programming at Theatre 36
Midsummer Night's Dream (play by Shakespeare) 112, 114
Mikiver, Mikk 50, 156
Miklossý, Katalin 223n9
Miller, Arthur 133, 134, 136
Ministeri murhataan (play by Pennanen) 97–98
Minister is Murdered, A *seeMinisteri murhataan* (play by Pennanen)
Miss Julie (play by Strindberg) 128, 129, 209, 214
Miten kalat suutelevat (play by Katz) 102–103
Mnouchkine, Ariane 92, 161
modern dramatic classics 127; Anglo-American relationship drama 132–136; from Continental Europe 139–142; 'generation of Masters, A' 127–132; Nordic modern classics 129; social commentary dramas 137–139
Molière's plays in Finnish National Theatre 118; *Hypochondriac, The* 118, 120–121; *School for Wives, The* 118–120, *119*

Index

Molotov-Ribbentrop pact 107
monologues 166, 169
Monsieur Is Hunting! (play by Feudeau) 189
More Stately Mansions (play by O'Neill) 133
Moring, Kirsikka 92, 141, 142, 162, 196, 213 *see also* Siikala, Kirsikka
Moscow Art Theatre 179
Mourning see *Suruaika* (play by Baran)
Mourning Becomes Elektra (play by O'Neill) 87, 136
Mr Iso-Heikkilä and his Man Kalle see *Iso-Heikkilän isäntä ja hänen renkinsä Kalle* (play by Brecht and Wuolijoki)
Mrozek, Sławomir 157, 204
Mr Puntila and his Man Matti (play by Brecht and Wuolijoki) 46, 72, 83–84, 85
Murrell, John 167
Mustonen, Olli 175
My Brother Federico (play by Bailes) 139
Myllymäki, Anita 136

Naapurilähiö 52n11
Naismetsä (play by Haavikko) 93
Nam nam (play by Virtanen) 200
national culture of Finland 111
national dramatic canon 72
national Finnish history in theatrical stages 96; historical characters 96–101; war history and contemporary politics 102–108
national house 54
national institution 6, 13, 22, 54, 61, 111
National Opera 45, 60, 189
national operations of Finnish National Theatre 25–27
National Stage, The (Kruger) 6
National Theatre see Finnish National Theatre
national theatres 5–6, 8, 19; in Finland 5; importance of buildings 53–54; as institution 9; "national" theatre programme 65
National Theatres in a Changing Europe (Wilmer) 8
native Finnish drama, lack of 68–69
Naumanen, Eeva-Liisa 192
Näyttämötaiteilijasta teatterityöntekijäksi (Kallinen) 39
Negendanck, Fred 140
Neil Simon Theater 109n28
Neither Fish Nor Flesh (play by Kroetz) 212
Nekrosius, Eimuntas 131
Nemteanu, Dan 113, 180
Nestroy, Johann 190

New American Drama, advocate of *see* Kivimaa, Arvi
'new folk theatre' 74
Niemi, Irmeli 30, 76
Niemi, Juhani 9
Niemi, Kaius 215
Nieminen, Markku 91
Night After The Last One, The (play by Maróti) 147–148
Niiniluoto, Marja 209
Niit, Ellen 157
Niskavuoren nuori emäntä (play by Wuolijoki) 86
No-Man's Land (play by Pinter) 136
Nordic premiere 219
Norén, Lars 165
Notes on the Folk Play (Brecht) 72
Nousiainen, Heikki 41, 83, 104, 113, 132, 137, 161, 168–169, 200
Nummisuutarit (play by Kivi) 80–82, 99, 214
Nuotio, Kurt 44, 114, 132, 174, 198
Nurmimaa, Seppo 192
Nyytäjä, Outi 39, 44–45, 55, 67–68, 90, 101

Offenbach, Jacques 190
Oktober (Swedish musical theatre) 164
'old folk drama' 72–73
Old Vic Company 211
Omapohja studio space 27, 34, 35, 53, 57, 60, 61, 127, 169, 200; artistic programming of 59–60; *Leningradin yö* staged at 202; opening of 196–198; playing *Suruaika* staged at 200; *see also* Main Stage building; Small Stage building; Willensauna stage
One Devil, One Angel see *Yks perkele, yks enkeli* (play by Salo)
O'Neill, Eugene 87, 133, 134
On Golden Pond (play by Thompson) 147, 163
On the Log River *see Tukkijoella* (play by Pakkala)
On the Yalta (play by Habeck-Adameck) 214
Öötöö (night work) 209
operetta(s) 187, 190–192; debate about Kajava's *Parisian Life* review 192–194; *Parisian Life* 190–192, *191*
Ordinary Life see *Arkielämää* (Jotuni)
Örkeny, István 148
Ormerod, Nick 116, 212
Orphans, The (play by Kessner) 198, 199, 214, 215
Orsmaa, Taisto-Bertil 179

Index

Orwell, George 211
Osborne, John 210, 211
Ostrobothnian pietism 89
Ostrovsky, Aleksandr 46, 48, 50, 122, 124, 125

Pääkkönen, Seppo 81, *82*, 100, *101*, 186
Paavolainen, Pentti 35, 36, 67, 73, 194
pacifism, dramas about 177; *Drums in the Night* 180; *Johnny Johnson* 177–180, 181, *178*; *King John* 180
Pacius, Karin *88*, 164, 170, *191*
Packalén, Markus 43, 79, 81, 83
Pakkala, Teuvo 82, 83, 191
Palace of Eternal Youth, The (Chinese classic play) 214
Palo, Jukka-Pekka 188
Panula, Terhi 132
Papin perhe (play by Canth) 78
Parisian Life (play by Offenbach) 173, 190–193, *191*
Parliament's Daughter, The (play by Wuolijoki) 86
Parraksen pakinat 32
Parras (pseudonym) see Veistäjä, Olavi
Parviainen, Jussi 197, 209
Pasanen, Pertti 52n11
Pasanen, Veijo 115, 116, 150
Paukkunen, Kari 136
Peltonen, Aulis 81
Peltonen, Juhani 108
Pelttari, Raija 194
Penciulescu, Radu 47, 180
Pennanen, Eila 97, 181, 182
Pennanen, Jotaarkka 36, 44, 114, 115–116
Pennington, Michael 212
Performance Studies Reader, The (Conquergood) 10
Perttu, Tapani 41, 107, 199
Pete Q 26, 181–182
Philoctetes (play by Sophocles) 111
physical storytelling 147
pietism 90
Pinello, Arthur 210–211
Pinter, Harold 136
Pinzka, Wolfgang 84
Pirskanen, Juhani 198
Pirttimaa, Paavo 174
Places of Performance (Carlson) 11
Play It Again, Sam (play by Allen) 48
Poems from Kanteletar 94
Poliakoff, Stephen 174
political prejudices of artists 38

Popovits, Sara 198
popular national theatre 6
Poquelin, Jean-Baptiste see Molière
Portrait (play by Mrozek) 157, 215
Postlewait, Thomas 9
'pounded token patriotism' 143
Pownall, David 174, 214, 215
press debates on National Theatre 187; from classic farce to folk theatre 187–190; criticism and crisis at public attention 192–195; operetta causes scandal 190–192; see also Finnish National Theatre
primadonna act 168
production photographs 12
productive reception 12, 32
programming of Finnish National Theatre 65, 177; chasing diversity and artistic merit 65–68; crossing border between high and low art 70–74; debates about development of domestic Finnish drama 68–70; 'smörgåsbord' approach 67, 68
Protest (play by Havel) 152–153
Puntilan isäntä ja hänen renkinsä Matti see *Mr Puntila and his Man Matti* (play by Brecht and Wuolijoki)
Puotila, Jukka 143, 197
Purgatory see Kiirastuli (Jylhä)
Puurunen, Sakari 106, 139, 167

Quinn, Michael L. 176n14
Qveflander, Anneli 45, 173

radical folk theatre 91
Raging Roses group see Raivoisat Ruusut group
Raittila, Hannu 202
Raivoisat Ruusut group 44, 168
Rajala, Panu 67, 90
Rame, Franca 166
Ranin, Matti 167–168
Rantasila, Mari *201*
Rätsep, Tõnis 209
Raudsepp, Hugo 210
Rausmaa, Heikki 158n24
Raw Youth, The (Dostoyevsky and Lyubinov) 124
Red Finnish People's Army 103
Red Line, The (opera by Sallinen) 151
Red River, The (play by Laville) 161
Reed, John 206
relationships and cultural caricature dramas 162–163; *Autumn and Winter*

165; *Bass Viola* 164; *In Celebration* 163;
Close of Play 163; *Forever Yours* 164; *On
Golden Pond* 163; *I'm Not Rappaport*
164–165; *True West* 163–164
'repertoire "find", A' concept 65
Retro (play by Galin) 146–147, 214
Richardson, Henry Robson 55
Riitolahti, Pentti 122
Rinne, Tiina 41, 93, 123, 136, 214
Rinne, Tommi 165, 189
Ritavuori, Heikki 97
Ritolahti, Pentti 197
River Flows, The poetry 209
Road to the Winter War, The *see Tie
talvisotaan* (play by Ylikangas)
Roine, Esko 188, 195n1
Rokem, Freddie 96, 148
Romanian drama 147
Romeo and Juliet (play by Shakespeare) 114
Roos, J. -P. 91–92
Rosencrantz and Guildenstern Are Dead
(play by Stoppard) 210
Roth, Seppo 33
Royal Dramatic Theatre (Dramaten),
Sweden's 115
Royal Shakespeare Company 204, 210
Rozovsky, M. G. 205
Ruby 213
Rummel, Hando 209
Ruohonen, Laura 200–201, 203n10
Ruotsalainen, Paavo 90
Russian classics 122–125, 208; *Bankruptcy*
124; *Diary of a Madman, The* 124–125;
Enough Stupidity in Every Wise Man
122–123; Government Inspector, The
122; *Idiot, The* 123–124; *Raw Youth,
The* 124; see also Soviet dramas
Russian Grand Duchy 1, 103

Saario, Esa 85, 147, 161, 180
Sallinen, Aulis 150–151
Sallinen, Petteri 198, 199
Salmelainen, Eino 45, 72, 73, 81, 84
Salo, Arvo 100, 101
Salonen, Esa-Pekka 191
Saluri, Rein 50, 155, 156, 214, 215
Sámi language 218, 223n2
Sämpy series 52n11
Samuel Kröll Prosecutor *see Kanneviskaali
Samuel Kröll* (play by Järnefelt)
Sandberg, Markus 121
Särkelä Itte (Turja) 91
Satanowski, Jerry 121
Saunders, James 210

Sauter, Willmar 10, 74n1
Savola, Kai 3, 5, 13, 20, *20*, 33, 36n4, 38,
40, 43, 46, 57–59, 65, 127, 137, 145,
178, 180, 187, 188, 204, 205, 214;
directorship of TNL 21; directorship of
TTT 21; hiring choices and decisions 45;
idea about dramatic theatre 25; inaugural
speech at Finnish National Theatre
65–66; interest in Eastern Europe drama
47; network of contacts 21; own artistic
choices 47; role of Director of Theatre
72; statement about domination of
television programming 67; as Theatre
Director 21–22
Savola, Terttu 46, 76, 86, 104, 147, 165,
170, 198, 198–199
Savonlinna's Opera Festival 91
Savutie, Maija 26, 32, 100, 115, 140, 188
Schiller, Friedrich von 121
Schlippe, Andrey von 124
Schnitzler, Arthur 50, 140–142
School for Wives, The (play by Molière)
118–120, *119*
Schwarz, L. 122
Seagull, The (play by Chekhov) 51, 132
Seitsemän veljestä (novel and stage
adaptions by Kivi) 80, 99
Selma is Plotting *see Selman juonet* (play by
Kivi)
Selman juonet (play by Kivi) 83
'semi-absurdist' *see* Havel, Vačlav
set designers in Finnish theatres 45–46
Sevänen, Erkki 9
Seven Brothers *see Seitsemän veljestä* (play
by Kivi)
Shaffer, Peter 171, 214
Shakespeare's plays in Finnish National
Theatre 111–112; *Comedy of Errors, The*
112, 113; *Julius Caesar* 112; *King John*
112, 113–114; *King Lear* 112, 113,
114–115, *116*; *Macbeth* 112, 113,
116–118, *117*; *Midsummer Night's
Dream* 112, 114; *As You Like It* 112
Shakespeare, William 48, 211
Shapiro, Adolf 130–131
Shaw, G. B. 133
Shepard, Sam 163, 164
Sherman, Martin 170, 171
Siikala, Kirsikka 31, 77, 123, 190 *see also*:
Moring, Kirsikka
Siikala, Ritva 44, 132, 134
Siimes, Paula 120
Siimes, Pentti 38, 41, 120, 123, 128, 134,
136, 163, 169, 174, *175*, 178, *178*, 179

242 Index

Siitonen, Seppo-Ilmari 132
Sillantaus, Teppo 142, 143
Sinervo, Elvi 84–85
Siren, Heikki 55, 56–57, 59
Siren, Kaija 55–57
Skalicky, Jan 51
Šlavkin, Viktor 206
'small Finnish classics' 82
Small Stage building 27, 34, 35, 53, 56, 61, 196, 219; artistic programming 56–57; dramas about relationships 76; *Foundation, The* staged at 169; Havel's plays in 151; *Idiot, The* staged at 123–124; *Justiina* staged at 86–87; *Lead Time* staged at 171; *Macbeth* staged at 116; *Machine Wreckers, The* staged at 91; new Finnish drama on 69; new generation of playwrights 198–202; *No-Man's Land* staged at 136; *Papin perhe* staged at 78; Savola's experimentation on 127; *Who's Afraid of Virginia Woolf* staged at 136; *see also* Main Stage building; Omapohja studio space; Willensauna stage
'smörgåsbord' approach 67, 68
social change in Finland 4
social commentary dramas: *Barbarians* 137, 139; *Mandat* 137; *Suicide, The* 137–138
social criticism 223
social upheaval dramas on national stage: environmental threat, dramas about 184–186; generational rebellion dramas 181–184; pacifism, dramas about 177–181
Soikkanen, Timo 4
solid stage directors 39
Sophocles 111
Sorescu, Marin 150
Source, The (play by Sorescu) 150
Soviet dramas 205; *Duck Hunting* 146; *Retro* 146–147; scarcity at National Theatre 146; *see also* Russian classics
stage directors in Finnish theatres 42–43; international 47–48; permanent 44, 45; visiting 44–46; women 44–45
Stanislavskian method 39
Stanislavski, Konstantin 42, 137, 182
'star theatres' era 41
"state theatre" 23
Stegars, Rolf 45
Stein, Peter 45, 50
Stockholm City Theatre 213
Stoppard, Tom 190, 210

Storey, David 163
Story of the Horse, The (Tolstoy) 206
Street (play by Cartwright) 198
Strehler, Giorgio 50, 92, 162
Strindberg, August 78, 127, 128, 209, 214; *Dance of Death, The* 128; *Erik XIV* 128; *Father, The* 128, 129; *Miss Julie* 128, 129
Stuff Happens (play by Hare) 105
Sturua, Robert 50, 207
Suicide, The (play by Erdman) 50, 137–138, 146, 214
Sukupolveni unta (Hämäläinen) 94
Sumera, Lepo 156
Summer (play by Bond) 174
Sundqvist, Harry 120
Suomalainen Teatteri *see* Finnish National Theatre
Suomen Kansallisteatteri *see* Finnish National Theatre
Suomen Sosialidemokraatti newspaper 32, 122
Suomen Teatteriliitto 21
Suruaika (play by Baran) 200
Süskind, Patrick 164
Suzuki, Tadashi 42
Svedberg, Lars 84, 100
Svenska Teatern of Helsinki 3, 41, 87, 223n3
Swedish tradition of court theatre 115, 116
Szakonyi, Károly 148

Taganka Theatre 48, 50, 205–207, 214
Taide-ja teatteripoliittinen ohjelma 221
Taide instituutiona ja järjestelmänä (Sevänen) 9
Taisto Veikkola (pseudonym) *see* Tolvanen, Taisto
Tales From the Vienna Woods (play by von Horváth) 50, 141
Tallinn Theatre 214
Tamminen, Simo 88
Tampere's Työväen Teatteri *see* TampereWorkers' Theatre (TTT)
Tampere University 24, 39
Tampere Workers' Theatre (TTT) 3, 5, 20–22, 25, 44, 66, 73, 77, 98, 137, 143, 145, 150, 163, 178
Tandefelt, Ernst 97
Tanskanen, Katri 203n10
Tarjanne, Onni 54–55
Tarkka, Pekka 185
Tartuffe (play by Molière) 206

Teatteri-Grilli (Theatre-Grill) 57
Teatterikomitea 1972 23
Teatteri magazine 33, 35, 40, 41, 44, 65, 67, 68, 69, 91–92, 194
Technical Arts College 45
Tempest, The (play by Shakespeare) 181
Ten Days That Shook the World (Reed) 206
Terttula, Eugen 43, 89, 104, 113, 124, 125, 128, 133, 147, 171
Theater Heute magazine 158n17
Theatr Cymru 210
Theatre & Nation (Holdsworth) 5–6, 7
Theatre Academy *see* Finnish Theatre School
theatre audiences: as critics 30; diversity of 31; general public as 33–36
Theatre Committee 1972 *see* Teatterikomitea 1972
theatre company visits from East and West 204–205; British theatrical culture 210–212; Gorki Theatre 205–207; Taganka Theatre 205–207; Western diversity and Far East traditions 212–214
theatre experience: audience member *vs.* critic 30; diversity of theatre critics 31–32; newspaper clippings as source material 30; theatrical opinions among experienced critics 32
Theatre of the Absurd, The (Esslin) 153–154
theatre professionals 38
theatrical actors in Finnish theatres 38–41
theatrical expression 6
theatrical nationhood 6–7
There Shall Be No Night (play by Sherwood) 106
Thirty Silver Coins *see* Kolmekymmentä hopearahaa (play by Ylikangas)
Thomas, Brandon 187–188
Thomas, Dylan 76
Thompson, Ernest 147, 163
Thorvaldsen, Bertel 182
Threepenny Opera (play by Brecht) 179
Three Sisters, The (play by Chekhov) 50, 130, 131–132, 205, 207
Tiedonantaja newspaper 32
Tie talvisotaan (play by Ylikangas) 105
Tiitu, Tapio 93
Tikkanen, Aino-Maija 94
Timon of Athens (play by Shakespeare) 112
Tiusanen, Timo 100, 115, 134, 147, 162

Tohtori Karellin vaikea yö (play by Kross) 50, 156–157
Tohvelisankarin rouva (play by Jotuni) 79–80, *80*
Toikka, Oiva 45, 114, 140
Tola, Heini 165
Tola, Olli 161, 162
Toller, Ernst 91
Tolvanen, Taisto 153
Tompkins, Joanne 10
Tormis, Lea 156, 215
Tovstonogov, Georgi 46, 47, 122, 123, 130, 188, 205
Towards the Heart of the World *see Kohti maailman sydäntä* (play by Peltonen)
Traces of Colonialism: The Centre, the Periphery, and Finland *see* Kolonialismin jäljet: keskustat, periferiat ja Suomi (Lehtonen and Löytty)
traditional classics in Finnish National Theatre: *Arkielämää* 76–77; *Numisuutarit* 80–81; *Kanneviskaali Samuel Kröll* 77; *Kauppaneuvoksen härkä* 82–83; *Kultainen vasikka* 78–79; *Lehtolapsi* 77–77; *Papin perhe* 78; *Selman juonet* 83; *Seven Brothers* 80; *Tohvelisankarin rouva* 79–80, *80*
transnationalism 220
Trifonov, Yuri 207
True West (play by Shepard) 163–164
Tsagarett, A. 205
TTT *see* Tampere Workers' Theatre (TTT)
Tukkijoella (play by Pakkala) 178, 179, 191
Tuomarila, Ilpo 36, 100, 197
Tuovinen, Kai 124, 129
Turja, Ilmari 91, 103, 104
Turkka, Jouko 25, 39, 42, 45, 74, 77, 91–93, 186, 197, 209, 222
Turku's City Theatre 25, 34, 39, 69, 84; playing *Seirtsemän veljestä* in 80; *Romeo and Juliet* in 114
Turku Swedish Theatre *see* Åbo Svenska Teater
Turun Sanomat newspaper 32, 189
Tüür, Erkki-Sven 155, 215
Tuuri, Antti 98–99
Twelfth Night (play by Shakespeare) 211
Työväen Näyttämöiden Liitto (TNL) 21, 145

Uexküll, Sole 31, 84, 103
Ugala Theatre 209

244 Index

Uibo, Toomas 209
Uibo, Väino 209
Uncle Vanya (play by Chekhov) 129, 131, 132
Under Milkwood (Thomas) 76, 210
Union of Workers' Stages *see* Työväen Näyttämöiden Liitto
University Theatre 21
Unknown Soldier, The (Linna) 102
Unsettling Space (Tompkins) 10
Unt, Mati 50, 155, 157, 208, 210, 215
Unveiling (play by Havel) 15n13, 151, 152
Uusi Suomi newspaper 31–32, 120, 123, 154, 163, 193, 211

Väänänen, Kari 109n21
Vaarik, Andrus 210
Valheita (play by Turkka) 74, *88*, 91, 186, 222
valuation of drama 74
Vampilov, Aleksandr 146
Vanemuine Theatre of Tartu 209, 215
Vares, Vesa 4
Vasiliev, A. 206
Vastaanotto (play by Havel) 151, *152*
Vast Domain, The (play by Schnitzler) 50, 141–142
Veistäjä, Olavi 32, 45, 46, 81, 123, 134, 179, 193–194
Veltheim, Katri 31, 32, 77, 120, 123, 154, 163, 180, 192
verse drama 121
Vicar's Family, The *seePapin perhe* (play by Canth)
Victor, or Power to the Children (play by Vitrac) 142–143
Viennese Performing Arts School 212
Vietnam War 4, 177
Viherjuuri, Mikko 168
Viiding, Juhan 209
Viimeiset kiusaukset (opera by Kokkonen) 90, 91
Viimeistä seuraava yö (play by Maróti) 149
Viron historia 208
Virtanen, Matti 4, 42, 52n6, 200
Vitrac, Roger 142
Volanen, Eeva-Kaarina 41, *85*, 93, 94, 114, 134, 147, 150, 167–168, 214
von Trotta, Margarethe 171
Vysotsky, Vladimir 207

Wager, Leif 41, 119, 164, 174, *175*
war history and contemporary politics 102; *Jääkäri Ståhl* 103–105;
Käännekohdat Suomen historiassa 106–108; *Kohti maailman sydäntä* 108; *Kolmekymmentä hopearahaa* 106; *Miten kalat suutelevat* 102–103; *Stuff Happens* 105; *Tie talvisotaan* 105, 105, 106; *Unknown Soldier, The* 102; see also historical character's depiction
Warsaw National Theatre 47, 48
War Veteran Association of Helsinki 108
Wecksell, J. J. 100
Weill, Kurt 177–178, 191
Weiss, Peter 125
Western dramas at Finnish National Theatre 71, 160; about abuses of power 169–171; dramatic and stage celebrities from 165–169; historic moments of stardom in 171–175; played on Main Stage 161–162; relationships and cultural caricatures in 162–165
When Grandfather Skied to Finland (Katz) 102
Who's Afraid of Virginia Woolf (play by Albee) 136
Wicked Duchess, The (play by Girandoux) 188–189, 191
Wikström, Riitta 121, 124, 132, 137, 165, 213
Wilde, Oscar 143
Wiles, David 7
Willensauna stage 27, 34, 35, 53, 57, *58*, 61, 127, 164, 169, 181, 200, 202, 208; artistic programming of 58–59; *Autumn and Winter* staged at 165; *Betrayal* staged at 136; *Caligula* staged at 181, 182; *Death of a Salesman, The* staged at 134, *135*; featured in KOM theatre company 62n17; founding of 59; *Kohti maailman sydäntä* staged at 108; *Life of Alexander März, The* staged at 170; *Lintu vai kala* staged at 200–201; *Masterclass* staged at 174–175; *Nam nam* staged at 200; new Finnish drama at 69–70; opening of new stage 66; *Philoctetes* staged at 111; *Bent* staged at 170; *Source, The* staged at 150; *see also* Main Stage building; Omapohja studio space; Small Stage building
Williams, Raymond 127, 129
Williams, Tennessee 133
Wilmer, S. E. 5, 8
Wilson, Woodrow 179
Winter's Tale, The (play by Shakespeare) 112, 113, 212

Winter War 98, 102, 105, 106
Witikka, Jack 43, 44, 57, 128, 136, 146, 173
women stage directors in Finland 44–45
Woods, Michelle 154, 158n22
Writers' Guild of Finland *see* Finnish Dramatists' Union
Wuolijoki, Hella 72–74, 75n24, 75n28, 83–84, 86–87, 89, 95n20
Wymark, Jane 211

Year of Soviet Drama' (1977–1978) in Finland 146
Yks perkele, yks enkeli (play by Salo) 100, 101
Yleisradio 43, 167

Ylikangas, Heikki 89, 90, 105, 106, 108
Yliruusi, Tauno 209
Yössä Gehennan (play by Tuomarila) 36, 100
Young Lady of Niskavuori, The *see* *Niskavuoren nuori emäntä* (play by Wuolijoki)
Youth Theatre of Tallinn 210, 215
Yuki, Magosaburo 213–214
Yukiza Marionette Theatre 213
YYA treaty *see* Agreement of Friendship, Cooperation, and Assistance

Zaniewska, Xymana 121
Zetterberg, Seppo 106, 208
Zilliacus, Benedict 107–108

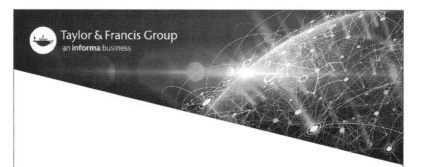

Printed in the United States
by Baker & Taylor Publisher Services